A Guide to

USED BOOK DEALERS
OF THE MID-ATLANTIC

Covering Portions of Pennsylvania, New Jersey, Delaware, Maryland, Virginia and Washington, D.C.

Philip and Meg Burns

Cover and interior artwork by Jasper Burns

Turtle Hill Books
Ellicott City, Maryland

Copyright © 1993 by Philip A. Burns and Meg Burns. Printed and bound in the United States of America. Published by Turtle Hill Books, 3420 Sylvan Lane, Ellicott City, Maryland 21043, (410) 465-7213.

The publisher does not assume and hereby disclaims any liability to any party for any loss or damage caused by errors or omissions in *A Guide to Used Book Dealers of the Mid-Atlantic*, whether such errors or omissions resulted from negligence, accident or any other cause.

This book contains no paid advertising.

All rights reserved. No part of this book may be reproduced in any form or by any electronic or mechanical means including information storage and retrieval systems without permission in writing from the publisher, except by a reviewer, who may quote brief passages in a review.

Cover and interior artwork by Jasper Burns

Publisher's Cataloging in Publication Data
Burns, Philip A.
    A guide to used book dealers of the mid-Atlantic: covering portions of Pennsylvania, New Jersey, Delaware, Maryland, Virginia and Washington, D.C./Philip and Meg Burns

    Includes indexes.
    1. Antiquarian booksellers - Middle Atlantic States - Directories. 2. Bookstores - Middle Atlantic States - Directories. 3. Booksellers and bookselling - Middle Atlantic States - Directories. 4. Book collecting - Middle Atlantic States - Directories. 5. Middle Atlantic States - Description and travel - Guidebooks. 6. Out-of-print books. I. Burns, Meg. II. Title.
Z475.B87   1993   070.5'025'74   93-93812
ISBN 0-9634481-1-0

To our parents and grandparents

Table of Contents

Introduction: How to Use This Book	vii
Abbreviations for Professional Affiliations	x
Pennsylvania	2
Philadelphia	3
Region 1	16
Region 2	30
Region 3	44
Delaware	56
New Jersey	60
Maryland	70
Baltimore	71
Region 1	80
Region 2	90
Region 3	113
Washington, D.C.	116
Virginia	128
Region 1	129
Region 2	138
Farther Afield	149
Indices	
Complete List (of all dealers contacted)	151
Specialty Index	167
By Appointment Dealers	174
Mail Order Service	175
General Index	176
Order Information	179

Introduction: How to Use This Book

A Guide to Used Book Dealers of the Mid-Atlantic contains detailed information on over 270 used book dealers in the mid-Atlantic states: information designed to help you zero in on the most likely sources for your current collecting interests. Dealer listings are arranged geographically, and a map showing dealer locations precedes the listings for each state.

The information in this book was collected during 1992 by means of questionnaires sent to every book dealer we could locate in the region that is covered by this guide. From these, 272 dealers responded to the questionnaire. The information presented includes useful information such as type of shop, hours, major categories, specialty categories, number of books and breakdowns according to paperback, hardback, in-print, out-of-print and rare, mail order service and catalogs, floor area, special items and services (such as searches and appraisals), directions, owners' names and professional affiliations, and miscellaneous information such as handicap access and nearby dining.

The first index in the back of the book gives a complete list of the over 400 dealers which were queried, along with their addresses. If your favorite book dealer does not appear in the text of the book, he or she may be listed in the complete list as one of the dealers who did not respond to our questionnaire. Used book dealers were located through telephone directory listings, *AB Bookman's Weekly* and *Yearbook*, the *American Book Trade Directory* (Bowker, 37th edition), *BookQuote* (Spoon River Press), various advertisements, and the regional information pamphlets available at many used bookstores.

Many of these sources include only dealers who pay a fee. In order to make this guide as complete as possible, inclusion in this guide was free to all dealers.

The reader is cautioned that the information contained in this guide is subject to change. In particular, the subject categories, approximate number of volumes and approximate breakdown (rare, out-of-print, in-print) are subject to constant change and fluctuation. Likewise, store hours are also subject to change, and we strongly recommend that you call ahead before visiting in order to verify that the listed hours are still current, especially if your visit takes you out of the way.

The questionnaire asked each dealer to list major categories in which his/her shop had at least 100 titles. These categories are listed below.

List of All Major Categories

Americana	Gardening	Paperback
Antiques	Geography	Philosophy
Art	Health-fitness	Poetry
Aviation	History	Political Science
Business	Hobbies & Crafts	Rare Books
Children's	Medicine	Religion
Collectibles	Military History	Romance
Cooking	Music	Science Fiction
Do-it-yourself	Mystery	Science/Technology
Education	Mythology	Social Science
Exploration	Nature	Spectator Sports
Fiction	Nautical	Travel
Folklore	Outdoor Recreation	

A sample entry is shown below. Note that the list has been arranged so that a given category is always in the same column. For example, the category "History" will only be found in the second column. Likewise, "Travel" will only be found in the third column. While structuring the lists in this fashion does not always lead to compactness and clean appearance, it does facilitate the chore of scanning the lists when the reader is looking through the entries for a particular category.

Sample Entry

Major Categories represented by at least 100 titles:

Americana	History	Paperback
Art	Medicine	Poetry
Fiction		Political Science
		Travel

To further assist the bibliophile in locating books in a particular subject, a specialty index is included. This index lists dealer specialties by subject, with page numbers for location in the text. It also distinguishes dealers who are true specialists (i.e. specialists only) from those who are general book dealers with specialty areas. Three additional indices are found at the rear of the book: a general index of the dealers arranged alphabetically (with page numbers), a list of dealers who operate by appointment, and a list of dealers who offer mail order service.

The general order of the entries is shown in the table of contents. Pennsylvania, Maryland and Virginia are each subdivided into smaller regions; New Jersey, Delaware, and Washington, D.C. are not. Within a region, the used book dealers appear alphabetically by city. Within a city, the dealers appear in order of increasing zip code. Within a zip code, the sequential order of dealers is at random in order to minimize the inconvenience of entries being carried over to another page.

Each entry ends with a solid line. Therefore, if there is no line at the end of a page, go to the next page to see the rest of the entry for that particular dealer. Regions within a state are separated by a double solid line. The double solid line on page 30, for instance, marks the end of Pennsylvania - Region 1, and the beginning of Pennsylvania - Region 2.

Although we have tried to make this directory as complete and as accurate as possible, we are human and therefore subject to error. Please let us know of any errors which you find, any dealers which you would like to see included in subsequent editions, or any comments you have about the book.

Whether you are a dealer, a browser or a collector, we hope that you will find this guide to be a helpful asset in your quest for books and fine reading.

Happy book hunting!

Abbreviations for Professional Affiliations

A.B.A.	American Booksellers Association
A.B.A.A.	Antiquarian Booksellers of America
A.B.N.J.	Antiquarian Booksellers of New Jersey
A.O.U.	American Ornithologists' Union
A.P.I.C.	American Political Items Collectors
A.P.H.S.	American Photo Historical Society
A.S.A.	American Society of Appraisers
A.S.I.D.	American Society of Interior Designers
C.R.A.B.S.	Chesapeake Regional Area Book Sellers
D.S.	Daguerrean Society
I.L.A.B	International League of Antiquarian Booksellers
I.S.A.	International Society of Appraisers
M.A.B.A.	Mid-Atlantic Booksellers Association
N.E.A.A.	New England Appraisers Association
N.J.B.A.	New Jersey Booksellers Association
N.S.A.	National Stereoscopic Association
P.B.F.A.	Provincial Booksellers Fairs Association
T.A.M.S.	Token and Medal Society
U.A.C.C.	Universal Autograph Collectors Club
W.A.B.A.	Washington Antiquarian Booksellers Association
W.O.S.	Wilson Ornithological Society

EXOTICA

Nat. Hist. Co.

1

MUSINGS

MISC. AUTHORS

Red Eft Pub., Inc

2 Pennsylvania

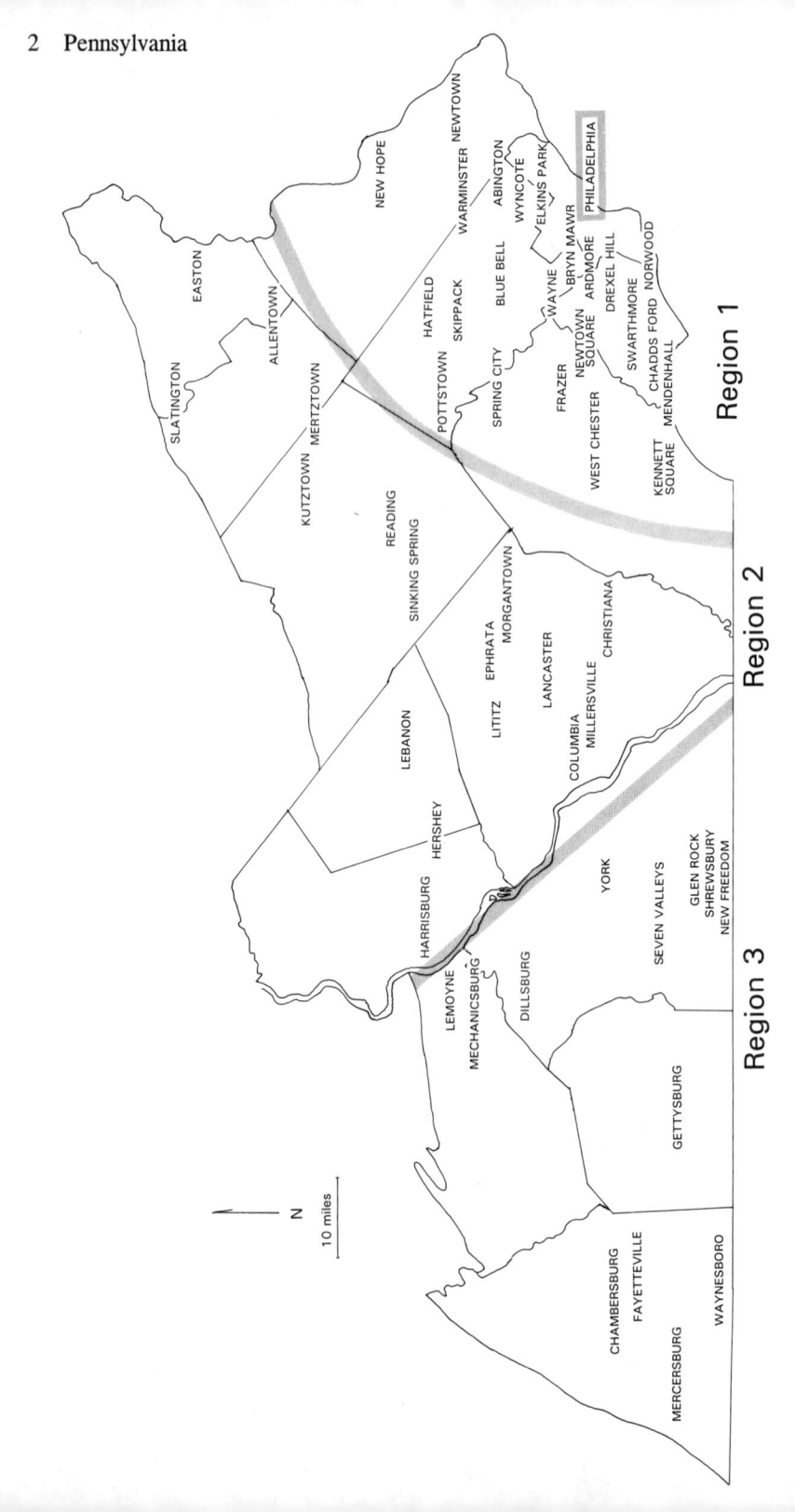

W. Graham Arader III
1308 Walnut Street
Philadelphia, PA 19017
(215) 735-8811
Owner(s): W. Graham Arader III
Type of Shop: Antiquarian
Major Categories represented by at least 100 titles:
```
Exploration      Geography         Rare Books
                 Nautical          Travel
```
Other major categories: Natural history.
Approximate number of volumes: --
        paperback: --
        hardback : 10,000
Special Items and Services: Appraisals, book searches.
Additional information: Founded in 1971. "Always interested in buying, highest prices paid." Other shops in New York, Chicago and San Francisco.

Miriam and William Crawford Books
P.O. Box 42587
Philadelphia, PA 19101
Owner(s): Miriam I. and William H. Crawford
Type of Shop: Mail-order used books, including pamphlets.
Major Categories represented by at least 100 titles:
```
Americana        History           Paperback
Art              Medicine          Poetry
Fiction                            Political Science
                                   Religion
                                   Science/Technology
                                   Travel
```
Other major categories: African-American literature, labor, radical materials.
Approximate breakdown: rare: 5%
        out-of-print: 85%
        in-print: 10%
Special Items and Services: Posters, postcards and pamphlets.

David J. Holmes, Autographs
230 South Broad Street, 3rd floor
Philadelphia, PA 19102
(215) 735-1083 FAX (215) 732-8151
Hours: Mon-Fri:9-5 by appointment.
Owner(s): David J. Holmes
Professional Affiliations: A.B.A.A., U.A.C.C., I.L.A.B.
Type of Shop: Autograph shop, rare books.
Major Categories represented by at least 100 titles:
```
Art              Mystery           Poetry
Children's                         Rare Books
Collectibles                       Romance
Fiction                            Social Science
```

Other major categories: English and American literature of the 18th-20th centuries, original drawings.
Specialty Categories: Autograph letters, manuscripts, rare books, presentation copies, archives and original drawings of English & American literary figures and artists of the 18th-20th centuries.
Approximate number of volumes: 1,500
                paperback: 1%
                hardback : 99%
Approximate breakdown: rare: 65%
                out-of-print: 35%
                in-print: --
Catalog issued 4 times per year at $5 or $10.
Special Items and Services: Autograph letters, manuscripts, archives, postcards, posters, prints, etc. Appraisals.
Directions: Located at northwest corner of Broad & Locust Streets in Center City Philadelphia; parking available everywhere.
Additional information: Founded in 1984. Began book trading 21 years ago in Boston. At least seven other bookshops or autograph shops and many good restaurants within walking distance. Various museums reasonably nearby. Handicap access. 1,200 sq. ft. shop area.

William H. Allen, Bookseller
2031 Walnut Street
Philadelphia, PA 19103
(215) 563-3398
Hours: Weekdays:8-5 Sat:8:30-1
Owner(s): George R. Allen
Professional Affiliations: A.B.A. (International)
Type of Shop: Antiquarian books in the humanities.
Major Categories represented by at least 100 titles:

Americana	History	Philosophy
Art	Medicine	Poetry
Exploration	Military History	Political Science
Folklore		Rare Books
		Religion
		Travel

Other major categories: Books on literature, history and philosophy in all languages.
Approximate number of volumes: --
                paperback: --
                hardback : 30,000
Approximate breakdown: rare: 2%
                out-of-print: 98%
                in-print: --
Catalog issued 5 times per year.
Special Items and Services: Appraisals.
Directions: Center City Philadelphia, on Walnut Street between 20th and 21st Streets. Metered parking and nearby parking lots.

Additional information: Founded in 1918. Located in west Philadelphia until 1941; present location since then. Good dining, museums and other book stores nearby. Street level entrance.

Catherine Barnes
2031 Walnut Street, 3rd floor
Philadelphia, PA 19103
(215) 854-0175
Hours: Mon-Fri by appointment.
Owner(s): Catherine Barnes
Professional Affiliations: Manuscript Society, U.A.C.C.
Type of Shop: Autographs and signed books.
Major Categories represented by at least 100 titles:

Americana	History	Science/Technology
	Medicine	

Other major categories: Presidential.
Approximate number of volumes: 300-400 items
Free catalog issued about twice a year.
Directions: Located in Center City Philadelphia. On-street parking and parking lots nearby.
Additional information: Founded in 1985. Located in same building as William H. Allen, Bookseller.

Book Mark
2049 West Rittenhouse Square
Philadelphia, PA 19103
(215) 735-5546
Hours: Daily:10-5 Sat:12-5
Owner(s): Valerie Polin and Robert Langmuir
Professional Affiliations: Library Co. of Philadelphia, Ephemera Society
Type of Shop: General used & rare books, specialty in architecture.
Major Categories represented by at least 100 titles:

Americana	Gardening	Philosophy
Art	Medicine	Poetry
Children's	Music	Rare Books
Fiction	Nature	Travel
Folklore		

Other major categories: Many categories handled, but in quantities of 20-50 titles.
Specialty Categories: Architecture.
Approximate number of volumes: --
   paperback: none
   hardback : 5,000-8,000
Approximate breakdown: rare: 5-15%
   out-of-print: 85-95%
   in-print: --
Catalog issued once or twice a year at $3.
Special Items and Services: Ephemera, prints, architectural renderings. Appraisals.

6 Pennsylvania - Philadelphia

Directions: Located between 20th and 21st Streets and between Locust and Spruce Streets in Center City Philadelphia. Parking on street and parking lot on same block as shop.
Additional information: Founded in 1978. Several other bookshops in a four to five block radius; fine dining, private museums. Shop located on first floor only.

Philadelphia Drama Bookshop
2209 Walnut Street
Philadelphia, PA 19103
(215) 981-0777
Hours: Mon-Sat:9-5
Owner(s): Madeleine Kelly
Type of Shop: Specialty - drama, music, film.
Specialty Categories: Film, drama.
Approximate breakdown: rare: 10%
　　　　　　　　　　　　out-of-print: 40%
　　　　　　　　　　　　in-print: 50%
Free annual catalog.
Special Items and Services: Cards, posters, sheet music, CDs, theatre memorabilia, T-shirts, sweats, mugs, jewelry. Store also carries new books in area of specialty. Book searches.
Directions: West on Walnut to 22nd Street, 3rd door of row houses on right.
Additional information: Founded in 1989. Offers "area's largest selection of theatre and performing arts books." Another used bookstore on same block. 1,000 sq. ft. shop area.

John F. Warren, Bookseller
124 South 19th Street
Philadelphia, PA 19103
(215) 561-6422
Hours: Mon-Fri:10-5
Owner(s): John Warren
Type of Shop: Specialty antiquarian - art books and anything dealing with visual arts.
Major Categories represented by at least 100 titles:
　　Antiques
　　Art
　　Collectibles
Specialty Categories: American art, art history, catalogues raisonnés, exhibition catalogs.
Approximate number of volumes: 10,000
　　　　　　　　　　　paperback: 4,000
　　　　　　　　　　　hardback : 6,000
Approximate breakdown: rare: 10%
　　　　　　　　　　　　out-of-print: 80%
　　　　　　　　　　　　in-print: 10%

Catalog issued twice per year at $3 each.
Special Items and Services: Prints of the W.P.A. period, American etchings & lithographs. Appraisals.
Directions: Located between Samson & Walnut Streets - 2nd floor. Centrally located in downtown Philadelphia.
Additional information: Founded in 1979. One of the few bookshops outside of New York City specializing exclusively in art books. 1,200 sq. ft. shop area.

Rittenhouse Medical Book Store
1706 Rittenhouse Square
Philadelphia, PA 19103
(215) 545-6072   FAX (215) 735-5633
Hours: Mon-Fri:9-5   Sat:10-5
Owner(s): Richard W. Foster
Type of Shop: Specialty antiquarian - medical books.
Specialty Categories: Out-of-print, old, rare medical titles & all sub-specialties of medicine.
Approximate number of volumes: --
      paperback: 2%
      hardback : 98%
Approximate breakdown: rare: 30%
            out-of-print: 70%
            in-print: 0%
Free catalog issued about twice per year.

House of Our Own
3920 Spruce Street
Philadelphia, PA 19104
(215) 222-1576
Hours: Mon-Thurs:10-6:30   Fri-Sat:10-6
Owner(s): Greg Schirm and Deborah Sanford
Professional Affiliations: A.B.A.
Type of Shop: General
Major Categories represented by at least 100 titles:

Children's	History	Paperback
Fiction		Philosophy
		Poetry
		Political Science
		Religion
		Science/Technology
		Social Science

Other major categories: Literature, biography, literary criticism.
Approximate number of volumes: 20,000
         paperback: 75%
         hardback : 25%
Directions: From Schuylkill Expressway (I-76), exit at University Avenue west on

8   Pennsylvania - Philadelphia

38th Street to Spruce Street, left on Spruce, 1 1/2 blocks to 3920 Spruce. Meter parking on Spruce in front of store.
Additional information: Founded in 1971. Bookstore also has 15,000 new books specializing in social and political issues. Specialty categories include African-American, feminist, cultural theory, third world and environmental. Located near University of Pennsylvania campus, University Museum (archeology & anthropology) and Annenberg Theatre. 1,000 sq. ft. shop area.

Bob's Book Shop
206 South 13th Street
Philadelphia, PA 19107
(215) 546-7015
Hours: Mon-Fri:12-6:30   Sat:12-5
Owner(s): Bob Waxler
Type of Shop: Collectible magazines and general stock.
Major Categories represented by at least 100 titles:

```
Art                 History              Paperback
Business            Mystery              Religion
Cooking             Nature               Science Fiction
```

Other major categories: Large selection of collectible magazines - all kinds.
Specialty Categories: Rare magazines - store and warehouse supply.
Approximate number of volumes: 100,000
             paperback: 40%, and 40% magazines
             hardback : 20%
Approximate breakdown: rare: 40%
             out-of-print: 30%
             in-print: 30%
Special Items and Services: Records & tapes. Book searches.
Directions: Rt 76 to Central Philadelphia (Vine Street Expressway). Take Vine to Twelfth, make right turn, store is on 13th between Walnut and Locust Streets.
Additional information: Founded in 1985. Many book stores in area. 450 sq. ft. shop area plus warehouse space.

George S. MacManus Company
1317 Irving Street
Philadelphia, PA 19107
(215) 735-4456
Hours: Mon-Fri:9-5
Owner(s): Clarence Wolf
Professional Affiliations: A.B.A.A.
Type of Shop: Antiquarian
Major Categories represented by at least 100 titles:

```
Americana           Military History     Rare Books
Exploration
```

Other major categories: Americana, American literature and English literature - all of the 18th and 19th centuries.

Approximate number of volumes: 23,000
Free catalog issued irregularly.

Russakoff's Books and Records
259 South 10th Street
Philadelphia, PA 19107
(215) 592-8380
Hours: Mon-Sat:11-7
Owner(s): Jerry & Shassy Russakoff
Type of Shop: General
Major Categories represented by at least 100 titles:
    ALL CATEGORIES.
Approximate number of volumes: --
        paperback: 50%
        hardback : 50%
Special Items and Services: Large variety of used records. Will trade.
Directions: Store is located in Center City, 10th Street, between Spruce & Locust Streets. Meter parking.
Additional information: This location founded in 1982. Owners have been in business at various locations for approximately 40 years. Located near historic district and a few blocks from new Convention Hall. 700 sq. ft. shop area.

Reedmor Magazine Company, Inc.
1229 Walnut Street, 2nd floor
Philadelphia, PA 19107
(215) 922-6643
Hours: Mon-Fri:11-5
Owner(s): David & Elaine Bagelman
Type of Shop: Comics, magazines back to 1780.
Major Categories represented by at least 100 titles:
    Art   Military History   Paperback
    Cooking   Rare Books
    Fiction   Science Fiction
                                                Travel
Specialty Categories: Science fiction.
Approximate number of volumes: 2,000,000 magazines.
Directions: Center City - next to corner of 13th & Walnut Streets. Parking lots close by.
Additional information: Founded in 1928 by present owner. Performs book searches. Good dining and museums nearby. Elevator with limited access. 10,000 sq. ft. shop area including warehouse.

The Book Shop
3828 Morrell Avenue
Philadelphia, PA 19114
(215) 632-7835
Hours: Mon,Tues,Sat:10-4:30   Wed,Fri:10-6:30   Closed Thursday & Sunday.
Owner(s): Kathleen and Bill Schlarp
Type of Shop: General - used paperbacks & hardbacks, some new books.
Major Categories represented by at least 100 titles:

Americana	Gardening	Paperback
Art	Health-fitness	Philosophy
Business	History	Poetry
Children's	Medicine	Political Science
Cooking	Military History	Religion
Do-it-yourself	Music	Romance
Fiction	Mystery	Science Fiction
	Nature	Science/Technology
		Social Science
		Spectator Sports
		Travel

Other major categories: Westerns and historical fiction. Horror, true crime, psychology/self-help, classics, reference.
Approximate number of volumes: 40,000
  paperback: 85%
  hardback : 15%
Approximate breakdown: rare: none
  out-of-print: 30%
  in-print: 70%
Special Items and Services: Maps, some posters, audiotapes, bookmarks. Requests and book swaps. Will mail books.
Directions: 9900 Frankford Avenue - northeast Philadelphia. Parking in front of store in Morrell Park Center.
Additional information: Founded in 1976. 1,000 sq. ft. shop area.

The Philadelphia Print Shop, Ltd.
8441 Germantown Avenue
Philadelphia, PA 19118
(215) 242-4750
Hours: Mon-Sat:9-5 Wednesday till 8.
Owner(s): Donald H. Cresswell and Christopher W. Lane
Type of Shop: Antiquarian
Major Categories represented by at least 100 titles:

Americana	Geography	Travel
Antiques		
Art		
Exploration		

Other major categories: Historical prints and historical cartography.
Approximate number of volumes: --
  paperback: --
  hardback : 5,000

Approximate breakdown: rare: 40%
out-of-print: 20%
in-print: 40%
Catalog available for $4, or $18 for a subscription of six.
Special Items and Services: Paper conservation, museum-quality framing and appraisals.
Directions: From Penn. Turnpike: take exit 25 (Norristown), turn right towards Philadelphia on Germantown Pike. Continue south for about 5 miles. Road becomes Germantown Avenue as you enter community of Chestnut Hill. Located on third block after street turns to cobblestone; on the left at corner of Highland Avenue.

The Philadelphia Rare Books & Manuscripts Co.
P.O. Box 9536
Philadelphia, PA 19124
(215) 744-6734
Hours: By appointment.
Owner(s): David Szewczyk and Cynthis Davis Buffington
Professional Affiliations: A.B.A.A., I.L.A.B.
Type of Shop: Antiquarian
Major Categories represented by at least 100 titles:
```
                                                Rare Books
```
Specialty Categories: Early printed books, substantive manuscripts, New & Old World Hispanica, New World languages, law, histories, travels, Bibles and Americana - all before 1820.
Free sample catalog available. Further catalogs are free to active collectors.
Additional information: Founded in 1984. Call for directions. Appraisals offered. Four steps to enter shop.

Bookhaven
2202 Fairmount Avenue
Philadelphia, PA 19130
(215) 235-3226
Hours: Tues,Thurs,Fri:11-7   Wed:11-9   Sat:10:30-5:30   Sun:12-5:30
Owner(s): Ricci & Rolf Andeer
Type of Shop: General - hardback & paperback.
Major Categories represented by at least 100 titles:

```
Art                History              Paperback
Children's         Military History     Philosophy
Cooking            Mystery              Poetry
Exploration        Nature               Religion
Fiction                                 Science Fiction
                                        Social Science
                                        Travel
```
Other major categories: Anthropology, African-American studies, drama.
Approximate number of volumes: 40,000 - 50,000
paperback: 60%
hardback : 40%

Approximate breakdown: rare: --
out-of-print: 60%
in-print: 40%
Directions: Take 22nd Street exit north from I-676 (Vine Street Expressway) to Fairmount Ave (700 block of 22nd St.). Turn left, store is on south side of Fairmount Ave. Lots of free parking.
Additional information: Founded in 1987. Several restaurants nearby. Close to Philadelphia Museum of Art, Franklin Institute, Natural Science Museum. 950 sq. ft. shop area.

Kathleen Rais & Company
3901 Conshohocken Avenue, Suite 2310
Philadelphia, PA 19131
(215) 877-8656
Hours: By appointment.
Owner(s): Kathleen Rais
Type of Shop: Antiquarian
Specialty Categories: Dogs.
Approximate number of volumes: 1,000
paperback: 5%
hardback : 95%
Approximate breakdown: rare: 60%
out-of-print: 30%
in-print: 10%
Free catalog issued once or twice per year.
Special Items and Services: Art (all dog-related): original paintings & graphics, jewelry, greeting cards. Antiques and collectibles relating to purebred dogs. Appraisals, book searches, minor repair & restoration, and consultant services for collection development and major restoration.
Directions: City Line Avenue (Rt 1 south) to Monument Avenue, left at second light (Conshohocken Avenue), left at second light to Greenbriar Club, Lobby #1. Ring for #2310.
Additional information: Founded in 1978 in Bloomington, Indiana, the day owner graduated from Indiana University. Located minutes from the Art Museum and various attractions of Fairmount Park. Only a few miles from historic Center City Philadelphia and from the Main Line. Original shop cat still in residence. Handicap access: elevator to third floor. 180 sq. ft. shop area.

Carmen D. Valentino, Rare Books & Manuscripts
2956 Richmond Street
Philadelphia, PA 19134
(215) 739-6056
Hours: By appointment only.
Owner(s): Carmen D. Valentino
Professional Affiliations: Manuscript Society, U.A.C.C.
Type of Shop: Rare books & manuscripts.

Pennsylvania - Philadelphia   13

Major Categories represented by at least 100 titles:

Americana	Geography	Rare Books
Antiques	History	Religion
Art	Medicine	Science/Technology
Aviation	Military History	Social Science
Business	Music	Travel
Exploration	Nautical	
Folklore		

Other major categories: Local history.
Specialty Categories: Manuscripts, ephemera.
Approximate number of volumes: --
        paperback: --
        hardback : 50%
Approximate breakdown: 100% rare and out-of-print.
Catalog available on occasion.
Special Items and Services: Manuscripts, ephemera, trade catalogs. Appraisals - mainly for gift tax and insurance.
Directions: Near Allegheny exit off I-95.
Additional information: Founded in 1977 by current owner. Located close to Center City Philadelphia.

Richard T. Rosenthal
4718 Springfield Avenue
Philadelphia, PA 19143
(215) 726-5493
Hours: By appointment.
Owner(s): Richard T. Rosenthal
Professional Affiliations: A.P.H.S., N.S.A., D.S.
Type of Shop: Specialty - rare books and photography.
Approximate number of volumes: 200
        paperback: 10%
        hardback : 90%
Approximate breakdown: rare: 40%
        out-of-print: 60%
        in-print: --
Free catalog available on request.
Special Items and Services: Rare 19th and 20th century photographs. Appraisals and book searches.

Art Carduner Booksearch
6228 Greene Street (Box 4197)
Philadelphia, PA 19144
(215) 843-6071
Hours: By appointment.
Owner(s): Art Carduner
Type of Shop: General antiquarian.

14   Pennsylvania - Philadelphia

Major Categories represented by at least 100 titles:
```
Americana        History            Philosophy
Art              Military History   Poetry
Business         Music              Political Science
Cooking          Mystery            Religion
Fiction          Nature             Spectator Sports
                 Nautical
```
Approximate number of volumes: --
        paperback: 500
        hardback : 25,000
Approximate breakdown: rare: --
        out-of-print: 100%
        in-print: --
Free catalog issued four times per year.
Additional information: Founded in 1949. Book searches. Call for directions. Easy parking. 1,500 sq. ft. shop area.

Factotum Books
1709 South Street
Philadelphia, PA 19146
(215) 985-1929
Hours: 12-6   Closed Monday.
Owner(s): Paul Reuther
Type of Shop: Antiquarian
Major Categories represented by at least 100 titles:
   Antiques
   Art
Other major categories: Decorative arts, architecture, scholarly books in history, literature, music and art.
Specialty Categories: Philadelphia, German art of all periods, and Eastern European and Russian art of the 19th and 20th centuries.
Approximate number of volumes: 15,000 out-of-print
Directions: Located four blocks south of Rittenhouse Square; Center City Philadelphia.
Additional information: Founded in 1980. Book searches. May have catalog in future.

The Book Trader
501 South Street
Philadelphia, PA 19147
(215) 925-0219
Hours: 10 to midnight, 365 days.
Owner(s): Peter C. Hiler
Type of Shop: General
Major Categories represented by at least 100 titles:
   ALL CATEGORIES.
Specialty Categories: Fishing, Spanish history, quilting, rare books, Civil War, stamp collecting.

Approximate number of volumes: --
        paperback: 100,000
        hardback : 75,000
Approximate breakdown: rare: 10%
        out-of-print: 70%
        in-print: 30%
Special Items and Services: Cards, posters, prints, CDs, LPs, cassettes.
Additional information: Founded in 1976. Excellent nearby dining. Located on ground level. 4,800 sq. ft. shop area.

Ninth Street Market Books & Records
1022 South 9th Street
Philadelphia, PA 19147
(215) 922-2352
Hours: Tues-Fri:10:30-5:30 Sat:9:30-5:30 Sun:9:30-2:30 Closed Mon.
Owner(s): Robert Dickie and Molly Russakoff
Type of Shop: Used books and records.
Major Categories represented by at least 100 titles:

Antiques	Gardening	Paperback
Art	Geography	Philosophy
Aviation	Health-fitness	Poetry
Business	History	Political Science
Children's	Hobbies & Crafts	Religion
Collectibles	Medicine	Romance
Cooking	Military History	Science Fiction
Do-it-yourself	Music	Science/Technology
Fiction	Mystery	Social Science
Folklore	Mythology	Spectator Sports
	Nature	Travel

Other major categories: Physics, occult, holistic health.
Specialty Categories: Cookbooks, black interest.
Approximate number of volumes: thousands
        paperback: 50%
        hardback : 50%
Approximate breakdown: rare: --
        out-of-print: 90%
        in-print: --
Special Items and Services: Offers great selection of used & rare LPs and 45s. Buys quality used books.
Directions: From I-95: take Washington Ave. exit west, take right onto 9th Street. Store located 1/2 block on the left.
From Rt 76 (Schulkyll Expressway): take Rt 76 to Rt 676, take 8th Street exit, follow 8th Street south to Washington Ave. and take right. Go west on Washington Ave. to 9th Street, make a right - store is one-half block on left.
Additional information: Founded in 1985. Store is located in heart of Philadelphia's historic Italian Market, the country's oldest outdoor market, which offers a unique shopping experience with six blocks of open air fruit and produce stands and great specialty shops. Famous for quality food at unbelievably low prices. Molly and Bob are husband and wife. Molly has a long history with

bookstores, is a writer, and has published poems in various literary magazines. Bob is one of Philadelphia's most prominent record experts, jazz enthusiast, and musician with many record credits. Two steps leading to store.

Abby's Book Case
1915 Susquehanna Road
Abington, PA 19001
(215) 885-2232
Hours: Mon-Thurs:10-8 Fri:10-7 Sat:11-6
Owner(s): Abby Fern Cohen
Major Categories represented by at least 100 titles:

Art	Gardening	Paperback
Business	Health-fitness	Philosophy
Children's	History	Religion
Cooking	Hobbies & Crafts	Romance
Do-it-yourself	Military History	Science Fiction
Fiction	Mystery	Spectator Sports
	Nature	Travel
	Outdoor Recreation	

Approximate number of volumes: 15,000
    paperback: 50%
    hardback : 50%
Approximate breakdown: rare: 1%
    out-of-print: 70%
    in-print: 30%
Special Items and Services: Records, cassettes, CDs. Limited booksearch.
Directions: Just off old York Rd (Route 611). Five minutes from Willow Grove Mall and PA turnpike. Three parking spots in front, additional parking in back, and street parking around corner on Church Rd.
Additional information: Store founded in 1988. Located one-half hour from Center City, Philadelphia. Are "carrying a little of just about everything at very reasonable prices. There is a discount for dealers." 1,200 sq. ft. shop area.

Mystery Books
42 Rittenhouse Place
Ardmore, PA 19003
(215) 642-3565
Hours: Wed-Fri:11-8 Sat:11-5 Sun:11-4
Owner(s): Robert M. Nissenbaum and Norma R. Frank
Type of Shop: Specialty - mystery.
Specialty Categories: Mysteries, detective fiction, espionage, adventure/suspense, and true crime.
Approximate number of volumes: 25,000
Approximate breakdown: rare: 5%
    out-of-print: 15%
    in-print: 80%
Special Items and Services: Mystery games and store-logo t-shirts.

Pennsylvania - Region 1   17

Directions: From PA Turnpike: Take exit 24 (Valley Forge) and continue on I-76 East (Schuylkill Expressway) to first exit, Gulph Mills (also Rt 320), down ramp, exit on right (east). Stay on Rt 320 when it turns right after 1 1/2 miles until it crosses Lancaster Pike (Route 30). Turn left at Route 30. Go 5 miles to Rittenhouse Place and turn right (at Main Line Bank) in town of Ardmore. From US Rt 1: Go south to US Rt 30, Lancaster Ave., turn left, go 2 1/2 miles to Rittenhouse Place (in Ardmore) and turn left at Main Line Bank. Angle parking and numerous public lots in area.
Additional information: Store founded in 1990. Many restaurants in different price ranges and several used and new bookstores in the neighborhood. No steps in or leading to store. 850 sq. ft. shop area.

Paperback Trader
Whitpain Shopping Center, 1502 DeKalb Pike
Blue Bell, PA 19422
(215) 279-8855
Owner(s): Todd P. Ziegler
Type of Shop: Paperback, comics.
Major Categories represented by at least 100 titles:

Children's	History	Romance
Fiction	Mystery	Science Fiction

Other major categories: Thriller, horror, series romance, western.
Approximate breakdown: 100% paperback.
Special Items and Services: New paperbacks discounted. Magazines.
Directions: Located between Germantown Pike & Rt 73 on Rt 202 (DeKalb Pike).
Additional information: Founded in 1978. 900 sq. ft. shop area. One step required.

The Owl Bookshop
801 Yarrow Street
Bryn Mawr, PA 19010
(215) 525-6117
Hours: Tues,Thurs,Fri:1-5 Sat:10-3
Owner(s): Bryn Mawr College Alumnae Association
Type of Shop: General - used, out-of-print, rare.
Major Categories represented by at least 100 titles:

Americana	Gardening	Paperback
Art	History	Philosophy
Children's	Military History	Poetry
Cooking	Music	Rare Books
Fiction	Mystery	Religion
	Nature	Romance
	Nautical	Science Fiction
		Science/Technology
		Social Science
		Travel

Approximate number of volumes: 50,000
  paperback: 20%
  hardback : 80%

18   Pennsylvania - Region 1

Approximate breakdown: rare: 10%
                            out-of-print: --
                            in-print: --
Special Items and Services: Postcards, records and prints. In-shop book searches. Will notify a customer if a wanted book comes in.
Directions: Located on corner of the Bryn Mawr College campus. Call for directions. Free parking on site.
Additional information: Store founded in 1971 and is run by volunteers for the sole benefit of the Bryn Mawr College Regional Scholarship Fund. All books are donated.

Epistemologist, Scholarly Books
P.O. Box 63
Bryn Mawr, PA 19010
(215) 527-1065
Hours: By appointment (call first).
Owner(s): Rob Wozniak
Type of Shop: Specialty antiquarian and used.
Other major categories: Psychology, psychiatry, philosophy and related fields.
Approximate number of volumes: 3,000
                         paperback: --
                         hardback : 100% (except for scholarly monographs in paper)
Approximate breakdown: rare: 2,000
                            out-of-print: 1,000
                            in-print: --
Free catalog issued three times a year.
Special Items and Services: Ephemera having to do with the history of psychology, psychiatry and philosophy. Appraisals (for stated fields only).
Additional information: Founded in 1974. At current location since 1980. Located near Bryn Mawr & Haverford Colleges. Two other used bookstores (Titlepage & Owl), many fine restaurants, about 20 minutes by car from Center City, Philadelphia.

Doe Run Valley Books
640 Baltimore Pike
Chadds Ford, PA 19317
(215) 388-2826
Hours: Thur-Sun:10-5 Mon:by appointment.
Owner(s): Judith Shaw Helms
Type of Shop: General antiquarian
Major Categories represented by at least 100 titles:
    Americana   Military History   Rare Books
    Children's
    Fiction
Other major categories: Sporting, including fishing, hunting, fox hunting.

Approximate number of volumes: 3,000
                paperback: 0%
                hardback : 100%
Approximate breakdown: rare: 50%
                out-of-print: 50%
                in-print: 0%
Special Items and Services: Ephemera. Appraisals.
Directions: West on Route 1 through Chadds Ford approximately 2 miles towards Longwood Gardens. Shop is in small building next to Chadds Ford Winery on south side of Route 1. Plenty of parking.
Additional information: Founded in 1980. Shop is small with a limited stock, but very high in quality. There is something for everyone without a lot of junk to sort through. There is lots to do in a one- to two-mile radius, with other bookstores, museums, restaurants, antiques, etc. Handicap access.

Sottile's Books (located at The Ardmart)
Lansdowne Ave. & State Road
Drexel Hill, PA 19026
(P.O. Box 528, Concordville, PA 19331)
(215) 789-6742
Hours: Thurs-Sun:11-6 Fri:11-9
Owner(s): J. Robert Sottile
Type of Shop: General
Major Categories represented by at least 100 titles:

Americana	History	Paperback
Antiques	Military History	Science Fiction
Art	Music	Spectator Sports
Aviation	Mystery	Travel
Children's	Nature	
Collectibles	Nautical	
Cooking		
Exploration		

Other major categories: Vintage paperback, theatre arts.
Specialty Categories: Local history - Philadelphia, Pennsylvania, New Jersey and Delaware. Children's books. Illustrators (N. C. Wyeth, Howard Pyle, Jessie Willcox Smith, others of the Brandywine School).
Approximate number of volumes: 8,000-10,000
                paperback: --
                hardback : 99%
Approximate breakdown: rare: --
                out-of-print: most
                in-print: --
Special Items and Services: Interesting and unique paper collectibles of most varieties. Appraisals.
Directions: Located less than one mile from U.S. Rt 1. Parking lot. Call for directions.
Additional information: Founded in 1975. Located in a very spacious antique mall housing about 35 dealers. "This location has been compared to some of the London antique malls. Come visit and enjoy." Fine, moderately priced restaurant next door. 650 sq. ft. shop area. Handicap access.

Motorsport Miscellania
913 Jenkintown Road
Elkins Park, PA 19117
(215) 884-8314
Hours: Weekdays:10-6   Sat:10-4
Owner(s): Jim Leary
Type of Shop: Specialty/theme store, automotive related.
Specialty Categories: Automotive - history, biography, photo, out-of-print, back date magazines.
Approximate number of volumes: 2,500
> paperback: 30%
> hardback : 70%

Approximate breakdown: rare: --
> out-of-print: 20%
> in-print: 80%

Special Items and Services: Collectible models, automobilia, cards, posters. Book searches, want lists, book/model (automotive) collections bought.
Directions: Located one block north of Pa. Rt 73, two miles west of Philadelphia. Parking in adjacent lot.
Additional information: Founded in 1983. Motorsport Miscellania is one of a very few stores in the country devoted solely to automotive books, hobbies and collectibles. Four steep steps required into store. 350 sq. ft. shop area.

Chester Valley Old Books
489 Lancaster Avenue (Box 1228)
Frazer, PA 19355
(215) 251-9500
Hours: Tues,Thur,Sat:10-5 Wed,Fri:10-8 Sunday & Holidays:12-5 Closed Mon.
Owner(s): Alicia W. Goodolf
Type of Shop: General
Major Categories represented by at least 100 titles:

Americana	Gardening	Paperback
Children's	Health-fitness	Philosophy
Cooking	Military History	Poetry
Do-it-yourself	Music	Religion
	Nature	Science Fiction
	Nautical	

Approximate number of volumes: 65,000
> paperback: 30%
> hardback : 70%

Approximate breakdown: rare: very few
> out-of-print: mostly
> in-print: good number

Special Items and Services: Will call people when wanted books are found, but no active advertising.
Directions: Located on the north side of Route 30, west of Route 401 and east of Route 202. This is located north of West Chester. Parking in front, back or across street.

Additional information: Founded in 1986. Original store (Gwynedd Valley Bookstore) was founded in 1964 and was located in Gwynedd Valley, Montgomery Co., PA. Books on two floors. There are also nearly a dozen good used bookstores 15 to 20 minutes away.

Jean's Books
Box 264
Hatfield, PA 19440
(215) 362-0732
Owner(s): Jean Kulp
Type of Shop: Specialty, antiquarian.
Major Categories represented by at least 100 titles:
```
Americana         History            Rare Books
Children's        Medicine
Cooking           Military History
```
Specialty Categories: 18th & 19th century Americana, manuscripts, account books & diaries.
Approximate number of volumes: 10,000
Approximate breakdown: rare: 35%
out-of-print: 100%
in-print: --
Special Items and Services: Posters, prints, broadsides. Appraisals and book searches.
Additional information: Founded in 1975. Please call for directions.

Thomas Macaluso Rare and Fine Books
130 South Union Street
Kennett Square, PA 19348
(215) 444-1063
Hours: Tues-Fri:1-5 Sat:11-5
Owner(s): Thomas and Brenda Macaluso
Professional Affiliations: Penn. Country Antiquarian Booksellers Association.
Type of Shop: General antiquarian.
Major Categories represented by at least 100 titles:
```
Americana         Gardening          Philosophy
Antiques          History            Poetry
Art               Medicine           Rare Books
Children's        Military History   Religion
Collectibles      Nature             Science/Technology
Cooking           Nautical           Social Science
Exploration                          Travel
Fiction
```
Other major categories: Illustrated books.
Specialty Categories: Illustrated and children's books, arts, literature, Americana.
Approximate number of volumes: 16,000
paperback: --
hardback: 100%

Approximate breakdown: rare: 75%
                        out-of-print: 25%
                        in-print: --

Free catalog issued roughly twice per year.
Special Items and Services: Many old prints and maps. Engravings, lithographs, occasional manuscripts, autographs, photographs. Appraisals and searches.
Directions: From Rt 1 take Rt 82 (Union Street) south into Kennett Square. Located at second traffic light (Cypress St.). Free parking behind store and in public lot across street.
Additional information: Founded in 1975. "A charming, clean, well-lit, and well-organized shop. All stock has been carefully selected and categorized." Two fine restaurants and a luncheonette within walking distance. Located one mile from Longwood Gardens. Near Winterthur, Hagley and Brandywine museums. Two good used book stores within a few miles. 1,500 sq. ft. shop area.

William Hutchison
P.O. Box 909
Mendenhall, PA 19357
(215) 388-0195
Hours: Most weekends (soon to have regular hours).
Owner(s): Bill Hutchison
Type of Shop: General antiquarian.
Major Categories represented by at least 100 titles:

Americana	Gardening	Philosophy
Antiques	History	Rare Books
Art	Nature	Travel
Children's	Nautical	
Cooking	Outdoor Recreation	
Exploration		
Fiction		

Specialty Categories: Americana, architecture, decorative arts, sporting, literature, fishing, mountain climbing, Civil War, rare books.
Approximate number of volumes: --
            paperback: 0
            hardback : 7,000
Approximate breakdown: rare: 35%
                            out-of-print: 65%
                            in-print: --
Special Items and Services: Prints. Appraisals.
Directions: Route 52, two miles south of US Rt 1, 12 miles north of I-95. Next to railroad.
Additional information: Founded in 1988. Longwood Gardens, Winterthur Museum, Brandywine River Museum, and good dining nearby. 1,000 sq. ft. shop area.

Bridge Street Old Books
129 West Bridge Street
New Hope, PA 18938
(215) 862-0615
Hours: Sat-Sun:11-6 & by appointment.
Owner(s): Diane & Merritt Whitman
Type of Shop: General antiquarian.
Major Categories represented by at least 100 titles:

Americana	Gardening	Philosophy
Antiques	Geography	Poetry
Art	History	Political Science
Aviation	Hobbies & Crafts	Rare Books
Business	Medicine	Religion
Children's	Military History	Romance
Collectibles	Music	Science Fiction
Cooking	Mystery	Science/Technology
Exploration	Mythology	Social Science
Fiction	Nature	Spectator Sports
Folklore	Nautical	Travel
	Outdoor Recreation	

Other major categories: Local history: Bucks County PA, Philadelphia.
Specialty Categories: Fishing and Civil War.
Approximate number of volumes: 7,000
   paperback: --
   hardback : 7,000
Approximate breakdown: rare: 5%
   out-of-print: 95%
   in-print: 0%
Special Items and Services: Prints and maps. Appraisals.
Directions: Located on Route 179 (old 202) across from the high school outside the main business district in New Hope. Route 179 is one of two main streets in New Hope. Small lot for parking and additional parking across the street.
Additional information: Founded in 1985 and is the owners' fourth bookstore. Previously owned Footnote in Lahaska, PA. The current location is in a picturesque area on the Delaware River. The area is known for its antiques and art galleries. There are many quaint bed & breakfasts, fine restaurants and old fashioned barge and train rides. Five minutes from Peddler's Village and Bucks County Winery. 700 sq. ft. shop area. There is another used bookstore three minutes away.

Newtown Book & Record Exchange
102 S. State Street
Newtown, PA 18940
(215) 968-4914
Hours: Mon-Sat:10-6   Fri:10-8   Sun (in December):12-4
Owner(s): Barbara W. Lewis
Type of Shop: Paperback exchange.

24   Pennsylvania - Region 1

Major Categories represented by at least 100 titles:
Business	Gardening	Paperback
Children's	History	Philosophy
Cooking	Medicine	Poetry
Education	Mystery	Political Science
Fiction		Religion
		Romance
		Science Fiction

Approximate number of volumes: 28,000-30,000
        paperback: 99.9%
        hardback : --
Special Items and Services: Used records, new and used tapes and CDs.
Directions: Exit from I-95 onto Penn. Rt 332 west. Approximately two miles to center of Newtown. State Street is the main street in town.
Additional information: Founded in 1981. Located in historic Colonial Newtown. 2 steps required with handrail (no ramp). 1,500 sq. ft. shop area

---

S & C Najarian
852 Milmar Road
Newtown Square, PA 19073
(215) 353-5165
Hours: By appointment only.
Owner(s): Steve & Chris Najarian
Type of Shop: General and antiquarian.
Major Categories represented by at least 100 titles:
Americana	Music	Rare Books

Specialty Categories: 19th century sheet music.
Additional information: Founded in 1973. Good dining and museums nearby. Offers prints. Call for directions.

The Bookworm
510 Chester Pike
Norwood, PA 19074
(215) 534-2446
Hours: Mon,Wed,Thur,Sat:10-4   Tues,Fri:1-4   Mon,Thur evenings:6:30-8:30
Type of Shop: Paperback
Major Categories represented by at least 100 titles:
Children's	Mystery	Paperback
Fiction		Romance
		Science Fiction

Other major categories: Current popular fiction.
Approximate number of volumes: 20,000+
        paperback: 99%
        hardback : 1%
Approximate breakdown: rare: --
              out-of-print: 30%
                in-print: 70%

Special Items and Services: Book searches.
Directions: Store is located on US Route 13 off I-95 in Delaware County (near the Philadelphia airport). Free on-street parking.
Additional information: Store founded in 1968. Atmosphere with "good vibrations." 800 sq. ft. shop area.

The Americanist
1525 Shenkel Road
Pottstown, PA 19464
(215) 323-5289
Hours: April-December:Mon-Sat:9:30-5:30   January-March: By appointment.
Owner(s): Michal Kane and Norman Kane
Professional Affiliations: A.B.A.A.
Type of Shop: General & antiquarian second-hand stock.
Other major categories: Carries a "good size stock in a good size area." Owners generally do not carry new books or paperbacks at this time.
Catalog issued sporadically.
Special Items and Services: Appraisals. Book auctions (Kane Antiquarian Auction).
Directions: A rural bookstore about two miles from Pottstown in northern Chester County. Call for directions.
Additional information: Founded in the 1950s, and at present location for past 30 years. Located near French Creek State Park and Hopewell Village. Hopewell Village is a "Federal reconstruction of an iron-working village." Lots to do and see.

S. F. Collins' Bookcellar
266 Concord Drive
Pottstown, PA 19464
(215) 323-2495
Hours: Mail order and appointment only.
Owner(s): Suzanne F. Collins
Professional Affiliations: Wizard of Oz Club, LCSNA, Bibliophiles Society
Major Categories represented by at least 100 titles:
   Children's   Mythology   Rare Books
Other major categories: Illustrated and fine press.
Specialty Categories: L. F. Baum, Arthur Rackham, Peter Newell, etc., including most illustrators of the 19th & 20th centuries.
Approximate number of volumes: 300
            paperback: --
            hardback : all
Approximate breakdown: rare: 80%
            out-of-print: 20%
            in-print: --
Catalog may be available in future.
Additional information: Founded in 1979.

The Book Place
Rt 73 & Rt 113 (P.O. Box 236)
Skippack, PA 19474
(215) 584-6966
Hours: Tues-Sun: 11-5
Owner(s): Bannie M. Stewart and Lane Rogers
Type of Shop: General stock including paperback.
Major Categories represented by at least 100 titles:

Art	Gardening	Paperback
Children's	Geography	Poetry
Cooking	History	Political Science
Do-it-yourself	Hobbies & Crafts	Religion
Fiction	Military History	Science Fiction
	Music	Science/Technology
	Mystery	Social Science
	Nature	

Approximate number of volumes: --
    paperback: 10,000
    hardback: 10,000
Special Items and Services: Prints, old ads, a few magazines, booklets.
Directions: Rts 113 & 73 - southwest corner. Great parking, access from both routes.
Additional information: Store founded in 1984. Good dining, many antique and craft stores nearby. 1,500 sq. ft. shop area.

Indian Path Books
Route 23 & Bethel Church Road
Spring City, PA 19475
(215) 495-3001
Hours: Mon-Sat:9-9 Sun:9-5
Owner(s): Joyce Watson and William Hornikel
Type of Shop: General
Major Categories represented by at least 100 titles:

Americana	Gardening	Paperback
Antiques	History	Philosophy
Art	Hobbies & Crafts	Poetry
Aviation	Military History	Religion
Business	Music	Romance
Children's	Mystery	Science Fiction
Collectibles	Mythology	Science/Technology
Cooking	Nature	Travel
Do-it-yourself	Nautical	
Exploration	Outdoor Recreation	
Fiction		
Folklore		

Approximate number of volumes: --
    paperback: 5,000
    hardback: 10,000
Approximate breakdown: rare: 3%
    out-of-print: 47%
    in-print: 50%

Pennsylvania - Region 1   27

Directions: Located 15 miles west of Valley Forge Park.
Additional information: Founded in 1990. Handicap access. 1,500 sq. ft. shop area.

BOOKSOURCE, LTD
15 S. Chester Road (P.O. Box 43)
Swarthmore, PA 19081
(215) 328-5083   FAX (215) 328-6875
Hours: Mon-Sat: 10-5
Owner(s): Patrick & Constance Flanigan
Type of Shop: General, out-of-print, scholarly.
Major Categories represented by at least 100 titles:

Americana	Gardening	Philosophy
Antiques	Geography	Poetry
Art	Health-fitness	Political Science
Aviation	History	Religion
Business	Hobbies & Crafts	Science Fiction
Children's	Medicine	Science/Technology
Collectibles	Military History	Social Science
Cooking	Music	Travel
Education	Mystery	
Fiction	Nature	
	Nautical	

Other major categories: Pennsylvania & local history, maps.
Approximate number of volumes: 15,000
    paperback: 0%
    hardback : 100%
Approximate breakdown: rare: 5%
    out-of-print: 85%
    in-print: 10%
Free catalog 2-3 times a year, plus special lists.
Special Items and Services: Out-of-print search service.
Directions: Center of Swarthmore, near college.
Additional information: Store founded in 1975. 1,500 sq. ft. shop area. Handicap access.

Volume Control
955 Sandy Lane
Warminster, PA 18974
(215) 674-0217
Owner(s): Jack Hatter
Type of Shop: Mail order only - World War II exclusively.
Approximate number of volumes: 4,000
    paperback: 5%
    hardback : 95%
Approximate breakdown: rare: 2%
    out-of-print: 63%
    in-print: 35% (new books & used)

28   Pennsylvania - Region 1

Catalog issued six times per year at $4.
Additional information: Founded in 1984. Free book searches.

Beattie Books
105 West Wayne Avenue
Wayne, PA 19087
(215) 687-3347
Hours: By appointment.
Owner(s): Jim Beattie
Type of Shop: Antiquarian
Major Categories represented by at least 100 titles:

Gardening	Rare Books
Medicine	Travel

Other major categories: Architecture, archeology, fine bindings.
Specialty Categories: Architecture.
Approximate number of volumes: 2,200
        paperback: --
        hardback : 2,200
Approximate breakdown: rare: 80%
        out-of-print: 20%
        in-print: --
Catalog issued monthly at $2.
Special Items and Services: Prints. Appraisals, book searches.
Directions: From Rt 30, go north on Wayne Avenue. Parking lot on right, shop on second floor.
Additional information: Founded in 1989. Hours by chance or by appointment. Other used book stores, good dining and museums nearby. 700 sq. ft. shop area.

Konigsmark Books
309 Midland Avenue, Box 543
Wayne, PA 19087-0543
(215) 687-5965
Hours: By appointment only.
Owner(s): Jocelyn Konigsmark
Type of Shop: General antiquarian and out-of-print.
Major Categories represented by at least 100 titles:

Americana	History	Philosophy
Art	Music	Poetry
Children's	Nature	Religion
Collectibles		Travel
Fiction		

Other major categories: Literature: first & fine editions. Illustrated books, fine bindings, 19th century publication bindings, fine printing, university press books.
Approximate number of volumes: --
        paperback: --
        hardback : 15,000

Approximate breakdown: rare: 10%
out-of-print: 90%
in-print: --
Special Items and Services: Appraisals and book searches.
Directions: One block south of Rt 30. From Lancaster Avenue (Rt 30), turn south on Aberdeen, at first street - Midland Avenue - turn left. House is second one on left. Located about four blocks from Rts 476 & 30. (Rt 476 goes from Penn. Turnpike to I-95.)
Additional information: Founded in 1980. "Miniscule" bed & breakfast (one room and bath) for book people only. Located two blocks from commuter train to Philadelphia. Near many restaurants, shopping, movies, etc. Books stored in two large rooms in house and barn in back.

Maiden Voyage Rare Books
120 East Virginia Avenue
West Chester, PA 19380
(215) 430-0529
Hours: By phone only.
Owner(s): Rick Robotham
Type of Shop: Rare books - first editions.
Major Categories represented by at least 100 titles:
```
Collectibles                    Rare Books
Fiction
```
Specialty Categories: Specialty in making up/building up/assembling first edition & rare book collections. Highlight collection of 20th century books, mostly signed and inscribed by authors.
Approximate number of volumes: 5,000
paperback: --
hardback : 100%
Approximate breakdown: rare: 100%
out-of-print: --
in-print: --
Catalog issued from 2 to 4 times per year at $3 to $5.
Additional information: Founded in 1976 (originally in New York City). Call for directions. Appraisals. Collections assembled.

Elizabeth L. Matlat - Antiques
Rt 202, Brandywine Summit Center (P.O. Box 3511)
West Chester, PA 19381
(215) 358-0359
Hours: Mon-Sat:9-5
Owner(s): Elizabeth L. Matlat
Type of Shop: Antiquarian
Major Categories represented by at least 100 titles:
```
Americana          History
Antiques
```
Other major categories: In- and out-of-print publications on antiques & architecture.

Approximate number of volumes: --
        paperback: --
        hardback : 1,500-2,000
Special Items and Services: 19th century maps of Chester County, Pa.
Directions: Six miles south of West Chester, Pa. Two miles east of Chadds Ford, Pa. Five miles north of Wilmington, Del.
Additional information: Founded in 1968. Brandywine River Museum and Winterthur Museum in close proximity.

David C. Lachman
127 Woodland Road
Wyncote, PA 19095
(215) 887-0228
Hours: By appointment.
Owner(s): David C. Lachman
Type of Shop: Specialty - antiquarian and second-hand theology, Bibles.
Specialty Categories: Rare & valuable Bibles and theology.
Approximate number of volumes: 5,000-8,000
        paperback: --
        hardback : 99+%
Approximate breakdown: rare: 50%
        out-of-print: 50%
        in-print: --
Free catalog issued 5 to 6 times per year to purchasing customers.
Special Items and Services: Offers related items. Appraisals and searches.
Additional information: Founded in 1979. Call for directions. Business is primarily mail order from owner's home. Customers are welcome to view stock, both secondhand and antiquarian, by appointment only. Owner specializes in Protestant Christian theology (primarily Reformed), particularly books printed before 1700, and always has a substantial stock of old Bibles.

Book Bargains
14 North 8th Street
Allentown, PA 18101
(215) 439-1552
Hours: Mon-Sat:9:30-5
Owner(s): Les & George Barley
Type of Shop: General, paperback, comics.
Major Categories represented by at least 100 titles:

Americana	Gardening	Paperback
Antiques	Health-fitness	Romance
Art	History	Science Fiction
Aviation	Hobbies & Crafts	Spectator Sports
Collectibles	Medicine	Travel
Cooking	Military History	
Do-it-yourself	Mystery	
Fiction	Mythology	
Folklore	Nature	

Other major categories: Back-date magazines.
Approximate number of volumes: --
    paperback: 50%
    hardback : 50%
Approximate breakdown: rare: --
    out-of-print: 50%
    in-print: 50%
Directions: Located 200 feet north of Main Street (Hamilton Mall), old movie house.
Additional information: Founded in 1977. Offers records (45s and LPs). Street-level access. 1,600 sq. ft. shop area.

Cap's Comic Cavalcade
1980 Catasauqua Road
Allentown, PA 18103
(215) 264-5540
Hours: Mon-Thurs:11-8 Fri:9-9 Sat:10-6 Sun:12-5
Owner(s): Dan Walter
Type of Shop: Comic (80% out-of-print).
Major Categories represented by at least 100 titles:
    Collectibles   Hobbies & Crafts   Science Fiction
Additional information: Founded in 1981. Located at intersection of US 22 & Airport Road, one block from ABE International Airport. Handicap access. 1,500 sq. ft. shop area.

Back Room Books
2 South Bridge Street
Christiana, PA 17509
(215) 593-7021
Hours: By chance or appointment. Usually open Sat:9-5, Sun:9-2. Call in advance.
Owner(s): Charles & Michele Bender
Type of Shop: Specializing in books on 17th, 18th & early 19th century American decorative arts.
Major Categories represented by at least 100 titles:
    Antiques
    Art
Approximate number of volumes: 5,000
Approximate breakdown: rare: 10%
    out-of-print: 80%
    in-print: 10%
Free catalog available.
Special Items and Services: Book searches, appraisals, library development.
Additional information: Founded in 1987. Located in Pennsylvania Dutch country, only 20 minutes from Lancaster. Call ahead for directions. 1,000 sq. ft. shop area.

Antonio Raimo Fine Books
401 Chestnut Street
Columbia, PA 17512
(717) 684-4111
Hours: Mon-Fri:9-5 Other times by appointment.
Owner(s): Antonio Raimo
Professional Affiliations: A.B.A.A., American Association of the History of Dentistry.
Type of Shop: Antiquarian
Major Categories represented by at least 100 titles:
```
Children's       Medicine           Rare Books
                 Nature             Science Fiction
                                    Social Science
```
Specialty Categories: Dentistry, fore-edge paintings, leather-bound sets.
Approximate number of volumes: --
        paperback: --
        hardback : 10,000
Approximate breakdown: rare: 10,000
        out-of-print: --
        in-print: --
Catalog issued quarterly at $1.
Directions: Located between York and Lancaster, PA, just off Rt 30.
Additional information: Founded in 1989. Located in a restored Victorian mansion decorated with period brass chandeliers, rare book cases and statuary, furniture and rugs. National Clock Museum around corner, fine dining and excellent B&B across the street. Handicap access. 5,000 sq. ft. shop area.

RAC Books in Partners' Antique Center
403 North Third Street
Columbia, PA 17512
(717) 684-5364
Hours: Open seven days 10-5
Owner(s): Anne P. Muren and Robin L. Smith
Type of Shop: General
Major Categories represented by at least 100 titles:
```
Children's       Military History    Paperback
Cooking          Mystery
Fiction
```
Other major categories: Biography
Approximate number of volumes: 1,800
        paperback: 20%
        hardback : 80%
Approximate breakdown: rare: --
        out-of-print: 90%
        in-print: 10%
Special Items and Services: Sheet music, cookbook pamphlets. Store also stocks new reference books on antiques and collectibles as well as used books. Book searches, including reading copies and paperbacks.

Directions: Penn. Rt 30 to Columbia/Marietta exit, turn right at stop sign, turn left at next stop sign to go south on Rt 441 (N. Third Street). Shop is one block on left in an old pretzel factory. Free parking on street.
Additional information: Columbia location founded in 1990. Located in historic Lancaster County within view of the Susquehanna River and is an easy commute from or to Amish country. Mall houses 20+ antique dealers with a book room. Other dealers also carry some books. Antonio Raimo Books located two blocks away. Columbia Clock and Watch Museum, Susquehanna Glass Company, and many antique shops in area. Map is available at Partners' Antiques. Book fair in Lancaster in June of each year. 200 sq. ft. shop area. Two steps into building. Owners have books on display at two other antique/book malls in York, Pa., as well as selling by mail order (direct mail to Box 296, RD #2, Seven Valleys, PA 17360).

Quadrant Book Mart
20 North Third Street
Easton, PA 18042
(215) 252-1188
Hours: Mon-Sat:9:30-5:30 Fri:9:30-8
Owner(s): Richard & Barbara Epstein
Type of Shop: General stock of out-of-print books.
Major Categories represented by at least 100 titles:

Americana	Gardening	Paperback
Art	Geography	Philosophy
Aviation	Health-fitness	Poetry
Children's	History	Political Science
Collectibles	Medicine	Rare Books
Cooking	Military History	Religion
Exploration	Music	Science/Technology
Fiction	Mystery	Social Science
Folklore	Mythology	Spectator Sports
	Nature	Travel
	Nautical	
	Outdoor Recreation	

Other major categories: Local history & literature.
Specialty Categories: Pennsylvania.
Approximate number of volumes: --
     paperback: 3,000
     hardback : 50,000
Approximate breakdown: rare: 20%
          out-of-print: 80%
          in-print: --
Special Items and Services: Appraisals & searches.
Directions: Off Center Square in heart of downtown Easton (2 blocks from Delaware River and the New Jersey border). Parking on street and in private lot behind buildings.
Additional information: Founded in 1977. Restaurants nearby. Canal Museum also nearby and about one mile from Larry Holmes' training camp. 4,000 sq. ft. shop area. Three steps from sidewalk to front door.

Clay Book Store
2450 West Main Street
Ephrata, PA 17522-9731
(717) 733-7253
Hours: Mon,Tues,Thurs,Fri:8-9 Wed,Sat:8-5
Type of Shop: New & used books; large selection of new maps.
Major Categories represented by at least 100 titles:

```
Children's        Gardening           Paperback
Cooking           Geography           Poetry
Education         Health-fitness      Religion
Fiction           History
                  Music
                  Nature
                  Outdoor Recreation
```
Approximate number of volumes: (used)
        paperback: 10,000
        hardback : 50,000
Directions: In the village of Clay between Ephrata and Brickerville.
Additional information: Present location since 1980. 1,500 sq. ft. shop area for used and new books. Handicap access. Family-owned business. "Largest used book store in the area."

The Bookworm Bookstore (two locations)
Box 1341
Harrisburg, PA 17105
(717) 657-8563
Owner(s): Samuel G. Marcus
<u>East Shore Location</u>
Colonial Park Markets
5101 Jonestown Road (Rt 22)
Hours: Thurs:9-8 Sat:9-4
<u>West Shore Location</u>
Carter's Silver Spring Market
6416 Carlisle Pike (Rt 11)
Hours: Sundays only:8-3
Type of Shop: General, which includes only antiquarian, out-of-print, paperbacks, maps & prints.
Major Categories represented by at least 100 titles:
ALL CATEGORIES.
Other major categories: Maps & prints, occult/mysticism, western, Indian, black history, Judaica, feminist, true crime, Pennsylvania, sets, hunting/fishing.
Specialty Categories: Good-quality literature, civil and military history, religion, science fiction, children's, low-priced good paperbacks.
Approximate number of volumes: East Shore ---- West Shore
        paperback: 12,000 ---- 30,000
        hardback :   3,000 ---- 20,000
Approximate breakdown: rare: 10% (breakdown is for hardbacks only)
        out-of-print: 90%
        in-print: very few hardbacks.

Pennsylvania - Region 2   35

Special Items and Services: Prints, maps and total selection of National Geographics & related items. Book searches, bookbinding, investment counseling, appraisals, paperback trading, 24-hour phone service. Takes part in six shows a year.
Additional information: West shore store founded in 1980 and east shore store founded in 1991. Both shops are located in antique/farmers/flea/craft markets. Both locations offer ample parking and are easily accessible for the handicapped. 2,200 sq. ft. shop area (west shore) and 400 sq. ft. shop area (east shore).

Paperback Exchange
3988 Jonestown Road
Harrisburg, PA 17109
(717) 545-6199
Hours: Mon,Wed,Thurs,Fri:10-5:30   Tues:10-7   Sat:10-4
Owner(s): Kathleen Graham
Type of Shop: Paperback (95%) and comics (5%)
Major Categories represented by at least 100 titles:

Children's	Mystery	Paperback
Fiction		Romance
		Science Fiction

Other major categories: Many of the major categories not shown above are represented by less than 100 books.
Approximate number of volumes: 60,000
   paperback: 100%
   hardback : --
Approximate breakdown: rare: --
   out-of-print: 40%
   in-print: 60%
Special Items and Services: New children's books discounted 20%. Keeps a special request list and will call customer if/when book comes in.
Directions: I-83 north to exit 30W (Progress), turn right, go 2 blocks, store located on right in plaza.
Additional information: Founded in 1983. Gives 1/4 cover price for trade-ins if in good condition and if needed by store. Books in store are all half-price. Also has rack of new books (latest best sellers) discounted 20%. 1,200 sq. ft. shop area. Owner operates another store in Lemoyne, Pa.

R. F. Selgas, Sporting Books
P.O. Box 227
Hershey, PA 17033
(717) 534-1868
Hours: 9-5
Owner(s): R. F. Selgas
Type of Shop: Mail order only - out-of-print angling.
Specialty Categories: Fresh and salt water angling - fly fishing only - and trout.
Special Items and Services: Angling prints. Appraisals and searches within specialty.

Rebecca of Sunnybook Farm
P.O. Box 209
Hershey, PA 17033
(717) 533-3039
Hours: By appointment.
Owner(s): Rebecca Greason
Type of Shop: Specialty - 20th century children's books, Golden Books.
Specialty Categories: Golden Books of all series, but especially Little Golden Books; pop-ups, mechanicals, Christmas books, illustrated books.
Approximate number of volumes: 4,000
        paperback: --
        hardback : 100%
Approximate breakdown: rare: 10%
        out-of-print: 85%
        in-print: 5%
Special Items and Services: *Tomart's Illustrated Guide to Golden Book Collectibles* - "a comprehensive coverage of nearly 5 decades of Golden Books", by Rebecca Greason, fully illustrated, 240 pgs., 8 1/2 x 11 inches.
Directions: Pa. Rt 743, 4 miles north of Hershey. Number 379 on mailbox, house on left. Or, 3 miles south of exit 28 off I-81. Residential parking. Please call in advance.
Additional information: Founded in 1982. Chocolate Town, USA! Five antique malls and many shops within 5 miles.

The Used Book Store
474 West Main Street
Kutztown, PA 19530
(215) 683-9055
Hours: Tues,Wed,Fri:2-6 Sat:10-5
Owner(s): James H. Tinsman
Type of Shop: General used books (hardcover/paper)
Major Categories represented by at least 100 titles:

Art	Gardening	Paperback
Business	Health-fitness	Philosophy
Children's	History	Poetry
Cooking	Hobbies & Crafts	Political Science
Education	Military History	Religion
Exploration	Mystery	Romance
Fiction	Nature	Science Fiction
		Science/Technology
		Social Science
		Travel

Other major categories: Biography, western, horror.
Specialty Categories: Detective mystery, science fiction/fantasy.
Approximate number of volumes: 50,000
        paperback: 60%
        hardback : 40%
Directions: Next to Kutztown University, top of hill on Main Street (south side, west end of town). Park on street or go around to alley, parking lot.
Additional information: Founded in 1979. Handicap access by rear of building. 1,200 sq. ft. shop area.

Pennsylvania - Region 2   37

The Book Haven
146 North Prince Street
Lancaster, PA 17603
(717) 393-0920
Hours: Mon-Fri:10-5   Fri eve:6-9   Sat:10-4
Owner(s): Kinsey Baker
Type of Shop: General antiquarian.
Major Categories represented by at least 100 titles:
    ALL CATEGORIES.
Specialty Categories: Civil War, Pennsylvania imprints, illustrated books, Pennsylvania and local history, Pennsylvania Dutch/German/Amish.
Approximate number of volumes: 75,000
    paperback: 1%
    hardback : 99%
Approximate breakdown: rare: --
    out-of-print: (including rare) 80%
    in-print: 20%
Special Items and Services: Prints, posters, maps, postcards, ephemera. Appraisals and book searches.
Directions: From Rt 30, take Fruitville Pike exit, go south. Fruitville Pike is Prince Street. Located approx. 8 blocks south on right side.
Additional information: Founded in 1978. Other used book stores, good dining nearby. 2,000 sq. ft. shop area.

Book Bin Bookstore
14 West Orange Street
Lancaster, PA 17603
(717) 392-6434
Hours: Mon-Thur & Sat:10-6   Fri:10-9   Sun:12-5
Owner(s): Jane Shull
Type of Shop: General
Major Categories represented by at least 100 titles:

Art	Gardening	Paperback
Cooking	History	Poetry
Fiction	Military History	Religion
	Music	Science Fiction
	Mystery	Social Science
		Travel

Specialty Categories: Foreign language and natural history.
Approximate number of volumes: 25,000
    paperback: 50%
    hardback : 50%
Approximate breakdown: rare: 10%
    out-of-print: 40%
    in-print: 50%
Special Items and Services: Valentines, trade cards, postcards, advertising catalogs. Book searches.

Directions: Rt 30 to Fruitville Pike exit, south into town on Prince Street. Park in garage at Prince and Orange Streets, or lots entered from Prince past Orange or entered from King Street 1/2 block east of Prince. Walk east on Orange 1/2 block.
Additional information: Founded in 1988. Two other used book stores within one block. Farmer's market, specialty shops, several restaurants, visitor's center and museum within easy walking distance. Handicap access with "curbing" accessible at corner. 1,600 sq. ft. shop area.

Chestnut Street Books
11 West Chestnut Street
Lancaster, PA 17603
(717) 393-3773
Hours: Mon-Sat:10-6   Fri:10-8
Owner(s): Warren Anderson
Type of Shop: General
Major Categories represented by at least 100 titles:

Business	History	Paperback
Children's	Military History	Philosophy
Cooking	Music	Poetry
Fiction	Mystery	Religion
	Nautical	Science Fiction

Specialty Categories: Baseball.
Approximate number of volumes: --
    paperback: 4,000
    hardback : 13,000
Approximate breakdown: rare: 1%
        out-of-print: 85%
        in-print: 14%
Catalog issued 4 to 5 times per year at $2.
Directions: Downtown Lancaster, curb parking in front of store.
Additional information: Founded in 1991. Book searches offered. Two other used book stores within one block. Located two blocks from Lancaster's famous Central Market. 1,700 sq. ft. shop area.

Johnson & Roth Used Books
121 East Cumberland Street
Lebanon, PA 17042
(717) 272-2511
Hours: Daily:10-5   Fri:until 9   Other hours by appointment. Closed Sundays.
Owner(s): James F. Johnson
Type of Shop: General
Major Categories represented by at least 100 titles:

Americana	Health-fitness	Paperback
Art	History	Philosophy
Business	Military History	Religion
Children's	Music	Science/Technology
Cooking	Nature	Social Science
Fiction	Nautical	Spectator Sports
		Travel

Pennsylvania - Region 2   39

Other major categories: Offers a large selection of occult/metaphysics, moderate selection of hunting and fishing.
Approximate number of volumes: 20,000
        paperback: 15%
        hardback : 85%
Approximate breakdown: rare: 10%
        out-of-print: 90%
        in-print: --
Free catalog issued at irregular intervals.
Special Items and Services: Appraisals.
Directions: Located on US 422. Unmetered parking in front and private parking on the side.
Additional information: Founded in 1980. Good restaurant 1/2 block away. Three steps leading into store that can be managed in wheelchair. Call ahead to arrange assistance. 800 sq. ft. shop area.

Antiquarian Map & Book Den
217 East New Street
Lititz, PA 17543
(717) 626-5002
Hours: By appointment.
Owner(s): James E. Hess
Type of Shop: Antiquarian
Major Categories represented by at least 100 titles:
    Americana   Religion
    Exploration
Specialty Categories: Cartography.
Catalog issued annually at $2.
Special Items and Services: Rare maps. Map and book searches.
Additional information: Founded in 1986.

Charles Agvent
RD 2, Box 377A
Mertztown, PA 19539
(215) 682-4750
Hours: By appointment.
Owner(s): Charles Agvent
Type of Shop: Antiquarian
Major Categories represented by at least 100 titles:
    Americana   Poetry
    Fiction   Rare Books
Specialty Categories: Autographed books, Mark Twain, modern & 19th century first editions.
Approximate number of volumes: 4,000
        paperback: --
        hardback : 100%

Approximate breakdown: rare: 80%
out-of-print: 20%
in-print: --

Catalog issued twice per year at $3.
Special Items and Services: Photographs. Appraisals, book searches, collection development.
Additional information: Located in Pennsylvania Dutch country with fine dining, many antique shops, a few museums, and other attractions in the area. Handicap access.

Mosher Books™

P.O. Box 111
Millersville, PA 17551-0111
(717) 872-9209
Hours: By appointment.
Owner(s): Philip R. Bishop
Professional Affiliations: Delaware Bibliophiles.
Type of Shop: Select antiquarian books, fine bindings, private press and fine printing.
Major Categories represented by at least 100 titles:

Americana	Military History	Philosophy
Children's		Poetry
		Rare Books
		Travel

Other major categories: Literature and books about books.
Specialty Categories: Rare books (16th - early 19th century), Mosher Books, and books from important personal libraries (Hoe, Poor, etc.).
Approximate number of volumes: 500-1,000
Approximate breakdown: rare: 100%
out-of-print: --
in-print: --

Lists available. Ads run in AB Weekly 5-10 times per year. Catalog available in future.
Special Items and Services: Co-author of "Thomas Bird Mosher and the Art of the Book", a catalogue of a centennial exhibition of Mosher's work.
Additional information: Founded in 1991. Located 3 miles from Lancaster, PA.

Walter Amos, Bookseller

The Market Place, Rts 10 & 23 (RD 1, Box 205)
Morgantown, PA 19543
(215) 286-0510
Hours: Mon-Sat:10-5
Owner(s): Walter L. Amos, Jr.
Type of Shop: General
Major Categories represented by at least 100 titles:

Americana	Geography	Paperback
Antiques	Medicine	Religion
Business	Mystery	Science Fiction
Cooking		Science/Technology
		Spectator Sports

Approximate number of volumes: 65,000
paperback: 15%
hardback : 85%
Approximate breakdown: rare: 1%
out-of-print: 60%
in-print: 39%
Directions: Penn. turnpike exit 22, south on Rt 10 to Rt 23, west on Rts 10 & 23 to Market Place on left. Plenty of free parking.
Additional information: Founded in 1980. Aisles wide enough for wheel chairs; however, recommend days other than Friday and Saturday due to heavy patronage. 3,000 sq. ft. shop area.

CML Books
Rts 23 & 10 South at the Market Place
Morgantown, PA 19543
(215) 286-7297
Hours: Mon,Wed,Thurs:10-5 Fri:10-7 Sat:10-6 Sun:11-3
Owner(s): Carolanne Lulves
Type of Shop: General
Major Categories represented by at least 100 titles:

Fiction	History	Paperback
	Military History	Political Science
	Mystery	Religion
		Science Fiction
		Spectator Sports

Other major categories: Literature.
Specialty Categories: Literature, military, Catholicism.
Approximate number of volumes: --
paperback: 500
hardback : 7,000
Directions: Located in west wing of "The Market Place" in Morgantown, Pa.
Additional information: Founded in 1990. Dealers stress quality of condition and quality of content. Another used book dealer two doors away. Outlet shopping mall in Morgantown. Very good little restaurant next door (Morganview Restaurant). 1,000 sq. ft. shop area.

Larry W. Soltys
330 South 17 1/2 Street
Reading, PA 19602
(215) 372-7670
Hours: 10-2
Owner(s): Larry W. Soltys
Type of Shop: Mail order
Major Categories represented by at least 100 titles:

Americana	History	Rare Books
Folklore	Military History	

Other major categories: Pennsylvania history (mainly southeastern Pa.), county history, Civil War, Native American.

42   Pennsylvania - Region 2

Approximate number of volumes: --
        paperback: --
        hardback : 100%
Approximate breakdown: rare: 20%
        out-of-print: 80%
        in-print: --
Additional information: Offers appraisals, Berks County postcards.

Whale of a Bookstore
1001 Oley Street
Reading, PA 19604
(215) 373-3660
Hours: Tues-Sat:10-5:30
Owner(s): Robert Smith
Type of Shop: General
Approximate number of volumes: --
        paperback: 10%
        hardback : 90%
Approximate breakdown: rare: --
        out-of-print: 99%
        in-print: --

Dell's Book Outlet
1018 Windsor Street
Reading, PA 19612-3156
(215) 376-7957
Hours: Tues-Sat:11-5   Closed Sunday and Monday.
Owner(s): Bernie & Evelyn Dell
Type of Shop: General, paperback, comics.
Major Categories represented by at least 100 titles:

Cooking	Music	Paperback
Fiction	Mystery	Rare Books
		Religion
		Romance
		Science Fiction

Approximate number of volumes: --
        paperback: 5,000
        hardback : 5,000
Approximate breakdown: rare: 20%
        out-of-print: 40%
        in-print: 40%
Advertises in "The Paper and Advertising Collector" monthly, with a list of items for sale by mail order.
Special Items and Services: Postcards, movie posters and prints.
Directions: Downtown factory outlet area.
Additional information: Founded in 1977. Good dining, museums and other used book stores only two blocks away. 10,000 sq. ft. shop area.

Thomas S. DeLong
RD 6, Box 336
Sinking Spring, PA 19608
(215) 777-7001
Hours: By appointment.
Owner(s): Thomas S. DeLong
Type of Shop: General
Major Categories represented by at least 100 titles:

Americana	History	Travel
Children's	Military History	
Collectibles	Nature	
Cooking	Nautical	
Exploration		
Fiction		

Specialty Categories: Gene Stratton Porter, Zane Grey & Stewart Edward White.
Approximate number of volumes: 5,000
  paperback: --
  hardback : 5,000
Approximate breakdown: rare: 10%
  out-of-print: 90%
  in-print: --
Special Items and Services: Located on a rural route in the countryside. Call for directions.
Additional information: Founded in 1990. Located in Pennsylvania Dutch area. Handicap access. 500 sq. ft. shop area.

Meadowbrook Hollow Books & Bits
8842 Furnace Road
Slatington, PA 18080
(215) 767-7542
Hours: By chance or appointment.
Owner(s): Margaret J. Anthony & Gail Haldeman
Type of Shop: General - 95% out-of-print hardbacks, 5% paperbacks & collectibles.
Major Categories represented by at least 100 titles:

Business	Gardening	Paperback
Children's	Health-fitness	Poetry
Cooking	History	Religion
Do-it-yourself	Medicine	Travel
Education	Mystery	
Fiction	Nature	

Other major categories: Small amounts of art, music, science fiction, and a little of all other categories.
Specialty Categories: Out-of-print children's, fiction.
Approximate number of volumes: --
  paperback: 2,500
  hardback : 12,000
Approximate breakdown: rare: 5%
  out-of-print: 75%
  in-print: 10%

Special Items and Services: Paper memorabilia. Book searches.
Directions: Located 6 1/2 miles east of Rt 309, 5 3/4 miles west of Rt 248. Take Rt 309 north past Scott & Fred's Lumber Co. to base of mountain. Take right onto Mountain Rd. Go approximately 6 miles to the 4th full crossroad and turn left onto Furnace Rd. Go to 9th mailbox and turn left. Located in a rural area with plenty of parking on owner's property.
Additional information: Founded in 1984. Good dining nearby (Penn. Dutch cooking). Other used book stores in nearby towns. Site built brand new by present owners in a very scenic rural setting in Penn. Dutch area. Handicap access.

Cloak & Dagger Books
Chambersburg Antique & Flea Market
868 Lincoln Way West
Chambersburg, PA 17201
(717) 267-0886
Hours: Sun-Sat:10-5
Owner(s): Robert M. Wynne
Type of Shop: Specialty - mystery & suspense, hardback & paperback.
Approximate number of volumes: 1,000-1,500
   paperback: 25%
   hardback : 75%
Approximate breakdown: rare: 45%
   out-of-print: 50%
   in-print: 5%
Free monthly listings of books in storage (over 3,000 titles).
Special Items and Services: Posters and framed cartoons. Book searches.
Directions: Located two miles north on Lincoln Way West from Square in Chambersburg. Left side, parking lot.
Additional information: Booth established at market in 1990. Owner operates booths at two other antique malls.

Cesi Kellinger, Bookseller
735 Philadelphia Avenue
Chambersburg, PA 17201
(717) 263-4474
Hours: By appointment.
Type of Shop: Old and rare books.
Major Categories represented by at least 100 titles:

Americana	History	Poetry
Art		Political Science
		Rare Books

Other major categories: Dance and women artists.
Specialty Categories: Art.
Approximate number of volumes: --
   paperback: --
   hardback : 10,000

Approximate breakdown: rare: 40%
out-of-print: 60%
in-print: --
Catalog issued twice a year - available on request.
Additional information: Founded in 1970. Other bookshops in Chambersburg.

Mason's Rare & Used Books
115 South Main Street
Chambersburg, PA 17201
(717) 261-0541
Hours: Mon-Sat:10-5 Closed Sunday.
Owner(s): Jon D. & Susan L. Mason
Professional Affiliations: Association of Mammonites
Type of Shop: Antiquarian and used.
Major Categories represented by at least 100 titles:
  ALL CATEGORIES except: education, geography, mythology
Other major categories: Pennsylvania.
Specialty Categories: Freemasonry, black Americana.
Approximate number of volumes: 25,000
paperback: 10%
hardback : 90%
Approximate breakdown: rare: 1%
out-of-print: 60%
in-print: 39%
Lists of 10-50 titles on specific subject areas issued every 2-3 months.
Special Items and Services: Appraisals & book searches.
Directions: Main Street is U.S. 11. Shop is located near intersection of U.S. 11 & U.S. 30. Parking in front of store.
Additional information: Founded in 1988. Seventeen years in business - 13 years in Wabash, Indiana. Nice Indonesian restaurant two doors away. 750 sq. ft. shop area. No stairs.

The Book House
Village Shops, Rt 15
Dillsburg, PA 17019
(717) 432-2720
Hours: Sat-Tues(1st & 3rd Sun only):10-4 Wed-Thurs:10-6 Fri:10-7:30
Owner(s): Larry & Joanne Klase
Professional Affiliations: American Booksellers Association.
Type of Shop: General hardcovers & paperbacks - new & used.
Major Categories represented by at least 100 titles:

Americana	Gardening	Paperback
Children's	History	Poetry
Collectibles	Military History	Political Science
Cooking	Mystery	Religion
Fiction	Nature	Romance
	Outdoor Recreation	Science Fiction

Specialty Categories: Pennsylvania history, Civil War, mystery, science fiction, juvenile series, vintage paperbacks, movie & TV "tie-ins"
Approximate number of volumes: 25,000
Special Items and Services: Maintains file of customer wants. Will mail order books. Paperback trade in recent titles.
Directions: Located in a small strip mall along Interstate Rt 15. Parking on lot.
Additional information: Founded in 1976. "Has always been a husband & wife operation. We're avid book-readers, -lovers, and -collectors. Daughter, now 8 years old, spent infant years in playpen in shop. She's a reader and thinks one copy of each children's book should be hers." 700 sq. ft. shop area. Aisles too narrow for wheel chairs but are happy to help.

Robert Wynne Books
Fayetteville Antique & Flea Market
3653 Lincoln Way East
Fayetteville, PA 17222
(717) 352-8485
Hours: Sun-Sat:10-5
Owner(s): Robert M. Wynne
Type of Shop: Specialty - natural history, geography, exploration and travel.
Approximate number of volumes: 500
    paperback: 95%
    hardback : 5%
Approximate breakdown: rare: 45%
    out-of-print: 50%
    in-print: 5%
Special Items and Services: Posters, prints & records. Book searches.
Directions: Four miles east of I-81 on Lincoln Way. Right side, parking lot.
Additional information: Booth set up in 1990. Owner operates booths at two other antique malls.

Stan Clark Military Books
915 Fairview Avenue
Gettysburg, PA 17325
(717) 337-1728
Hours: By appointment.
Owner(s): Stan Clark
Type of Shop: Specialty - military history.
Specialty Categories: U.S. Marine Corps, Civil War, Revolutionary War, War of 1812, Mexican War, WWI, WWII, Korean War, Vietnam, military biographies, campaign histories, memoirs, reminiscences, unit histories, Gettysburg Battlefield, Spanish-American War, U.S. military documents & autographs.
Approximate number of volumes: 10,000
    paperback: 5%
    hardback : 95%

Approximate breakdown: rare: 5%
out-of-print: 50%
in-print: 45%
Catalog issued periodically, free to buyers.
Special Items and Services: Military-related autographs and documents, unit (regimental and division) histories. Postcards, recruiting posters, limited edition prints; any military-related items (especially U.S. Marine Corps). Appraisals, some search services.
Additional information: Founded in 1985. Mail order only. "Located in Gettysburg, Pa.: military mecca of the United States." 2,500 sq. ft. shop area.

Robert Wynne Books
Mel's Antiques
Rear 103 Carlisle Street (P.O. Box 3503)
Gettysburg, PA 17325
(717) 334-9387
Hours: Fri-Sun:10-5
Owner(s): Robert M. Wynne
Type of Shop: Specialty - religion, biography, art, children's and sports.
Approximate number of volumes: 500
  paperback: 95%
  hardback : 5%
Approximate breakdown: rare: 45%
  out-of-print: 50%
  in-print: 5%
Special Items and Services: Posters, records and prints. Book searches.
Directions: One-half mile north of Square in Gettysburg on Carlisle Street (and right after railroad tracks through Revco Service Station).
Additional information: Booth set up in 1990. Owner operates booths at two other antique malls.

The Family Album
RD 1, Box 42
Glen Rock, PA 17327
(717) 235-2134
Owner(s): Ron Lieberman
Professional Affiliations: A.B.A.A.
Type of Shop: Antiquarian
Major Categories represented by at least 100 titles:

Americana	Medicine	Rare Books
Antiques	Military History	
Collectibles		

Other major categories: Early printed books and manuscripts, German-American imprints, incunabula, fore-edge paintings, early and/or unusual Bibles and editions of the Koran. Fine books relating to African, Arabic and Asian studies. A diverse list of current areas of interest is too long to include here in full, but includes atomic

science, books on books, bull terriers & dogfighting, and chromolithographs & Daguerrotypes.
Approximate number of volumes: 40,000
Additional information: Founded in 1969. Performs appraisals. "We are engaged in active collection development programs that embrace many diverse disciplines and nourish a clientele of eclectic tastes." Call or write for directions. 4,000 sq. ft. shop area. Catalog issued infrequently.

Paperback Exchange
1005-A Market Street
Lemoyne, PA 17043
(717) 761-2430
Hours: Mon-Wed & Fri:10-5:30   Thurs:10-7   Sat:10-4
Owner(s): Kathleen Graham
Type of Shop: Paperback (95%) and comics (5%)
Major Categories represented by at least 100 titles:

    Children's   Mystery   Paperback
    Fiction   Romance
                                               Science Fiction

Other major categories: Many of the major categories not shown above are represented by less than 100 books.
Approximate number of volumes: 60,000
            paperback: 100%
            hardback : --
Approximate breakdown: rare: --
                out-of-print: 40%
                in-print: 60%
Special Items and Services: New children's books discounted 20%. Keeps a special request list and will call customer if/when book comes in.
Directions: I-83 north to Lemoyne exit, turn right on 3rd Street, proceed to Market Street, turn left, store located on right at 10th & Market Streets.
Additional information: Founded in 1982. Owner operates another store in Harrisburg, Pa. Gives 1/4 cover price for trade-ins if in good condition and if needed by store. Books in store are all half-price. Also has rack of new books (latest best sellers) discounted 20%. 1,200 sq. ft. shop area.

William Thomas - Bookseller
P.O. Box 331
Mechanicsburg, PA 17055
(717) 766-7778
Hours: By appointment only.
Owner(s): William Thomas
Type of Shop: Specialty - Americana and Pennsylvania
Approximate number of volumes: --
            paperback: --
            hardback : 5,000
Approximate breakdown: rare: 40%
                out-of-print: 60%
                in-print: --

Windsor Park Books & News
5252 Simpson Ferry Road
Mechanicsburg, PA 17055
(717) 795-8262
Hours: Mon-Sat:7-9 Sun:7-5
Professional Affiliations: A.B.A.
Type of Shop: Independent bookstore/newsstand, with a section of used books in back of store, general stock.
Approximate number of volumes: 3,000 used books
        paperback: 40%
        hardback : 60%
Directions: One mile west of Rt 15, take Wesley Drive exit and go 1 mile to stoplight at Simpson Ferry Road (Mobil station on corner). Turn left and go 200 yards. Windsor Park Shopping Center on left, store located in center of strip plaza.
Additional information: Founded in 1989. Used book section is fairly low-level; mostly just decent second-hand material as inexpensive reading material, but not much in the way of collectors' items. Also small amount of old ephemera, posters, newspapers. 5,000 new books: 80% paperback, 20% hardback. 2,100 sq. ft. shop area.

Light of Parnell Bookshop
3362 Mercersburg Road
Mercersburg, PA 17236
(717) 328-3478
Hours: By appointment.
Owner(s): Nathan O. Heckman
Type of Shop: General
Major Categories represented by at least 100 titles:
    Americana   History
    Collectibles
    Cooking
    Fiction
Other major categories: Civil War.
Approximate number of volumes: --
        paperback: --
        hardback : 10,000
Special Items and Services: Book searches, appraisals, mail order.
Directions: Located on Rt 416, 12 miles west of Chambersburg, PA.
Additional information: Founded in 1972. Other used book stores in nearby towns within a twenty-mile radius. Also plenty of good restaurants, motels, etc. Handicap access. 850 sq. ft. shop area.

Miscellaneous Man
Box 1000
New Freedom, PA 17349
(717) 235-4766
Hours: Mon-Fri:10-6
Owner(s): George Theofiles
Type of Shop: Mail order - select graphic ephemera and paper collectibles.
Major Categories represented by at least 100 titles:
>   Americana   Military History   Travel
>   Art
>   Aviation
>   Collectibles

Specialty Categories: Rare out-of-print graphics and advertising art. Posters, books, trade cards, magazine covers, etc.
Approximate number of volumes: 1,000+
Approximate breakdown: rare: 50%
>   out-of-print: 50%
>   in-print: --

Catalog issued semi-annually.
Special Items and Services: Vintage posters and advertising. Searches.
Additional information: Founded in 1970. 4,200 sq. ft. shop area.

RAC Books
Box 296, RD #2
Seven Valleys, PA 17360
(717) 428-3776
Hours: Mail order only
Owner(s): Anne P. Muren and Robin L. Smith
Type of Shop: General
Major Categories represented by at least 100 titles:

>   Americana   Gardening   Paperback
>   Antiques   Medicine   Religion
>   Business   Military History   Science Fiction
>   Children's   Mystery   Science/Technology
>   Cooking   Spectator Sports

Other major categories: Biography.
Approximate number of volumes: 7,000
>   paperback: 50%
>   hardback : 50%

Approximate breakdown: rare: --
>   out-of-print: 90%
>   in-print: 10%

Special Items and Services: Book searches (even for reading copies and paperbacks).
Additional information: Founded in 1987. Business is mail order only at this location, with books on display at three book/antique malls. Owners also do 10+ book shows a year and will gladly fill orders for reading copies as well as for paperbacks, particularly in the areas of mystery and science fiction.

Kenton & Audrey Broyles Historical Collections
P.O. Box 42
Waynesboro, PA 17268
(717) 762-3068
Owner(s): Kenton H. Broyles
Professional Affiliations: A.P.I.C., TAMS.
Type of Shop: Mail order only.
Specialty Categories: Ku Klux Klan.
Special Items and Services: Political campaign memorabilia (no books in this area).

McIlnay's Books
306 West Market Street
York, PA 17401
(717) 846-0315
Hours: Wed-Sat:10-4
Owner(s): Mary Ann McIlnay
Major Categories represented by at least 100 titles:
Americana	History	Philosophy
Fiction	Music	Poetry

Other major categories: Language & rhetoric.
Specialty Categories: History, literature.
Approximate number of volumes: --
          paperback: --
          hardback : 5,000
Approximate breakdown: rare: 20%
          out-of-print: 80%
          in-print: --
Directions: Located on the main street of York. Free parking in rear of store.
Additional information: Founded in 1984. Present location since 1985. Good dining, another used book store nearby and historic restoration one block away. Offers book searches. 1,000 sq. ft. shop area.

RAC 8 Books in First Capitol Books & Antiques
343 West Market Street
York, PA 17401
(717) 846-2866
Hours: Wed-Sat:10-5 Sun:12-5 Closed Monday and Tuesday.
Owner(s): Anne P. Muren and Robin L. Smith
Type of Shop: General
Major Categories represented by at least 100 titles:
Children's	History	Paperback
Cooking	Military History	Religion
Fiction	Mystery	Science Fiction

Other major categories: Biography.

Approximate number of volumes: 3,000
        paperback: 50%
        hardback : 50%
Approximate breakdown: rare: --
        out-of-print: 90%
        in-print: 10%
Special Items and Services: Book searches including reading and paperback copies - especially mysteries and science fiction.
Directions: West on Philadelphia Street, turn left on Penn Street, take next left onto Market Street (one way). Store and free parking at lot on left.
Additional information: Founded in 1987. Located in large warehouse building with 10+ book dealers - books everywhere. McIlnay's Books across street. Two booksellers in York Antique Mall four blocks away. Farmer's Market across street. Owners have books on display at two other antique/book malls, as well as selling by mail order (direct mail to Box 296, RD #2, Seven Valleys, PA 17360). Two steps required into building. 140 sq. ft. shop area.

First Capitol Books & Antiques
also known as First Capitol Antiquarian Book & Paper Market
343 West Market Street
York, PA 17401
(717) 846-2866
Hours: Wed-Sat:10-5 Sun:12-5
Owner(s): Gwyn L. Irwin & Gary L. Robey, Sr.
Type of Shop: Multi-dealer shop of 18 dealers.
Major Categories represented by at least 100 titles:
    ALL CATEGORIES.
Other major categories: Pennsylvania, Civil War, theology & religion.
Approximate number of volumes: 250,000+
        paperback: constantly varies
        hardback : --
Approximate breakdown: rare: --
        out-of-print: constantly varies
        in-print: --
Special Items and Services: Posters, prints, trade cards, ephemera (in limited numbers). Appraisals. Limited amount of mail order. For travelling dealers, appointments can be made for times shop is normally closed.
Directions: From I-83 take George Street to West Philadelphia Street (one-way going west), take a left on Penn Street, go one block to Market, left on Market to middle of block on left side (Market is one-way going east.) Large off-street parking lot in front of building.
Additional information: Founded in 1984 by present owners. Each March & October during weeks of Historic York Book & Paper Fair all market dealers have sales with discounts ranging from 15% to 50%. Also there is a large room full of books at $1 each which go on sale at this time - 3 for $1. Another antiquarian bookstore (McIlnay's Books) across street. Blue Moon Cafe and Archie's each less than one block away. Two low steps at front entrance but have had no trouble with wheelchairs. 12,000 sq. ft. shop area.

Frank Fogleman/Bookseller
701 South Vernon Street
York, PA 17402
(717) 757-6977
Hours: Mail order only.
Owner(s): Frank Fogleman
Type of Shop: General
Major Categories represented by at least 100 titles:
Art	Mystery	Paperback
Children's	Mythology	Poetry
Fiction		Science Fiction
Folklore		

Other major categories: Biography; reference materials in science fiction & mystery fields.
Specialty Categories: Science fiction & fantasy; Sherlockian; and King Arthur fact, fiction, poetry.
Approximate number of volumes: --
  paperback: 35%
  hardback : 65%
Approximate breakdown: rare: --
  out-of-print: 70%
  in-print: 30%
Free catalog issued 2 to 3 times per year.
Additional information: Founded in 1984. Offers ephemera pertaining to science fiction & fantasy, Sherlock Holmes and King Arthur.

Comix Connection
Delco Plaza, 1201 Carlisle Road
York, PA 17404
(717) 843-6516
Hours: Mon-Sat:10-9   Sun:noon-5
Owner(s): Bill Wahl and Ned Senft
Type of Shop: Specialty - comic books.
Specialty Categories: Comic books, graphic novels, comic strip reprints, back issue comics.
Approximate number of volumes: 1,000
  paperback: 80%
  hardback : 20%
Approximate breakdown: rare: 10%
  out-of-print: 60%
  in-print: 30%
Special Items and Services: Posters, prints, portfolios. Searches.
Directions: Take Rt 30 to intersection of Rt 74. Take Rt 74 south 1/10 mile to Delco Plaza (on left). Acres of mall parking.
Additional information: Founded in 1988. "Efficient, friendly service; a haven for comic readers and collectors of all ages." 1,500 sq. ft. shop area.

54   Pennsylvania - Region 3

Inscribulus Books
c/o York Antique Mall
236 N. George Street (P.O. Box 2303)
York, PA 17405
(717) 845-7760
Hours: Seven days, 10-5
Owner(s): Josephine Hughes
Type of Shop: Booth at antique mall. Specialty - used & rare, art, antiques, children's, gardening and animals.
Major Categories represented by at least 100 titles:

Antiques	Gardening	Rare Books
Art	Mystery	
Children's	Nature	
Collectibles		

Approximate number of volumes: 10,000 total, 1,500 at mall
          paperback: few
          hardback : 100%
Approximate breakdown: rare: 25%
             out-of-print: 75%
             in-print: --
Will be distributing a catalog soon.
Special Items and Services: Free "ballpark" figures and informal searches.
Additional information: Business founded in 1981. Moved from Baltimore to present location in 1992. York Antique Mall houses over 40 antique and collectible dealers, as well as five other used book dealers.

RAC Books in York Antique Mall
236 North George Street
York, PA 17405
(717) 845-7760
Hours: Seven days, 10-5
Owner(s): Anne P. Muren and Robin L. Smith
Type of Shop: General
Major Categories represented by at least 100 titles:

Americana	Military History	Science/Technology
Children's		
Cooking		

Other major categories: Biography.
Approximate number of volumes: 1,500
             paperback: 10%
             hardback : 90%
Approximate breakdown: rare: --
             out-of-print: 90%
             in-print: 10%
Special Items and Services: Cookbook pamphlets & sheet music. Book searches including reading copies and paperbacks.
Directions: PA Rt 83 to Rt 30 west. Turn left on North George Street and right to free parking lot on North Street adjacent to mall.

Additional information: This location founded in 1990. This location is primarily an antique mall but it also houses five other book dealers among its 50+ dealers. Many of the antique dealers also carry books. Central Market (Farmers Market), Colonial Courthouse, Golden Plough Tavern (built 1741) are all within four blocks. First Capitol Books & Antiques and McIlnay's Books within four blocks. Book fairs are held in York during March and October. Owners have books on display at two other antique/book malls, as well as selling by mail order (direct mail to Box 296, RD #2, Seven Valleys, PA 17360). 180 sq. ft. shop area. Ramps for handicap access.

---

56 Delaware

YORKLYN
WILMINGTON
STANTON
NEW CASTLE

N

10 miles

DOVER

This portion of Delaware is
not included in this guide.

Delaware 57

The Bookseller
764 Townsend Blvd.
Dover, DE 19901
(302) 678-5935
Hours: Mon-Sat:10-6
Owner(s): Richard Satin
Type of Shop: General out-of-print stock and paperbacks.
Major Categories represented by at least 100 titles:

Americana	Health-fitness	Paperback
Business	History	Political Science
Children's	Mystery	Religion
Fiction	Nature	Romance
		Science Fiction

Approximate number of volumes: --
    paperback: 70%
    hardback : 30%
Special Items and Services: Book searches and special orders.
Additional information: Store founded in 1989. 2,000 sq. ft. shop area.

Oak Knoll Books
414 Delaware Street
New Castle, DE 19720
(302) 328-7232
Hours: Mon-Sat:9-5
Owner(s): Robert D. Fleck
Professional Affiliations: A.B.A.A.
Type of Shop: Antiquarian
Major Categories represented by at least 100 titles:
    Rare Books
Specialty Categories: Books about books, bibliographies, histories of papermaking, bookbinding, printing, illustrated books, etc.
Approximate number of volumes: --
    paperback: --
    hardback : 31,000
Approximate breakdown: rare: 95%
    out-of-print: --
    in-print: 5%
Twelve catalogs per year on antiquarian books, eight on new books about books per year, and one publishing catalog of Oak Knoll publications once per year.
Special Items and Services: Appraisals.
Directions: Located one hour north of Baltimore, 1 hour south of Philadelphia, 1/2 hour from Philadelphia airport, fifteen minutes from Wilmington Metroliner station. Store located in 3-story Victorian building on the main street.
Additional information: Founded in 1976. Previously located in Newark, DE. "Largest inventory in world" on stated subject area. Publishes about 12 titles each year concerning books about books. Six bed & breakfasts in the small town which is filled with colonial buildings. 3,000 sq. ft. shop area.

John P. Reid
307 Main Street
Stanton, DE 19804
(302) 995-6580
Hours: Wed-Sat:11-4
Owner(s): John P. Reid
Professional Affiliations: Abacis BookQuest
Type of Shop: Antiquarian books and antiques.
Major Categories represented by at least 100 titles:
   Americana
   Antiques
Other major categories: Some general readership books.
Specialty Categories: Delawareana books.
Approximate number of volumes: 3,000
   paperback: 1%
   hardback : 99%
Approximate breakdown: rare: 5%
   out-of-print: 95%
   in-print: --
Special Items and Services: Publishes the bi-monthly newsletter "Collecting Delaware Books", $18 per year for subscription. Affiliated with Abacis BookQuest, a computer database service linking book buyers and sellers worldwide.
Directions: Westbound Rt 4, 1 1/2 blocks east of Limestone Road.
Additional information: Founded in 1985 by present owner. Call for arrangements for handicap access. 600 sq. ft. shop area.

Aviation Books
705 West 38th Street
Wilmington, DE 19802
(302) 764-2427
Hours: By appointment.
Owner(s): Morris Glazier
Type of Shop: Specialty - aviation.
Specialty Categories: All types of aviation books and subjects. Also military history.
Approximate number of volumes: --
   paperback: 10%
   hardback : 90%
Approximate breakdown: rare: --
   out-of-print: 20%
   in-print: 70%
Catalog issued 4 times per year at $2.
Additional information: Founded in 1984. "Has been noted as having the best sales list and assorted aviation stock on the East Coast."

Delaware 59

Around Again Books
1717 Marsh Road
Wilmington, DE 19803
(302) 478-3333
Hours: Mon-Sat:10-5:30 Thurs evening till 7.
Owner(s): Helen Blanchard
Type of Shop: Paperback
Major Categories represented by at least 100 titles:

Business	Health-fitness	Paperback
Children's	History	Poetry
Cooking	Hobbies & Crafts	Political Science
Do-it-yourself	Mystery	Religion
Education		Romance
Fiction		Science Fiction
		Science/Technology
		Spectator Sports
		Travel

Approximate number of volumes: --
  paperback: 15,000
  hardback : 1,000
Directions: Located north of Wilmington in Brandywine Hundred. Parking front and back.
Additional information: Founded about 1980. Deals only in second-hand books, stock changes each day. 1,000 sq. ft. shop area.

Dale A. Brandreth, Books
P.O. Box 151
Yorklyn, DE 19736
(302) 239-4608
Hours: Mail order only.
Owner(s): Dale A. Brandreth
Type of Shop: Specialty - chess.
Major Categories represented by at least 100 titles:
  Rare Books
  Science/Technology
Other major categories: Mainly chess.
Approximate number of volumes: --
  paperback: 40%
  hardback : 60%
Approximate breakdown: rare: 10%
  out-of-print: 60%
  in-print: 30%
Catalog issued about 8 times a year. Price is $2 per year.
Special Items and Services: Appraisals.
Additional information: Founded in 1970. 800 sq. ft. shop area.

60 New Jersey

This portion of New Jersey is not included in this guide.

FLEMINGTON

LAMBERTVILLE
PRINCETON

WEST TRENTON
HAMILTON

HOWELL

AUDUBON
HADDONFIELD

MULLICA HILL

EGG HARBOR

BRIDGETON
MILLVILLE

N

20 miles

Galaxy Book Trader
121 West Merchant Street
Audubon, NJ 08106
(609) 546-6283
Hours: Mon-Thurs & Sat:10-6   Fri:10-8
Owner(s): Robert Sagirs
Type of Shop: Paperback & comic books.
Major Categories represented by at least 100 titles:
```
Children's        Mystery           Paperback
Collectibles                        Science Fiction
Fiction
```
Other major categories: Horror, comic books.
Approximate number of volumes: --
　　　　paperback: 15,000
　　　　hardback : 1,000
Approximate breakdown: rare: 10%
　　　　　　　　　　　out-of-print: 60%
　　　　　　　　　　　in-print: 30%
Special Items and Services: Silver Age comics, posters and comic supplies. Book and comic searches, and comic book subscriptions.
Directions: Located off Rt 30. Parking on street and a parking lot behind the store.
Additional information: Founded in 1985.

A Novel Idea
Dutch Neck Village, RD 2, Trench Road
Bridgeton, NJ 08302
(609) 451-3280
Hours: Mon-Sat:10-5   Sun:12-5
Owner(s): Linda M. Eisenberg
Professional Affiliations: New York Region/Mid-Atlantic Booksellers Assoc.
Type of Shop: Paperback, and some hardback. Large selection of romance. New books also.
Major Categories represented by at least 100 titles:
```
Children's         Hobbies & Crafts    Paperback
Cooking            Mystery             Romance
Fiction                                Science Fiction
```
Approximate number of volumes: 25,000
　　　　paperback: 75%
　　　　hardback : 25%
Approximate breakdown: rare: --
　　　　　　　　　　　out-of-print: 30%
　　　　　　　　　　　in-print: 70%
Free catalog (new books only), twice per year.
Special Items and Services: Cards, sounds-of-nature cassettes, and "Romantic Times" magazine. Book searches, responsive to customers' special preferences. Also offers latch hook rug kits, cross-stitch kits, and instruction.

Directions: Located two miles south of Bridgeton, off Rt 49 - follow signs to Dutch Neck Village. Free parking.
Additional information: Founded in 1984. Craft shows: first Saturday in June, first Saturday in October, Christmas Special first Friday and Saturday in December. Romance authors who have visited for book signings include Constance O'Day-Flannery, Colleen Quinn, Elaine Barbieri, Judith French, Colleen Faulkner, Ann Lynn and Donna Fletcher; also cookbook author Myra Chanin. Good dining nearby. 800 sq. ft. shop area. Handicap access.

Heinoldt Books
1325 W. Central Ave.
Egg Harbor, NJ 08215
(609) 965-2284
Hours: Call first.
Owner(s): Margaret Heinoldt
Professional Affiliations: N.J.B.A.
Type of Shop: Out-of-print Americana.
Major Categories represented by at least 100 titles:
   Americana   Nautical
   Exploration
Other major categories: New Jersey, New York, Pennsylvania, Indians, Revolution, Civil War, railroads, ocean liners, American West.
Approximate number of volumes: 5,000
        paperback: 4,800
        hardback : 200
Approximate breakdown: rare: 250
        out-of-print: 4,750
        in-print: --
Free catalog available.
Special Items and Services: Appraisals.
Directions: From Philadelphia: take Atlantic City Expressway to Egg Harbor exit. Left on Rt 50 towards Egg Harbor, about 1 1/2 miles to South Egg Harbor Fire House on left. Turn right on Central Ave. Red brick house on corner of second block.
Additional information: Started in business in North Plainfield in 1956. Present location since 1970. Visitors always welcome - just be sure we are home. Good dining nearby; casinos 13 miles away.

The People's Bookshop
160 Main Street
Flemington, NJ 08822
(908) 788-4953   Home (908) 369-4488
Hours: Noon to 5 pm daily (including weekends) & by appointment.
Owner(s): Rosemarie Beardsley
Professional Affiliations: N.J.B.A.
Type of Shop: General

Major Categories represented by at least 100 titles:

Americana	Gardening	Paperback
Business	Health-fitness	Philosophy
Children's	History	Poetry
Education	Medicine	Political Science
Fiction	Military History	Religion
	Music	Romance
	Mystery	Science Fiction
	Nature	Social Science
	Nautical	Spectator Sports

Other major categories: Foreign languages - German, French, etc.
Approximate number of volumes: --
    paperback: many
    hardback : at least 50,000
Approximate breakdown: rare: 10%
    out-of-print: 90%
    in-print: --
Special Items and Services: Few prints. Book search.
Directions: Behind Air Park Realty, across from Avanti Restaurant.
Additional information: Founded in 1979. Famous discount shopping nearby. Two new and two paperback bookshops nearby. Floor area approx 35'x20'.

Pollywog Paperback Bookswap
23 Church Street
Flemington, NJ 08822
(908) 782-6900
Hours: Sun:12:30-5   Mon & Fri:9-6   Sat:10-5
Owner(s): Richard C. Row
Type of Shop: General
Major Categories represented by at least 100 titles:

Business	Health-fitness	Paperback
Children's	History	Philosophy
Do-it-yourself	Hobbies & Crafts	Religion
Fiction	Military History	Romance
	Mystery	Science Fiction
		Science/Technology
		Social Science

Other major categories: Westerns, suspense (spy, etc.), horror, disaster, biography, occult.
Approximate number of volumes: --
    paperback: 70,000
    hardback : 1,500
Approximate breakdown: rare: --
    out-of-print: 10%
    in-print: 90%
Special Items and Services: Acceptable trade-in gives additional 20-25% discount on paperbacks. Hardbacks discounted up to 95% without trade-in.
Directions: Located 3/4 block west of traffic light at Main Street. Driveway on east side of building to parking in rear (on south side).
Additional information: Founded in 1974. Same owner since 1978. Outlet shopping centers within one block. 1,500 sq. ft. shop area.

64 New Jersey

Between the Covers Rare Books
132 Kings Highway East
Haddonfield, NJ 08033
(609) 354-7665
Hours: Open most days, call for hours.
Owner(s): Thomas & Heidi Congalton
Professional Affiliations: A.B.A.A., I.L.A.B., A.B.N.J.
Type of Shop: Antiquarian
Major Categories represented by at least 100 titles:

Americana	Gardening	Philosophy
Art	Military History	Poetry
Children's	Music	Rare Books
Exploration	Mystery	Science Fiction
Fiction		Travel

Specialty Categories: Wine books, literary first editions, African-American literature, signed books, and rare books in many fields.
Approximate number of volumes: 15,000
   paperback: 1%
   hardback : 99%
Approximate breakdown: rare: 50%
   out-of-print: 50%
   in-print: --
Free catalog issued five times per year.
Special Items and Services: Some vintage prints, posters and photographs. Appraisals.
Directions: Located on the main street in Haddonfield. Metered parking on street and in rear. Call for directions.
Additional information: Business founded in 1986, store in 1991. Two other book shops in proximity: Ray Boas and Caney Books. Lots of antique shops in town. 1,600 sq. ft. shop area. Handicap access.

Ray Boas, Bookseller
407 Haddon Avenue
Haddonfield, NJ 08033
(609) 795-4853
Hours: Wed-Sat:10:30-6   Mon-Tues: By chance or appointment.
Owner(s): Ray Boas
Professional Affiliations: New Jersey Antiquarian Booksellers Association
Type of Shop: Antiquarian & out-of-print.
Major Categories represented by at least 100 titles:
   ALL CATEGORIES except: paperback, romance.
Specialty Categories: General non-fiction, New Jerseyana, military, business history, children's.
Approximate number of volumes: 15,000
   paperback: --
   hardback : 100%
Approximate breakdown: rare: 15%
   out-of-print: 85%
   in-print: --

Directions: Exit 32 off I-295 to Haddonfield.
Additional information: Mail order since 1980; store founded in 1990. Located 10 minutes from center city Philadelphia. Handicap access to 1st floor. 1,500 sq. ft. shop area.

Old Cookbooks - H. T. Hicks
P.O. Box 462
Haddonfield, NJ 08033
(609) 854-2844
Hours: Mail order only.
Owner(s): H. T. Hicks
Professional Affiliations: Antiquarian Booksellers of New Jersey, Library Company of Philadelphia
Type of Shop: Specialty antiquarian
Specialty Categories: Pre-1918 cooking and related - scarce & rare.
Approximate number of volumes: 300 hardbacks (scarce & rare)
Catalog issued irregularly at $3.
Special Items and Services: Publishes *J. T. Hicks Collectors Guide to Old Cookbooks* (2nd Edition and Comprehensive Edition), as well as monographs about cookery books. Cookery guides contain information from major bibliographies, food histories, auction and dealer catalogs, and more. Guides are based on years of research and are available in different bindings at different prices.
Additional information: Founded in 1974.

Booktrader of Hamilton
104 Flock Road
Hamilton, NJ 08619
(609) 890-1455
Hours: Mon,Tues,Wed:10-6   Thurs-Fri:10-8 Sat:10-5
Owner(s): Joanne Perillo
Type of Shop: Paperback
Major Categories represented by at least 100 titles:

Business	Health-fitness	Paperback
Children's	History	Poetry
Cooking	Military History	Religion
Fiction	Mystery	Romance
		Science Fiction

Other major categories: Large selection of computer books at 50% off.
Approximate number of volumes: --
              paperback: 100%
              hardback : --
Approximate breakdown: rare: --
              out-of-print: 20%
              in-print: --
Special Items and Services: Carries "Cat's Meow" Village pieces (collectible wooden houses), public domain IBM software - over 800 selections ($3.50 per disk). New paperbacks discounted 15%.

Directions: Rt 195 (north or south), exit 65A (Sloan Ave.), come straight through light, then left into shopping center. Strip mall store - parking is no problem.
Additional information: Founded in 1986. Used books are 1/2 cover price. Gives 20% credit for paperbacks in good condition. Handicap access. 1,800 sq. ft. shop area.

Elisabeth Woodburn, Books
Booknoll Farm (P.O. Box 398)
Hopewell, NJ 08525
(609) 466-0522
Hours: By appointment only.
Owner(s): Bradford G. Lyon and Joanne Fuccello
Professional Affiliations: A.B.A.A.
Type of Shop: Specialist in horticulture, carrying old, rare and new books.
Specialty categories: Horticulture, gardening, herbs, landscape gardening, flowers.
Approximate number of volumes: 12,000
Catalog issued in various subject areas such as herbs, fruits, trees, etc. twice per year at $2.50.
Special Items and Services: Some ephemera such as plant and seed catalogs. Special searches.
Additional information: Founded in 1946. Previously owned by Elisabeth Woodburn, who died in November 1990. Brad Lyon, one of the current owners, worked with her since 1976.

Bookbizniz
58 Marc Drive
Howell, NJ 07731
(908) 901-8870
Hours: Mail order only.
Owner(s): Rusela Yap
Type of Shop: General antiquarian.
Approximate number of volumes: 5,000
        paperback: 5%
        hardback : 95%
Approximate breakdown: rare: --
        out-of-print: 80%
        in-print: 20%
Additional information: Book searches. Founded in 1989.

Phoenix Books
49 North Union Street
Lambertville, NJ 08530
(609) 397-4960
Hours: Mon, Wed, Thurs:11-5 Fri-Sun:11-6
Owner(s): Janet & Barry Novick; Joan & Michael Ekizian
Type of Shop: General antiquarian.

Major Categories represented by at least 100 titles:

Americana	Gardening	Philosophy
Antiques	History	Poetry
Art	Hobbies & Crafts	Political Science
Aviation	Medicine	Rare Books
Business	Military History	Religion
Children's	Music	Science Fiction
Collectibles	Mystery	Science/Technology
Cooking	Mythology	Social Science
Do-it-yourself	Nature	Spectator Sports
Fiction	Nautical	Travel
Folklore		

Other major categories: Cinema
Specialty Categories: Literature and literary criticism, art, cinema, history, first editions.
Approximate number of volumes: 30,000
        paperback: 2%
        hardback : 98%
Approximate breakdown: rare: 10%
        out-of-print: 80%
        in-print: 10%
Special Items and Services: Jazz and classical records.
Directions: From I-95 south: New Hope exit, approx. 10 miles north on Rt 32. From I-95 north: Lambertville/Trenton exit, approx. 10 miles north on Rt 29.
Additional information: Founded in 1987. Located across the river from New Hope, Pa., a major tourist area; numerous restaurants, antique shops, bed & breakfasts, etc. Two used book stores in immediate vicinity, eight more in 20-mile radius. Dealer discount available. 1,150 sq. ft. shop area.

Wind Chimes Book Exchange
210 N. High Street
Millville, NJ 08332
(609) 327-3714
Hours: Mon-Sat:11-5
Owner(s): Dave & Diann Ewan
Type of Shop: 48% paperback exchange, 48% remainders, 2% used hardback. Categories vary depending on availability of remainders, etc. Heavily into all how-to subjects. Carries about 80,000 paperbacks, mostly fiction; large sections of general fiction, romance, mystery, etc.
Approximate number of volumes: 90,000
        paperback: 90%
        hardback : 10%
Approximate breakdown: rare: --
        out-of-print: 80%
        in-print: 20%
Special Items and Services: Kites, cards, postcards, classical & jazz cassettes. Special orders.
Directions: One-half block south of the post office on High Street. Parking on street or on lot in back.
Additional information: Founded in 1976. At present location since 1982. Good hardware store next door. Catalog may be available in future. 1,750 sq. ft. shop area. No steps.

White Papers, c/o Wolf's Antiques
36 S. Main Street (P.O. Box 129)
Mullica Hill, NJ 08062
Home: (609) 467-2004   Store: (609) 478-4992
More likely to reach owner at home since store is co-op.
Hours: Tues-Sat:10-4   Sun:12-5
Owner(s): Joann V. White
Professional Affiliations: Antiquarian Booksellers of New Jersey
Type of Shop: Antiques
Major Categories represented by at least 100 titles:

Children's	History	Paperback
Cooking		Religion
Fiction		

Specialty Categories: Children's and children's series books.
Approximate number of volumes: 4,000-5,000
Approximate breakdown: rare: --
   out-of-print: 50%
   in-print: 50%
Special Items and Services: Postcards, sheet music, general ephemera. Book searches.
Directions: Mullica Hill is located at junction of Rts 322 & 45; east from exit 2 off NJ Tpk.; east from exit 11 off Rt 295; west from exit 50B off Rt 55.
Additional information: Mullica Hill is a small town. On-street parking usually not a problem. Several restaurants in town. Murphy's Loft (large bookstore) nearby. Other merchants also carry books & paper goods.

Bryn Mawr Book Shop
102 Witherspoon Street
Princeton, NJ 08542
(609) 921-7479
Hours: Tues-Sun:12-4
Owner(s): Margery R. Claghorn, business manager.
Type of Shop: Antiquarian and paperback.
Major Categories represented by at least 100 titles:

Americana	Gardening	Paperback
Antiques	History	Philosophy
Art	Music	Poetry
Children's	Mystery	Political Science
Cooking	Nature	Rare Books
Fiction		Religion
		Science Fiction
		Social Science
		Travel

Directions: Diagonally opposite Princeton Public Library.
Additional information: Founded in 1986. Offers postcards. All proceeds go for scholarships at Bryn Mawr College. Princeton University and two other used book stores nearby.

Autographs & Collectibles
124 Pickford Avenue
West Trenton, NJ 08628
(609) 530-1350
Hours: Seven days:9-5
Owner(s): Brian B. Kathenes
Professional Affiliations: A.B.N.J., U.A.C.C., I.S.A., Manuscript Society
Type of Shop: Specialty - manuscripts, autographs, documents and books
Major Categories represented by at least 100 titles:

```
Americana          History              Political Science
Aviation           Military History
Collectibles
```

Specialty Categories: Autographs, documents, biographies, Civil War, American Revolution.
Approximate number of volumes: 5,000
          paperback: --
          hardback : 100%
Approximate breakdown: rare: 20%
          out-of-print: 80%
          in-print: --
Catalog issued monthly at $10.
Special Items and Services: Autographs. Computerized want lists, professional court-defensible appraisals.
Directions: Rt 95 (exit 4) to Rt 31 south to Pickford Avenue.
Additional information: Founded in 1984. Credentialed appraiser/authenticator on site. Appraisal instructor for International Society of Appraisers. Authentication seminars. Nearby are Trenton Museum, Old Barracks, Washington Crossing, and eight bookstores within 10 miles. Handicap access. 600 sq. ft. shop area.

70 Maryland

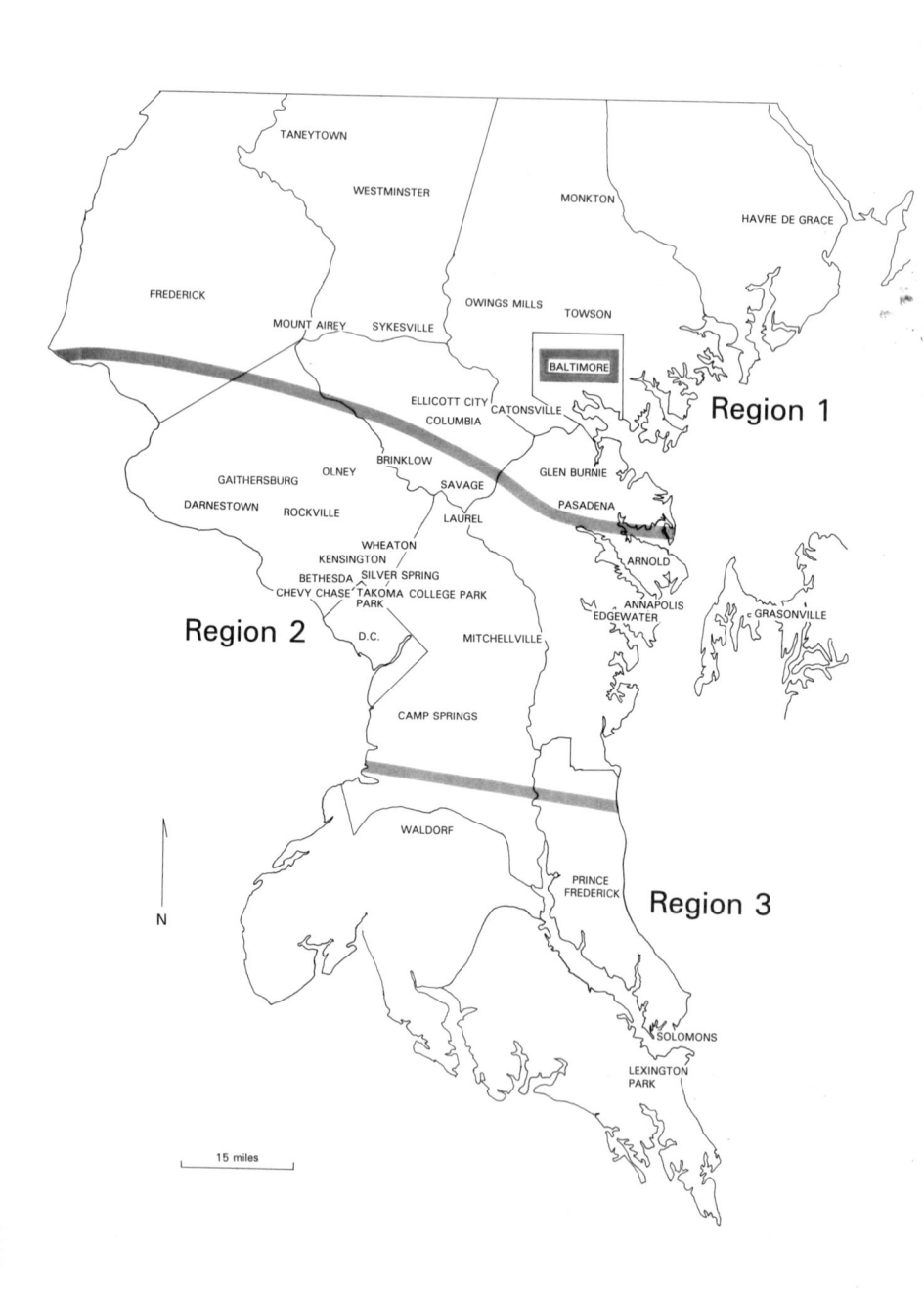

New Era Book Shop
408 Park Ave.
Baltimore, MD 21201
(410) 539-6364
Hours: Tues & Thur-Sat:10-6
Type of Shop: Specialty - new and used books on social change.
Major Categories represented by at least 100 titles:

Art	Health-fitness	Philosophy
Children's	History	Poetry
Cooking	Music	Political Science
Education	Mystery	Rare Books
Fiction		Religion
Folklore		Science Fiction
		Social Science

Specialty Categories: Books on the origin of classical Egyptian & Ethiopian great civilizations.
Approximate number of volumes: 5,000 volumes (80% new, 20% used)
Special Items and Services: Cards, posters, prints, CDs, audio tapes, etc. Appraisals and book searches.
Directions: Between Franklin and Mulberry Streets. Also close to the main Enoch Pratt Library on Cathedral Street.
Additional information: Founded in 1962. "In many ways, New Era Books is quite unique in that we relate to every progressive person who wants to change socio-economic relations worldwide. So we appeal to each progressive and revolutionary to come on down to New Era and see for yourself. We have something for everyone."

Drusilla's Books
859 North Howard Street
Baltimore, MD 21201
(410) 225-0277
Hours: Wed-Sat:12-5 and by appointment.
Owner(s): Drusilla P. Jones
Type of Shop: Specialty antiquarian.
Major Categories represented by at least 100 titles:

Children's	Hobbies & Crafts

Other major categories: Fine bindings and art nouveau trade bindings of the turn of the century.
Specialty Categories: Children's and illustrated - all sorts of children's books including art, biographies, foreign languages, cooking, mystery series books, crafts, fairy tales & folktales, song books, Little Golden Books, nature, travel, etc.
Approximate number of volumes: 5,000
 paperback: 0%
 hardback : 100%
Approximate breakdown: rare: 50%
 out-of-print: 40%
 in-print: under 10%
Catalog issued yearly (at least) on children's and illustrated books. Illustrations included. Catalog is $3 to new customers.

Special Items and Services: Greeting cards, posters (mostly children's), and antique prints. Book searches and appraisals for children's and illustrated books.
Directions: Metered parking on street all day long (quarters only). Light rail access at two stops north and south. Train passes directly in front of store which is located in Antique Row.
Additional information: Business founded in 1978 and present shop opened in 1985. The Antique Row in Mount Vernon Historic District features the Lyric and Meyerhoff Halls, many fine restaurants, the Walters Art Gallery, the Peabody Conservatory, Center Stage and more within easy walking distance. Owner participates in book shows regularly, mostly out of town. Shop located on second floor, entrance by steps only. 800 sq. ft. shop area.

Entry for **Lambda Rising** is on page 122.

Camelot Books
2403 Hillhouse Road
Baltimore, MD 21207
(410) 448-1015
Hours: By appointment.
Owner(s): James A. Kissko
Type of Shop: Antiquarian
Major Categories represented by at least 100 titles:
    Americana   Geography
    Exploration
Specialty Categories: U.S. maps & atlases and Western Americana.
Additional information: Founded in 1977.

Geppi's Comic World, Inc.
7019 Security Blvd.
Baltimore, MD 21207
(410) 298-1758
Hours: Mon, Fri, Sat:10-9   Tues-Thurs:11-8   Sun:11-6
Owner(s): Steve Geppi
Type of Shop: Specialty - comics and baseball cards.
Major Categories represented by at least 100 titles:
    Collectibles   Paperback
                                    Science Fiction
                                    Spectator Sports

The Perfect Ending
1004 Reisterstown Road
Baltimore, MD 21208
(410) 448-5340
Hours: Fri:11-4   Sat:10-10   Sun:10-5
Owner(s): Ms. Moyna D. Anderson
Type of Shop: Children's books, collectible (cartoon) toys, bears and Steiff animals.

Maryland - Baltimore 73

Major Categories represented by at least 100 titles:
```
Children's                        Rare Books
Collectibles
Fiction
Folklore
```
Other major categories: Disney art & titles especially. Little Golden Books.
Specialty Categories: Disney, Hanna Barbera, Warner Brothers, Golden Books, posters, movie standees.
Approximate number of volumes: --
    paperback: 10%
    hardback : 90%
Approximate breakdown: rare: 5%
    out-of-print: 70%
    in-print: 25%
Special Items and Services: Uncirculated posters, items never for sale, advertisement pieces, movie one sheets, movie standees, CDs and more related to animation. Appraisals (specialized). Will purchase books from customers, and help locate books by recommending other sources.
Directions: Pikesville exit off I-695 onto Reisterstown Road; head toward city to intersection of Reisterstown Road and Sherwood Avenue.
Additional information: Store founded in 1989. Previously located at the Antique Galleria on North Howard Street. Offers more in the way of animated collectibles than most others. Also carries collectible toys, holds book signings, contests, and gives great price breaks. Can open store on request during closed hours. Several specialty shops nearby including a record shop and vintage clothing store. Cultural Arts Center due to open across the street. Surrounded by restaurants: Jilly's, Puffin's, Mr. Chan's.

Book Arbor
P.O. Box 20885
Baltimore, MD 21209
(410) 367-0338
Owner(s): Judith M. Bloomgarden
Type of Shop: Specialty antiquarian.
Major Categories represented by at least 100 titles:
    Gardening
    Nature
Specialty Categories: Landscape architecture, garden history and design, agriculture.
Approximate number of volumes: --
    paperback: --
    hardback : 99%
Approximate breakdown: 99% rare and out-of-print
Free catalog issued two or more times per year, lists also available.
Special Items and Services: Will respond to inquiries.

ASABI International
4610 York Road
Baltimore, MD 21212
(410) 323-2355
Hours: 11-7
Owner(s): Gracye Johnson
Professional Affiliations: A.B.A.
Type of Shop: African-American culture items.
Other major categories: African & African-American history and culture.
Approximate number of volumes: --
        paperback: 1,000
        hardback : 3,000
Approximate breakdown: rare: 10%
        out-of-print: 20%
        in-print: 50%
Special Items and Services: Cards, postcards and prints. Searches.
Additional information: Founded in 1988. Next door to jazz record shop. Street parking. Handicap access. 700 sq. ft. shop area.

The Rug Book Shop
2603 Talbot Road
Baltimore, MD 21216
(410) 367-8194
Hours: By appointment only and mail order.
Owner(s): Paul Kreiss
Type of Shop: Specialty - new and used books about rugs.
Specialty Categories: Oriental rugs and Navajo blankets.
Approximate number of volumes: --
        paperback: 20% (new & used)
        hardback : 80% (new & used)
Approximate breakdown: rare: 10% (used)
        out-of-print: 40% (used)
        in-print: 50% (used)
Free catalog issued about 2-3 times per year.
Special Items and Services: Book searches and special orders.
Additional information: Founded in 1976. Many titles are imports from Europe.

Tales From the White Hart
3360 Greenmount Avenue
Baltimore, MD 21218
(410) 889-0099
Hours: Mon-Sat:Noon-9
Owner(s): Kathy & Leo Sands
Type of Shop: Specialty - science fiction, fantasy, horror. New and used.

Major Categories represented by at least 100 titles:
```
Children's                    Rare Books
Collectibles                  Science Fiction
Fiction
Folklore
```
Other major categories: Vampire & werewolf sub-specialties. Star Trek and other media fanzines.

Approximate number of volumes: --
>paperback: 20,000
>hardback : 2,000

Approximate breakdown: rare: 5%
>out-of-print: 75%
>in-print: 20%

Catalog on vampire and werewolf subjects available by sending self-addressed stamped envelope. Catalog is updated monthly.

Special Items and Services: Science fiction and fantasy folk music (known as "Filk music"), traditional/contempary folk music and world music. Appraisals and modified book searches and information on science fiction conventions. New books: science fiction, fantasy and horror, including many titles people might think are out-of-print (due to careful searching and ordering from many sources). Also a large collection of tarot decks and books and a reasonable number of esoteric books and music. New book ghettos include children's, medieval, media, gay & lesbian, vampire & werewolf.

Directions: From I-83 south: take 28th Street exit, turn left on Greenmount Avenue and park between 33rd and 35th Streets for on-street parking. There are two spaces in back of building.

Additional information: Store founded in 1975. "Largest selection of new & used science fiction in the Baltimore-Washington area." Located at north end of "Bookstore Mecca" in Baltimore. Four other used or specialty book stores in easy walking distance, four others within a mile. Great choice of oriental restaurants within a block. 400 sq. ft. shop area for used books and 750 sq. ft. shop area for new books, both filled floor-to-ceiling. Access to new book area requires three steps down - if people with wheelchairs call ahead, the store will arrange to have personnel on hand to lift person and chair down. Crutches also on hand. Used books are up a flight of stairs but employee will fetch desired material.

Baltimore Book Company, Inc.
2112 North Charles Street
Baltimore, MD 21218
(410) 659-0550
Hours: Mon-Fri:11-5
Owner(s): Chris Bready
Type of Shop: Antiquarian
Major Categories represented by at least 100 titles:
```
Americana        History           Paperback
Art              Mystery           Poetry
Children's                         Rare Books
Fiction                            Science Fiction
                                   Science/Technology
```

Approximate number of volumes: 2,000
       paperback: 10%
       hardback : 90%
Approximate breakdown: rare: 25%
       out-of-print: 70%
       in-print: 5%
Auction catalog five to six times per year.
Special Items and Services: Prints, photographs, documents. Appraisals.
Directions: On-street parking.
Additional information: Store founded in 1989. Primary business is book/autograph/photograph/print auctions - five to six times per year. Restaurant next door and other book stores three blocks away. 800 sq. ft. shop area.

The Kelmscott Bookshop
32 West 25th Street
Baltimore, MD 21218
(410) 235-6810
Hours: Mon-Sat:10-6
Owner(s): Donald & Teresa Johanson
Professional Affiliations: A.B.A.A., Baltimore Bibliophiles
Type of Shop: Antiquarian
Major Categories represented by at least 100 titles:

Americana	Gardening	Philosophy
Antiques	History	Poetry
Art	Medicine	Political Science
Aviation	Military History	Rare Books
Business	Music	Religion
Children's	Mystery	Science/Technology
Cooking	Mythology	Social Science
Education	Nature	Travel
Exploration	Nautical	
Fiction		
Folklore		

Other major categories: H. L. Mencken, Marylandia
Specialty Categories: Literature, travel, American and English literature, art & architecture, Marylandia, H. L. Mencken
Approximate number of volumes: 80,000
       paperback: 0.5%
       hardback : 99.5%
Approximate breakdown: rare: 33%
       out-of-print: 33%
       in-print: 33%
Lists on specific subjects are available periodically at no cost.
Special Items and Services: Appraisals, searches, book binding.
Directions: Parking available at rear of store, meter parking in front.
Additional information: Store founded in 1977. Near the Baltimore Museum of Art, Walters Art Gallery, and three other book stores on same block making a "Book Row." Handicap access by rear entrance. 5,760 sq. ft. shop area.

Maryland - Baltimore 77

Tiber Bookshop
8 West 25th Street
Baltimore, MD 21218
(410) 243-2789
Hours: Mon-Sat:10:30-6
Owner(s): Whit Drain and Bob Kotansky
Type of Shop: General
Major Categories represented by at least 100 titles:
  ALL CATEGORIES except romance.
Specialty Categories: Science/technology, religion and philosophy.
Approximate number of volumes: 80,000
        paperback: 10%
        hardback : 90%
Approximate breakdown: rare: --
        out-of-print: 50%
        in-print: 50%
Directions: North on Charles Street to 25th Street. Near northwest corner of Charles and 25th Street.
Additional information: Store founded in Ellicott City in 1984, and moved to present (much larger) location in 1987. Good dining nearby and three other book stores on same block. 3,500 sq. ft. shop area.

Second Story Books
3302 Greenmount Ave.
Baltimore, MD 21218
(410) 467-4344
Hours: Sun-Thur:11-7 Fri & Sat:11-9
Owner(s): Allan Stypeck (president)
Professional Affiliations: A.B.A.A., I.L.A.B., A.B.A., A.S.A.
Major Categories represented by at least 100 titles:
  ALL CATEGORIES.
Specialty Categories: Rare books.
Approximate number of volumes: 75,000
        paperback: 35%
        hardback : 65%
Approximate breakdown: rare: 25%
        out-of-print: 50%
        in-print: 25%
Catalog will be available in the future.
Additional information: Appraisals and expert witness. 2,800 sq. ft. shop area. Second Story Books has four locations in the Baltimore-Washington area.

78 Maryland - Baltimore

Cecil Archer Rush, Fine Books - Fine Arts
1410 Northgate Road
Baltimore, MD 21218-1549
(410) 323-7767
Hours: By appointment.
Owner(s): Cecil Archer Rush
Type of Shop: Antiquarian
Major Categories represented by at least 100 titles:

Art	Medicine	Paperback
	Mythology	Rare Books
	Nature	Religion

Other major categories: Fine press books, illustrated books and erotic art.
Specialty Categories: Art books and illustrated books in European languages - French, German and Italian.
Approximate number of volumes: --
    paperback: 10%
    hardback : 90%
Approximate breakdown: rare: 35%
    out-of-print: 50%
    in-print: 15%
Catalog issued about once per year at $3.
Special Items and Services: Fine arts paintings and statues (European & African). Also carries new books: fine press, limited editions, fine illustrated, literature, art books over $50 suggested list price. Appraisals and book searches.
Directions: Ask for directions when calling for appointment.
Additional information: Founded in 1942 and operated since under sole ownership. Business office located at 1410 Northgate Road, and stock and office located at 2605 North Charles Street.

Allen's Book Shop
416 East 31st Street, 2nd floor
Baltimore, MD 21218-3410
(410) 243-4356
Hours: Mon-Fri:1-6 Sat:11-5 (Closed Sun)
Owner(s): David S. Ray
Type of Shop: Antiquarian and out-of-print.
Major Categories represented by at least 100 titles:

Americana	History	Paperback
Antiques	Medicine	Philosophy
Art	Military History	Poetry
Business	Music	Rare Books
Children's	Mystery	Religion
Collectibles	Mythology	Science/Technology
Cooking	Nature	Spectator Sports
Do-it-yourself	Nautical	
Fiction		

Other major categories: Physics & math, psychology, literary biography & criticism.

Specialty Categories: Maryland, music, philosophy, railroads and cookbooks.
Approximate number of volumes: 25,000
        paperback: 25%
        hardback : 75%
Approximate breakdown: rare: 10%
        out-of-print: 60%
        in-print: 30%
Special Items and Services: Book searches.
Directions: One-half block off Greenmount Ave. Curb-side parking and lot in rear on Saturdays only.
Additional information: Founded in 1974. Two other book stores on same street.

D. R. Sandy
P.O. Box 15317
Baltimore, MD 21220
(410) 661-2974
Hours: By appointment.
Owner(s): D. R. Sandy
Professional Affiliations: Guild of Book Workers.
Type of Shop: By appointment in residence/office.
Major Categories represented by at least 100 titles:
                                          Rare Books
Other major categories: Fine bindings and limited small press.
Approximate number of volumes: 800
        paperback: 2%
        hardback : 98%
Free catalog issued occasionally.
Special Items and Services: Photographs and postcards. Hand bookbinding. Bookbinding is of primary interest.

The 19th Century Shop
1047 Hollins Street
Baltimore, MD 21223
(410) 539-2586
Hours: Mon-Fri:10-5
Owner(s): Stephan Loewentheil
Major Categories represented by at least 100 titles:

Americana	History	Poetry
Collectibles	Medicine	Rare Books
Fiction		Science Fiction
		Science/Technology

Specialty Categories: 19th century literary classics, Darwin, Twain, Franklin, Mencken.
Approximate number of volumes: --
        paperback: --
        hardback : 100%

80 Maryland - Baltimore, Region 1

Approximate breakdown: rare: 100%
out-of-print: --
in-print: --
Catalog issued at $5 to $10 dollars.

Butternut and Blue
3411 Northwind Road
Baltimore, MD 21234
(410) 256-9220
Hours: By appointment.
Owner(s): Jim McLean
Type of Shop: New and used books.
Specialty Categories: American Civil War, baseball.
Approximate number of volumes: 2,500
paperback: 5%
hardback : 95%
Approximate breakdown: rare: 5%
out-of-print: 50%
in-print: 45%
Catalog 5 times a year. $3 for first catalog.
Special Items and Services: Limited edition prints.
Additional information: Founded in 1983. 500 sq. ft.

The Castle Bookshop, Ltd.
611 Frederick Road
Catonsville, MD 21228
(410) 788-0207
Hours: Mon-Sat(except Wed):10-6 Wed:12-6 Closed Sundays.
Owner(s): Ed & Joann De Santis
Professional Affiliations: A.B.A., C.R.A.B.S., M.A.B.A.
Type of Shop: General used books, military history a specialty.
Major Categories represented by at least 100 titles:

Business	Health-fitness	Paperback
Children's	History	Religion
Cooking	Medicine	Romance
Do-it-yourself	Military History	Science Fiction
Fiction	Mystery	Science/Technology
	Nature	

Specialty Categories: Military history, collectible paperbacks.
Approximate number of volumes: 30,000 (and expanding)
paperback: 60%
hardback : 40%
Approximate breakdown: rare: --
out-of-print: 90%
in-print: 10%
Six catalogs per year ($5 per year) on military history.

Special Items and Services: Military postcards. Book searches.
Directions: One-half block east of intersection of Ingleside & Frederick Roads (or two blocks west of Frederick Road exit off I-695).
Additional information: Store founded in 1991. 1,540 sq. ft. shop area. Store capacity is 40,000 books when store is fully stocked. Handicap parking and wide aisles for wheel chairs.

Culpepper, Hughes & Head
9770 Basket Ring Road
Columbia, MD 21045
(410) 730-1484
Hours: Catalog only.
Owner(s): Betty M. Culpepper
Type of Shop: Specialty mail order - black studies.
Major Categories represented by at least 100 titles:
```
Children's          History           Political Science
Education                             Social Science
```
Approximate number of volumes: --
       paperback: --
       hardback : 10,000
Approximate breakdown: rare and out-of-print: 90%
       in-print: --
Free catalog issued quarterly.
Additional information: Founded in 1983. Book searches. Mail order only.

John Gach Books, Inc.
5620 Waterloo Road
Columbia, MD 21045
(410) 465-9023
Hours: By appointment.
Owner(s): John & Betty Gach
Professional Affiliations: A.B.A.A., I.L.A.B.
Type of Shop: Antiquarian
Major Categories represented by at least 100 titles:
```
                                      Rare Books
                                      Social Science
```
Other major categories: Psychology, psychiatry, psychoanalysis.
Specialty Categories: Freud, Reich, Jung.
Approximate number of volumes: 30,000
       paperback: --
       hardback : 100%
Approximate breakdown: rare: 20%
       out-of-print: 60%
       in-print: 20%
Catalog issued 4 to 6 times per year (free).
Special Items and Services: Appraisals, book searches.
Directions: Directions given when making appointment. Parking available.
Additional information: Founded in 1968. Started specialty in psychology in

1972. Has the "largest and best inventory in the world" on behavioral sciences with no language restrictions. Currently has books in 13 languages, preponderantly English, French and German. 2,000 sq. ft. shop area.

Second Edition Used Books
6490M Dobbin Road
Columbia, MD 21045
(410) 730-0050
Hours: Mon-Sat:10-7 Sun:12-5
Owner(s): Marty Looking Bill
Type of Shop: General paperback and hardback.
Major Categories represented by at least 100 titles:

Antiques	Gardening	Paperback
Art	Health-fitness	Philosophy
Business	History	Poetry
Children's	Hobbies & Crafts	Political Science
Cooking	Medicine	Religion
Do-it-yourself	Military History	Romance
Education	Music	Science Fiction
Fiction	Mystery	Science/Technology
		Spectator Sports
		Travel

Approximate number of volumes: 30,000
        paperback: 50%
        hardback : 50%
Approximate breakdown: rare: 5%
        out-of-print: 5%
        in-print: 90%
Special Items and Services: Book searches.
Directions: Route 95 south of Baltimore to Route 175 west (towards Columbia). Go approximately 1 mile to light at Dobbin Road, take left, go to second light and take right into Columbia Business Center.
Additional information: This store founded in 1989 after moving another store opened in 1984. The store is "clean, upscale and well categorized." 1,400 sq. ft. shop area. Handicap access.

Deeds Book Shop
8012 Main Street (P.O. Box 85)
Ellicott City, MD 21041
(410) 465-9419
Hours: Tues-Sun:12-5 and by appointment.
Owner(s): Jean M. Mattern
Professional Affiliations: Baltimore Bibliophiles.
Type of Shop: General
Major Categories represented by at least 100 titles:

Americana	Gardening	Philosophy
Antiques	History	Poetry

(LIST CONTINUED NEXT PAGE)

Art	Hobbies & Crafts	Rare Books
Aviation	Music	Religion
Children's	Mystery	Science/Technology
Collectibles	Mythology	
Cooking	Nature	
Do-it-yourself	Nautical	
Fiction		
Folklore		

Other major categories: Marylandia, local history.
Specialty Categories: Marylandia, poetry, literature and juvenile.
Approximate number of volumes: 9,000
        paperback: 5%
        hardback : 95%
Approximate breakdown: rare: 10%
        out-of-print: 60%
        in-print: 30%
Special Items and Services: Book searches and appraisals.
Directions: From Route 40 west or Route 29 north: follow signs to historic Ellicott City. There are four designated parking areas and some on-street parking.
Additional information: Store founded in 1970. Located in historic Ellicott City across from B&O Museum. Antique shops and several restaurants close by.

Turtle Hill Books
3420 Sylvan Lane
Ellicott City, MD 21043
(410) 465-7213
Hours: Mail order and by appointment only.
Owner(s): Phil & Meg Burns
Type of Shop: Specialty mail order - used fishing books.
Specialty Categories: Fishing, fly fishing, trout, fresh water, salt water.
Approximate number of volumes: 600 (essentially all hardback)
Approximate breakdown: All out-of-print, some rare.
Free catalog available upon request.
Additional information: Turtle Hill Books, the publisher of this guide to used book dealers, will be offering a wide selection of new guide books/maps to outdoor activities for the mid-Atlantic region, starting in April 1994. Activities covered will include hiking, camping, fishing, cross-country skiing, bicycling, canoeing, cliff-climbing, spelunking, touring, travel, fossil/mineral hunting, and birding. We also have two fishing titles under way which are scheduled to be published in March and May of 1994. This book is our second publication, the first being *P.B.'s Quick Index to Bird Nesting*. Please write or call if you would like to receive our free catalog covering new books (guide books to the mid-Atlantic), as well as Turtle Hill publications.
Wanted: We have a PERMANENT WANT for used/rare/scarce fishing books. We offer competitive prices and would be pleased to respond to your quotes. Please be descriptive including date, edition/printing, publisher, condition, defects, and presence/absence of dust jacket.

Wonder Book and Video
1306 West Patrick Street (Rt 40 West)
Frederick, MD 21702
(301) 694-5955
Hours: Mon-Sat:10-10   Sun:12-8   (closed Christmas and Thanksgiving)
Owner(s): Charles Roberts
Type of Shop: Used, rare, out-of-print, publisher's overstock, new/used/rare comics, used/new rental videos, used/new CDs and audio tapes.
Major Categories represented by at least 100 titles:
 ALL CATEGORIES.
Approximate number of volumes: 300,000
   paperback: 30%
   hardback : 70%
Approximate breakdown: rare: 10%
   out-of-print: 50%
   in-print: 40%
Special Items and Services: New and used CDs. Can special order any video not in stock. Out-of-print video searches. Book buyers are available Mon-Sat 10-5 or by appointment. Free out-of-print search service.
Directions: Easy to find. Store located less than 1 1/2 miles from I-70, I-270 and US 15. Route 40 is a main drag through Frederick.
Additional information: Store founded in 1980 and has moved and expanded three times. "Largest selection of used books in Baltimore-Washington region." Very well organized with category breakdown and store map to help locate books by subject. Great nearby restaurants. Civil War battlefield and skiing nearby. 11,000 sq. ft. shop area. Also a second Wonder Book and Video "Clearance Center" at 425 Jefferson Street (at US 15) in Frederick, MD 21701, phone (301) 662-2774.

Book Nook II
143 Delaware Avenue, N.E.
Glen Burnie, MD 21061
(410) 766-5758
Hours: Mon-Sat:10-5
Owner(s): Mary Monteith
Type of Shop: Used books - hardbacks, paperbacks and comics.
Major Categories represented by at least 100 titles:

Art	Gardening	Paperback
Business	Health-fitness	Poetry
Children's	History	Rare Books
Collectibles	Hobbies & Crafts	Religion
Cooking	Medicine	Romance
Do-it-yourself	Military History	Science Fiction
Fiction	Music	Science/Technology
	Mystery	Spectator Sports
	Nature	Travel
	Nautical	
	Outdoor Recreation	

Specialty Categories: Black history, women's studies, science fiction, new age & occult, horror.

Approximate number of volumes: 59,000
Special Items and Services: Books purchased ("we are selective").
Directions: Parking directly in front of store.
Additional information: Store founded in 1976. Close proximity to cinemas, American and ethnic dining, and shopping. 1,150 sq. ft. shop area. Handicap access. Ms. Monteith also owns the Book Nook in College Park.

Courtyard Bookshop
313 St. John Street
Havre De Grace, MD 21014
(410) 939-5150
Hours: Mon-Sat:10-6   Sun:12-5
Owner(s): Jack Kelly
Major Categories represented by at least 100 titles:

Americana	Geography	Paperback
Art	History	Romance
Aviation	Military History	Science Fiction
Children's	Mystery	
Do-it-yourself	Nature	
Fiction	Nautical	

Approximate number of volumes: 10,000
         paperback: 35%
         hardback : 65%
Approximate breakdown: rare: --
         out-of-print: 50%
         in-print: 50%
Directions: Located in downtown Havre De Grace with public parking just off I-95 & Rt 40.
Additional information: Founded in 1989. Offers book searches. Good dining nearby. Three museums in town: Decoy Museum, Lighthouse Museum, Lockhouse Museum. Plus U.S. Army Ordinance Museum 5 miles away at Aberdeen.

Eleanor C. Weller, Charlotte's Web Antiques
16135 Old York Road
Monkton, MD 21111
(410) 771-4239
Hours: By appointment.
Owner(s): Eleanor Weller
Professional Affiliations: A.S.I.D., A.B.A.
Type of Shop: Selected out-of-print titles on art, decorative arts, antiques, architecture, gardens & garden history, some sporting.
Major Categories represented by at least 100 titles:

Americana	Gardening	Rare Books
Antiques		
Art		

Other major categories: Garden history and historic gardens.
Approximate number of volumes: 2,000

Approximate breakdown: rare: 10%
out-of-print: 40%
in-print: 50%
Directions: Call for appointment and directions.
Special Items and Services: Sells an equal number of specialized titles in new books. Normally orders multiple copies of foreign, small press, and unusual books which are hard to get. Sometimes titles go out-of-print while still on inventory.
Additional information: Founded in 1979. Started as a sideline in an antique shop. Historic "Milton Inn" nearby.

B&B Smith, Booksellers
P.O. Box 158
Mount Airy, MD 21771
(410) 549-1227
Hours: Mon-Fri:10:30-5
Owner(s): William P. Smith
Professional Affiliations: A.B.A.
Type of Shop: Specialty mail order - new & used.
Specialty Categories: Owner deals only in classics (Greek & Latin), Mediterranean archeology, and ancient history, in all languages.
Approximate number of volumes: 8,000
paperback: 10%
hardback : 90%
Approximate breakdown: rare: 5%
out-of-print: 60%
in-print: 35%
Free catalog issued 3-4 times per year.
Special Items and Services: French & German special orders and "library jobber" in specialty subject area.
Additional information: Founded in 1981. Mail order only. Hopes to move later during 1992 and be open to the public. 1,200 sq. ft. area.

BookQuest
135 Village Queen Drive
Owings Mills, MD 21117
(410) 581-0394
Hours: 24 hours a day, every day.
Type of Shop: On-line computer information service which links booksellers, libraries, and collectors worldwide. Deals in all subjects.
Additional information: BookQuest has a database of over 650,000 books and serials entered by its customers worldwide. The computers automatically match books wanted with books for sale. Customers are informed of the matches and then contact the owner directly or through BookQuest's E-mail or fax systems. Other features include QuickQuote and QuickSearch services for bookstores and dealers, an on-line pricing guide, a listing of small press titles available, and a missing and stolen books database. For more information, call (410) 581-0394.

Books From X to Z
8513 Summit Road
Pasadena, MD 21122-3046
(410) 360-9602
Hours: Mail order.
Owner(s): Daniel & Janet Martin
Type of Shop: Mail order - social sciences and business.
Major Categories represented by at least 100 titles:
    Americana   History   Political Science
    Business   Social Science
Specialty Categories: Economics, psychology, business management, public administration.
Approximate number of volumes: 4,000
        paperback: 0%
        hardback : 100%
Approximate breakdown: rare: 30%
                      out-of-print: 70%
                      in-print: 0%
Eight to ten free catalogs issued annually on the topics listed under specialty categories.
Directions: Appointment only.
Additional information: Founded in 1988.

Jerome Shochet
6144 Oakland Mills Road
Sykesville, MD 21784
(410) 795-5879
Hours: Mail order only.
Type of Shop: Specialty - boxing.
Approximate number of volumes: 1,000
        paperback: 10%
        hardback : 90%
Approximate breakdown: rare: 20%
                      out-of-print: 70%
                      in-print: 10%
Free catalog issued every three to four months.
Special Items and Services: Boxing magazines, posters, programs, tickets, autographs, photos, etc.
Additional information: In operation for last 15 years.

Taneytown Antique Shoppes
7 Frederick Street
Taneytown, MD 21787
(410) 756-4262
Hours: Tues & Fri:11-5 Sat-Sun:10-6
Owner(s): Linda Bilo
Type of Shop: Antique shop.

Major Categories represented by at least 100 titles:
```
Americana          Medicine              Poetry
Cooking            Military History      Religion
Fiction
```
Specialty Categories: Civil War, U.S. and Maryland history, agriculture, children's series, biographies.
Approximate number of volumes: 6,000
        paperback: --
        hardback : 100%
Approximate breakdown: rare: 5%
        out-of-print: 95%
        in-print: --
Special Items and Services: Postcards, framed prints, ephemera, general line of antiques. Book searches.
Directions: From Washington, DC and Virginia: I-270 north to Rt 15 north (Frederick), exit at Rt 26 to Rt 194. Shop is on Rt 194 about 25 miles from Frederick.
Additional information: Founded in 1981. Location features 15 rooms of various antiques and collectibles. One room dedicated to books alone, with cases of books scattered about the house (i.e., all cookbooks in the kitchen).

E. Christian Mattson
1 Center Road A1
Towson, MD 21204
(410) 825-8967
Hours: By appointment only.
Type of Shop: Antiquarian
Major Categories represented by at least 100 titles:
    Children's
Specialty Categories: C. Dickens, A. C. Doyle, juvenile series books, fore-edge paintings.
Approximate number of volumes: 7,000
Approximate breakdown: rare: 50%
        out-of-print: 50%
        in-print: 0%
Catalog issued occasionally.
Special Items and Services: Appraisals, book searches.
Directions: Exit 27 off I-695, left on Goucher Blvd., right on Joppa Road, to Center Road.
Additional information: Business founded in 1961. Handicap access.

Jean-Maurice Poitras & Sons
107 Edgerton Road
Towson, MD 21204
(410) 821-6284
Hours: By appointment only.
Owner(s): Helen M. & Jean-Maurice Poitras
Type of Shop: Specialty - antiquarian medical only. Catalog mail order.

Approximate number of volumes: 50,000
Catalog issued twice a year. Price is $3.
Special Items and Services: Medical only: postcards, prints, photographs and medical equipment (but rarely put in catalog).
Additional information: First catalog issued in 1981. Towson Town Center about one mile away.

Smith College Club of Baltimore Used Book Sale
7300 York Road
Towson, MD 21204
(410) 821-6241
Hours: Annual sale in early spring.
Owner(s): Smith College Club of Baltimore
Type of Shop: General
Major Categories represented by at least 100 titles:

Americana	Gardening	Paperback
Antiques	Health-fitness	Philosophy
Art	History	Poetry
Business	Hobbies & Crafts	Political Science
Children's	Military History	Rare Books
Cooking	Music	Religion
Do-it-yourself	Mystery	Romance
Education	Nature	Science Fiction
Exploration	Outdoor Recreation	Science/Technology
Fiction		Social Science
		Travel

Other major categories: Archeology, humor, Marylandia, law development, personal & popular psychology, women, literature, reference.
Approximate number of volumes: 50,000-70,000
    paperback: 15%
    hardback : 85%
Approximate breakdown: rare: 5%
    out-of-print: 50-60%
    in-print: 35-40%
Special Items and Services: Ephemera, prints/art, silent auction (weird and/or collectible).
Directions: The annual book sale is located at the Towson Armory at Washington and Chesapeake Avenues. Ample parking in nearby parking garage but no free parking.
Additional information: Club founded in 1958. The club is a non-profit organization and all proceeds go to scholarships at the Smith College, Northampton, Mass. All books sold are from donations. May go to a bookstore format in the future - under consideration. Handicap access.

The Paperback Exchange Book Store
100 Manchester Avenue
Westminster, MD 21157
(410) 848-0828
Hours: Daily 10-5, closed Wed & Sun.
Owner(s): Karen Wantz
Type of Shop: Paperback
Major Categories represented by at least 100 titles:
> Children's   Mystery   Religion
> Fiction   Romance
>   Science Fiction

Specialty Categories: New and used.
Approximate number of volumes: --
> paperback: 30,000
> hardback : --

Special Items and Services: Mail order.
Directions: From Baltimore: I-795 to Rt 140 west to Westminster. After entering city limits, turn left at second stop light onto Gorsuch Road. Manchester Avenue starts at curve. Take right turn on Greenwood Avenue, and a right into parking lot.
Additional information: Store founded in 1981. Carroll County Farm Museum and Shellman House - Historical Society nearby. 1,800 sq. ft. shop area. Handicap access.

Briarwood Books
88 Maryland Ave.
Annapolis, MD 21401
(410) 268-1440
Hours: Mon-Sat:9:30-5:30   Sun:9-5
Owner(s): David Grobani
Type of Shop: General
Major Categories represented by at least 100 titles:
> Art   History   Paperback
> Exploration   Military History   Political Science
> Fiction   Mystery   Rare Books
>   Nautical   Science Fiction
>   Social Science
>   Travel

Approximate number of volumes: 10,000
> paperback: 3,000
> hardback : 7,000

Approximate breakdown: rare: 20%
> out-of-print: 60%
> in-print: 20%

Special Items and Services: Book searches. Special orders on new titles.
Directions: Maryland Ave. off of State Circle in downtown Annapolis. Park where you can.
Additional information: Founded in 1982. Maryland Avenue features many antique and craft stores. 1,000 sq. ft. shop area.

Elm Spy Books
Box 9753
Arnold, MD 21012
(410) 544-9014   FAX (410) 544-7670
Hours: By appointment and mail only.
Owner(s): Emil Levine
Type of Shop: Specialty - out-of-print mail order.
Specialty Categories: Non-fiction espionage, spy, military intelligence, cryptography, terrorism, guerrilla, escape, POW.
Approximate number of volumes: 1,500
          paperback: --
          hardback : 100%
Approximate breakdown: rare: --
          out-of-print: 100%
          in-print: --
Catalog issued quarterly. Price is $2 - refundable with purchase.
Special Items and Services: Book searches. Computerized reference - will suggest appropriate title for particular subject of interest or research.
Additional information: Founded in 1982. "Second largest dealer of non-fiction espionage in the Western Hemisphere!" Located one-half way between Baltimore and Annapolis. Business is primarily mail order, but will see special collectors evenings or weekends. Call for appointment.

Second Story Books
4836 Bethesda Ave.
Bethesda, MD 20814
(301) 656-0170
Hours: Everyday:10-10
Owner(s): Allan Stypeck (president)
Professional Affiliations: A.B.A.A., I.L.A.B., A.B.A., A.S.A.
Major Categories represented by at least 100 titles:
ALL CATEGORIES.
Specialty Categories: Rare books.
Approximate number of volumes: 75,000
          paperback: 35%
          hardback : 65%
Approximate breakdown: rare: 20%
          out-of-print: 60%
          in-print: 20%
Catalog will be available in the future.
Additional information: Appraisals and expert witness. 2,800 sq. ft. shop area. Second Story Books has four locations in the Baltimore-Washington area.

Iranbooks
8014 Old Georgetown Road
Bethesda, MD 20814
(301) 986-0079

Hours: Mon-Sat:10-6
Type of Shop: Specialty - books in Persian (Farsi) and about Iran (all subject areas) Annual catalog available for $3; seasonal catalog is free.
Special Items and Services: Book searches (relating to Iran) - "will find any book on Iran." Also carries a large selection of new books.
Directions: Please call for directions.
Additional information: Founded in 1979.

Mystery Bookshop Bethesda
7700 Old Georgetown Road
Bethesda, MD 20814
(301) 657-2665
Hours: Mon-Sat:10-7 Sun:Noon-5
Owner(s): Jean & Ron McMillen
Professional Affiliations: Malice Domestic Committee Members, Sisters in Crime, Mystery Readers International, A.B.A.
Type of Shop: Specialty - mystery, detective and spy fiction.
Approximate number of volumes: approx. 3,000 used books
  paperback: 5%
  hardback : 95%
Approximate breakdown: rare: 10%
  out-of-print: 70%
  in-print: 20%
Special Items and Services: Primarily stocks new books. Collection of 15,000 titles includes 12,000 new titles of mystery, horror, spy and thriller fiction. About 40% of these new titles are hardback. Annual catalog of fiction titles (not including children's mysteries or used books) is available, as well as a newsletter three times yearly.
Directions: From I-495 (Capital Beltway), take Old Georgetown Road toward Bethesda. From downtown Washington: take Wisconsin Avenue into the heart of Bethesda, turn left onto Old Georgetown Road, and go one block. Park in the indoor parking garage, or in public lot across the street.
Additional information: Founded in 1989. Good dining, numerous secondhand bookshops nearby and Olsson's general bookstore across the street. 1,000 sq. ft. shop area. Handicap access.

The Book Cellar
8227 Woodmont Ave.
Bethesda, MD 20814
(301) 654-1898
Hours: Mon-Fri:11-6 Sat:10-5 Sun:11-5
Owner(s): Don & Linda Bloomfield
Type of Shop: General antiquarian.
Major Categories represented by at least 100 titles:
  ALL CATEGORIES.
Other major categories: Foreign language books on language and literature.

Approximate number of volumes: 40,000
    paperback: 3,000
    hardback : 37,000
Approximate breakdown: rare: 4%
    out-of-print: 95%
    in-print: 1%
Special Items and Services: Prints, maps and postcards. Book searches.
Directions: One block west off Wisconsin Avenue (Route 355) and one door south of Battery Lane. Metered parking garage directly across street - free on weekends. Three blocks from Metro.
Additional information: Store founded in 1976. "Well-organized store with hundreds of subject categories, many of them arranged alphabetically by author's name." Two other used book stores within two blocks and dozens of restaurants nearby. 1,200 sq. ft. shop area.

Georgetown Book Shop
7770 Woodmont Ave.
Bethesda, MD 20814
(301) 907-6923
Hours: 7 days a week: 10-6
Owner(s): Andy Moursund
Type of Shop: General.
Major Categories represented by at least 100 titles:

Americana	History	Paperback
Antiques	Military History	Philosophy
Art	Music	Poetry
Business	Nature	Rare Books
Children's		Spectator Sports
Cooking		Travel
Fiction		

All of the categories shown on the questionnaire (see introduction) not shown above, are represented by less than 100 titles except for the following: do-it-yourself, education, health fitness, medicine, outdoor recreation, romance, science/technology, and social science.
Other major categories: Baseball, photography, vintage magazines (New Yorker, Life, Sport, etc.), film.
Specialty Categories: Very large art and military history selections. Also, very large collection of out-of-print baseball books.
Approximate number of volumes: 14,000
    paperback: 2,000
    hardback : 12,000
Special Items and Services: British children's postcards, and a few WWII and Gilbert & Sullivan posters. Want lists quoted to.
Directions: From the Washington Beltway (I-495): take the Wisconsin Ave. exit southbound. Go about 1 1/2 - 2 miles. Woodmont Ave. is the first right after the National Institute of Health (also on the right). Continue down Woodmont for five or six blocks, store on right. Municipal parking lot four doors past store: 50 cents/hour on weekdays, free on weekends.
Additional information: Store founded in 1984. Started in Georgetown and moved

to Bethesda in 1989. Inventory of books lies somewhere between a rare book shop and the "average" secondhand book shop. Several other used book shops within ten minute walk and many restaurants nearby. Handicap access and no stairs. 1,500 sq. ft. shop area.

Curious Books
7921 Norfolk Ave.
Bethesda, MD 20814
(301) 656-2668
Hours: Tues-Thur:11-7   Fri-Sat:Noon-9   Closed Sun-Mon
Owner(s): Nan Taylor
Type of Shop: General used and out-of-print.
Major Categories represented by at least 100 titles:
```
Americana          History            Paperback
Art                Music              Poetry
Children's         Mystery            Science Fiction
Fiction            Nature
```
Specialty Categories: Literary biography, criticism and essays.
Approximate number of volumes: 10,000
     paperback: 45%
     hardback : 55%
Directions: From Washington Beltway (I-495): south on Rt 355 (Wisconsin Ave.), right on Woodmont, right on Cordell Ave., left on Norfolk Ave. From DC: north on Wisconsin Ave, left on Old Georgetown Rd., right on St. Elmo, left on Norfolk. Metered on-street parking or parking garage on Cordell.
Additional information: Founded in 1988. Formerly the Old Forest Bookshop. Many restaurants (including foreign cuisine) and other used book stores within walking distance. Waverly Auctions (book auctions) one block away. Handicap access. 800 sq. ft. shop area.

Bartleby's Books
4823 Fairmont Avenue
Bethesda, MD 20814
(P.O. Box 15400, Chevy Chase, MD 20825)
(301) 654-4373
Hours: By appointment and open most Saturdays (best to call).
Owner(s): John Thomson and Karen Griffin
Type of Shop: General antiquarian.
Major Categories represented by at least 100 titles:
```
Americana                           Rare Books
Art
Fiction
```
Approximate number of volumes: 5,000
     paperback: --
     hardback : 100%
Approximate breakdown: rare: 25%
            out-of-print: 90% (including rare)
              in-print: --

Catalog issued approximately every other month in specific subject areas.
Directions: Downtown Bethesda - public parking garages.
Additional information: Founded in 1984. Was an open shop from 1984 to 1991 at a different location. Now a closed shop with more emphasis on Americana, general antiquarian, and mail order (by catalog). For those that visit, several other used book stores within two to three blocks. 500 sq. ft. area.

R. Quick, Bookseller
7155 Wisconsin Avenue (book stall in farm market)
Bethesda, MD 20815
(301) 654-5030
Hours: Wed & Sat:8-4 and by appointment
Owner(s): R. Quick
Major Categories represented by at least 100 titles:
    Americana   History
    Children's
    Fiction
Other major categories: Classics and world literature.
Approximate breakdown: rare: 10%
                       out-of-print: 30%
                       in-print: 60%
Special Items and Services: Located in Montgomery Farm Women's Co-op Market, 7155 Wisconsin Ave., in downtown Bethesda. Limited parking on market grounds. Plenty of pay parking in public lot in back (reasonable rates).
Additional information: Founded in 1985. Book stall in the "Village Marketplace." All on ground level - no steps.

Federal Circuit Div. of Shellenard, Inc.
7100 Crail Drive
Bethesda, MD 20817
(301) 229-7102
Hours: 8am-8pm (office hours - no open shop)
Owner(s): Leonard S. Blondes (chairman/president)
Type of Shop: Used law books specializing in Federal Practice large sets.
Special Items and Services: Appraisals and book searches.
Directions: Telephone only or visit by Mr. Blondes.
Additional information: Founded in 1952. "The most effective source dealing with used Federal Sets of law books."

Schweitzer Japanese Prints, Inc.
6313 Lenox Road
Bethesda, MD 20817
(301) 229-6574
Hours: By appointment.

Owner(s): Paul R. Schweitzer
Professional Affiliations: Society for Japanese Art (The Hague), Ukiyo-e Society of America
Type of Shop: Primarily Japanese art, history, culture, china, mysteries.
Approximate number of volumes: 600-700
                paperback: 10%
                hardback : 90%
Approximate breakdown: rare: 15%
                out-of-print: 84%
                in-print: 1%
Special Items and Services: Offers large stock of Ukiyo-e prints, Japanese graphics and woodblock books.
Directions: Located near River Road and Whittier Blvd. Near Kenwood Golf Club.
Additional information: Founded in 1965. Located close to other Bethesda used bookstores. Limited handicap access.

Continental Divide Trail Society
P.O. Box 30002
Bethesda, MD 20824
(301) 493-4080
Hours: By appointment only.
Owner(s): James R. Wolf
Professional Affiliations: Rocky Mountains Book Publishers Association.
Major Categories represented by at least 100 titles:
    Americana   Nature
                            Outdoor Recreation
Specialty Categories: Rocky Mountains and Southwest.
Approximate number of volumes: 1,000
                paperback: 10%
                hardback : 90%
Additional information: Bookselling is an outgrowth of guidebook publication activities. Predominant business is mail order.

Old Hickory Bookshop
20225 New Hampshire Avenue
Brinklow, MD 20862
(301) 924-2225
Hours: By appointment.
Owner(s): Johanna Grimes
Type of Shop: Antiquarian
Major Categories represented by at least 100 titles:
                Medicine   Science/Technology

Stewart's Used Bookstore
6504 Old Branch Avenue
Camp Springs, MD 20748
(301) 449-6766
Hours: Tues-Fri:11-5 Sat:10-4   (Closed Sun and Mon)
Owner(s): Frances M. Stewart
Professional Affiliations: Washington Antiquarian Booksellers Association
Type of Shop: General
Major Categories represented by at least 100 titles:
    Art   History   Paperback
    Aviation   Military History   Religion
    Cooking   Nautical
Specialty Categories: Military history.
Approximate number of volumes: 10,000
       paperback: 30%
       hardback : 70%
Approximate breakdown: rare: --
       out-of-print: 70%
       in-print: 30%
Special Items and Services: Stamps, covers and postcards.
Directions: From I-95 (Capital Beltway): take exit 7B to second traffic light, turn right and go one block to Old Branch Avenue, turn left.
Additional information: Founded in 1975. Easy on/off from Beltway; only 8 miles from U.S. Capitol. 1,000 sq. ft. shop area.

Ashe & Deane Fine Books
P.O. Box 15601
Chevy Chase, MD 20825
(301) 588-9590
Owner(s): Anita Macy
Type of Shop: Mail-order antiquarian.
Major Categories represented by at least 100 titles:
    Americana   History   Poetry
    Art   Mystery   Rare Books
    Children's   Travel
    Fiction
Other major categories: 19th and 20th century first editions, foreign language, illustrated.
Approximate number of volumes: 8,500
       paperback: --
       hardback : 95%
Catalog issued occasionally.
Additional information: Founded in 1986. Appraisals, book searches.

Book Nook
9933 Rhode Island Ave.
College Park, MD 20740
(301) 474-4060
Hours: Mon-Sat:10-5 Wed:10-7:30
Owner(s): Mary Monteith
Type of Shop: General - second-hand, used.
Major Categories represented by at least 100 titles:

Art	Gardening	Paperback
Business	Health-fitness	Poetry
Children's	History	Religion
Collectibles	Hobbies & Crafts	Romance
Cooking	Mystery	Science Fiction
Do-it-yourself	Nature	Science/Technology
Education		Spectator Sports
Fiction		

Other major categories: Black history & women's studies, foreign language, biographies, westerns, humor, classics, literature, occult/new age, horror.
Special Items and Services: Comics and small selection of books on tape. No formal searches per se, but will keep eye open for customers searching for specific titles.
Directions: Take exit 25B (College Park) off the Beltway (I-495), get in far left lane and turn left at first light onto Edgewood Road. At four-way stop, take left onto Rhode Island Ave. Go one block, store is on right. Large parking lot in front of store with free parking.
Additional information: Store founded in 1975. Store has occupied several locations on Rhode Island Ave. Present store is new, bright, and well laid out by subject. Easy to find what one is looking for. A "kiss and ride" stop on the Green Line is due to open 6-8 blocks away in a year or two. Good dining within two miles including ChiChi's, Fireside, Sir Walter Raleigh Inn, and Beefsteak Charlies. Ms. Monteith also owns the Book Nook II in Glen Burnie, Md. Three handicap parking spaces directly in front of store and a ramp. Aisles are 3 to 4 feet wide and the restroom has handicap bars and turn-around room. 1,500 sq. ft. shop area.

Steven C. Bernard - First Editions
15011 Plainfield Lane
Darnestown, MD 20874
(301) 948-8423
Hours: By appointment only.
Owner(s): Steven C. Bernard
Professional Affiliations: A.B.A.A., W.A.B.A.
Type of Shop: Mail-order antiquarian.
Major Categories represented by at least 100 titles:

Fiction	Mystery	Rare Books
		Science Fiction

Other major categories: Modern first editions and signed first editions.
Approximate number of volumes: 5,000
        paperback: 1%
        hardback : 99%

Approximate breakdown: rare: 70%
out-of-print: 30%
in-print: --
Catalog issued 5-6 times per year. Free to buyers - $3 for new customers.
Directions: 22 miles northwest of Washington, DC off Seneca Road between River Road and Rt 28. Residential off-street parking.
Additional information: Founded in 1974. Mail-order business has been operated from several former residences over the years.

The Book Shelf
57 Mayo Road
Edgewater, MD 21037
(410) 798-0595
Hours: Mon-Fri:10:30-5   Sat:10:30-4   Sun:Noon-4:00   (Closed Wed)
Owner(s): Cathy Toth
Type of Shop: General
Major Categories represented by at least 100 titles:

Children's	History	Paperback
Fiction	Mystery	Religion
	Nature	Romance
	Nautical	Science Fiction

Approximate number of volumes: 30,000
paperback: 65%
hardback: 35%
Approximate breakdown: rare: --
out-of-print: 15%
in-print: 85%
Additional information: Founded in 1989. London Towne Publik House nearby. Will buy/trade books. 1,400 sq. ft. shop area.

Book Alcove, Inc.
15976 Shady Grove Road
Gaithersburg, MD 20877
(301) 977-9166
Hours: Mon-Fri:10-8   Sat:10-6   Sun:12-5
Owner(s): Carl Sickles
Professional Affiliations: Washington Antiquarian Booksellers Association.
Type of Shop: General.
Major Categories represented by at least 100 titles:
    ALL CATEGORIES.
Special Items and Services: Appraisals by Ray Sickles.
Directions: Located in shopping center on Shady Grove Road between I-270 and Route 355.
Additional information: Store founded in 1974. Same location for past 15 years. Good dining nearby.

Chervyl's Cookbooks
18705 Capella Lane
Gaithersburg, MD 20877
(301) 977-8033
Hours: Mail order and catalog only.
Owner(s): Chervyl Hammerley
Type of Shop: A catalog of choice culinary comestibles for cooks and collectors.
Specialty Categories: Special section of household how-to titles. Of special interest in the catalog are many fine advertising cook booklets and leaflets put out over the years by various food companies and manufacturers.
Approximate number of volumes: 300
　　　　　paperback: 60%
　　　　　hardback : 40%
Approximate breakdown: rare: --
　　　　　out-of-print: 95%
　　　　　in-print: 5%
Catalog available. Price is $2 and is refundable with a $5 (or larger) order. Titles are fully described including date, condition, description of contents, etc.
Special Items and Services: Free book search service.
Additional information: Founded in 1991.

Olde Soldier Books, Inc.
18779-B North Frederick Road
Gaithersburg, MD 20879
(301) 963-2929
Hours: Mon-Fri:9-4 Sat:9-3
Owner(s): Dave & Chris Zullo
Type of Shop: Specialty - American Civil War
Approximate number of volumes: --
　　　　　paperback: --
　　　　　hardback : 16,000
Approximate breakdown: rare: 8,000 (rare & out-of-print)
　　　　　out-of-print: --
　　　　　in-print: 8,000
Free catalog issued monthly.
Special Items and Services: Letters, photos, documents, medals, ribbons and autographs. Appraisals and book searches.
Directions: Take I-495 (Capital Beltway) to I-270 north, exit 11. Turn left on Rt 355 (Frederick Road) and go 1.2 miles. Turn right on Game Preserve Road. Store located at first right.
Additional information: Store founded in 1975. Shopping mall with dining located one mile away. Handicap access. 1,500 sq. ft.

Doris Frohnsdorff
P.O. Box 2306
Gaithersburg, MD 20886
(301) 869-1256
Hours: By appointment.
Owner(s): Doris Frohnsdorff
Professional Affiliations: A.B.A.A., I.L.A.B.
Type of Shop: Antiquarian (rare books).
Major Categories represented by at least 100 titles:
```
    Children's                                  Rare Books
```
Other major categories: Fine bindings and miniature books.
Specialty Categories: Beatrix Potter.
Catalog issued 4 times per year. Founded in 1967.

Delmarva Book Shop
300 Drummer Drive   [Route 50-301, Exit 44B]
Grasonville, MD 21638
(410) 827-9400
Hours: Wed-Sun:10-5
Owner(s): Christopher Dobbyn
Type of Shop: General antiquarian and paperback.
Major Categories represented by at least 100 titles:
```
    Americana         Gardening            Paperback
    Business          Health-fitness       Rare Books
    Children's        Hobbies & Crafts     Romance
    Cooking           Mystery              Science Fiction
    Do-it-yourself    Nautical
    Education
    Fiction
```
Other major categories: Eastern Shore, Chesapeake Bay.
Specialty Categories: Wall Street (stock markets), yachting (sail & power, Chesapeake Bay), ships & voyages.
Approximate number of volumes: 35,000
           paperback: 20%
           hardback : 80%
Approximate breakdown: rare: 5%
                out-of-print: 85%
                    in-print: 10% (including new books)
Catalog available in January 1993.
Special Items and Services: Nautical prints with custom framing. "Books for the Beach."
Directions: Exit 44B from Rt 50-301, 100 feet to right on Drummer Drive., third building on right. Book shop is visible from east and westbound lanes of Rt 50-301. Parking for 26 cars, plenty of extra parking with easy turn-around for buses, trailers and RVs. Easy on/off Rt 50-301.
Additional information: Founded in 1992. Located in middle of upscale outlet stores (Bay Bridge to Queenstown). Many antique shops within five miles. Great local waterfront dining. Bookshop shares same property with flea market. Handicap access. 1,600 sq. ft. shop area.

Lionel Epstein - Bookseller
9909 Old Spring Road
Kensington, MD 20895
(301) 949-8622
Hours: By appointment
Owner(s): Lionel Epstein
Type of Shop: Specialty
Specialty Categories: Law, economics, American history.
Free catalog issued 3 to 4 times per year. Book searches.

Children's BookAdoption Agency
P.O. Box 643
Kensington, MD 20895-0643
(301) 565-2834   FAX (301) 585-3091
Hours: By appointment
Owner(s): Barbara B. Yoffee, B.S. M.S. Ed.
Type of Shop: Specialty - children's books.
Major Categories represented by at least 100 titles:
    Children's   Poetry
                                      Rare Books
Other major categories: African-American (adults' & children's books)
Specialty Categories: Late 19th century (1890-1900), early 20th century (1901-1940), modern (1941 to present).
Approximate number of volumes: 10,000
        paperback: 500
        hardback : 9,500
Approximate breakdown: rare: 750
        out-of-print: 8,250
            in-print: 1,000 (generally first editions or printings)
Free catalog issued 4 times per year.
Special Items and Services: Some unusual illustrated books, older travel guides, items of local interest in Md. & D.C., and early World's Fair memorabilia. Book searches, mail order.
Directions: Located on Md. Rt 192, directly north of the Mormon Temple.
Additional information: Founded in 1987 by present owner. The business was initially formed to provide inexpensive, high-quality children's books to nursery schools and day care centers. Owner is early childhood education specialist who is available at nominal charge (in some cases no charge) to advise such institutions on the development of libraries and reading readiness programs. Handicap access not difficult, no special arrangement. Located near Antique Row in Kensington. 750 sq. ft. shop area.

Comic Classics
365 Main Street
Laurel, MD 20707
(410) 792-4744
Hours: Mon-Fri:12-8 Sat:12-6 Sun:12-5

Maryland - Region 2   103

Type of Shop: Mostly comics, some paperback.
Specialty Categories: Comics and used paperbacks on science fiction, horror and fantasy.
Monthly catalog issued first Friday of each month ($1.25).
Special Items and Services: Items: Posters, T-shirts, sports and non-sports cards, price guides for sports, non-sports, comics (many more can be ordered), storage supplies for comics and cards, limited edition prints, imported video tapes and toys. Services: Subscriptions, mail order, military discounts, subscriber discounts, extensive back issue selection, layaway, gift certificates, appraisals, catalog to order in advance limited edition prints. Collections purchased.
Directions: Less than one mile off I-95. Take Route 216 Laurel exit, take left at second light on Main Street. Directly off Route 1 (west side). There is parking on Main Street and on side streets. Some parking lots are available for general public.
Additional information: Main Street has many antique stores, a dinner theatre and restaurants within walking distance. Another used bookstore and a coin dealer are also at Route 1 and Main Street. Handicap access. This is a comics specialty store which also carries used paperbacks. New shipments every week. Many items in store and additional items in catalog which are difficult to find elsewhere. Opened second location in 1991 in Frostburg, MD (203 E. Main Street, (301) 689-1823).

Attic Books
100 Washington Blvd.
Laurel, MD 20707
(301) 725-3725
Hours: Mon-Sat:10-7 (Closed Tues.)   Sun:1-5
Owner(s): Richard Cook
Major Categories represented by at least 100 titles:

Americana	History	Paperback
Art	Military History	Philosophy
Cooking	Music	Poetry
Fiction	Mystery	Religion
	Nature	Science Fiction
		Spectator Sports
		Travel

Other major categories: Drama, literary criticism.
Specialty Categories: Science fiction, military.
Approximate number of volumes: 25,000
        paperback: 25%
        hardback : 75%
Approximate breakdown: rare: 10%
        out-of-print: 60%
        in-print: 30%
Special Items and Services: Science fiction collection appraisals.
Directions: Corner of Route 1 south and Main Street in downtown Laurel, MD.
Additional information: Store founded in 1971 in Wheaton, MD. Located in Laurel since 1985. Founded by John Basilico, also founder of Second Story Books. Antique shops, dinner theatre and restaurants are all within walking distance. 1,200 sq. ft. shop area.

The Vintage Paperback Exchange
8821 Cardinal Court
Laurel, MD 20723
(301) 369-0484
Hours: Mail order and by appointment.
Type of Shop: Vintage paperback.
Major Categories represented by at least 100 titles:
    Fiction   Mystery   Paperback
                                            Rare Books
                                            Romance
                                            Science Fiction
                                            Spectator Sports
Other major categories: Westerns.
Specialty Categories: Old paperbacks and first printings.
Approximate number of volumes: 10,000
Free catalog issued roughly every month.
Special Items and Services: Buys vintage paperback collections.
Directions: Private residence.
Additional information: Founded in 1991.

Frazier Americana
10509 Water Point Way
Mitchellville, MD 20721
(301) 336-3616
Owner(s): William Frazier
Type of Shop: Mail order - Civil War books & prints.
Specialty Categories: Civil War and Presidential titles.
Approximate number of volumes: 1,000+
        paperback: 1%
        hardback : 99%
Approximate breakdown: rare: 10%
                      out-of-print: 80%
                      in-print: 10%
Catalog issued three times per year at $5.
Special Items and Services: Engravings and prints. Appraisals and book searches.
Additional information: Founded in 1986. Mail order and shows only.

T.A. Borden
17119 Old Baltimore Road
Olney, MD 20832
(301) 774-4669
Hours: By appointment.
Owner(s): Guy Gram and T. Borden
Type of Shop: General stock of out-of-print, antiquarian, and rare hardbacks.

Major Categories represented by at least 100 titles:
- Americana
- Art
- Fiction
- Nature
- Science/Technology
- Travel

Other major categories: Almost all major categories represented. Also a growing stock of out-of-print and enduring academic titles in all fields.
Specialty Categories: Orientalia.
Approximate number of volumes: 2,500-3,000
        paperback: 0%-1%
        hardback : 99%-100%
Approximate breakdown: rare: (over $100) 5-10%
        out-of-print: essentially all.
        in-print: --
Catalogs or lists available occasionally.
Special Items and Services: Offers consulting on collection development, especially in history and area studies.
Directions: Located three houses off Georgia Ave. (on east side). Parking in driveway.
Additional information: Founded in 1987. Olney Ale House on Rt 108, three minutes away, is famous for good brews, home-made soups, bread, sandwiches, and low prices.

Quill & Brush
Box 5365
Rockville, MD 20848
(301) 460-3700
Hours: By appointment only.
Owner(s): Patricia & Allan Ahearn
Professional Affiliations: A.B.A.A., I.L.A.B., A.B.A.
Type of Shop: Antiquarian
Major Categories represented by at least 100 titles:
- Fiction
- Mystery
- Poetry
- Rare Books
- Science Fiction
- Travel

Approximate number of volumes: 8,000 first editions.
Annual catalog - $10. Five others free.
Special Items and Services: Author price guides. Appraisals and book searches.
Directions: Residence off Bel Pre Road between Georgia Ave. and Norbeck Road (Rt 28). Route 28 east off I-270.
Additional information: Founded in 1976. 800 sq. ft. shop area.

Richard Alexander Books
5901 Montrose Road, # 807N
Rockville, MD 20852
(301) 816-2944
Hours: Mail order only.
Owner(s): Richard Alexander
Type of Shop: Mail order - out-of-print book searches.

Q. M. Dabney & Company
11910 Parklawn Drive
Rockville, MD 20852
(301) 881-1470
Hours: Mon-Fri:9-5:30 Saturday by appointment.
Professional Affiliations: A.B.A.A.
Type of Shop: Mail-order antiquarian (not a "browsing bookstore").
Major Categories represented by at least 100 titles:

Americana	History	Political Science
Aviation	Military History	Rare Books
	Music	
	Nautical	

Approximate breakdown: rare: --
out-of-print: 100%
in-print: --
Catalog issued 20 times per year at $1 to $3.
Directions: Beltway (I-495) to Bethesda, take Rockville exit, north on Rockville Pike, right on Randolph Road, right on Parklawn Drive (second signal) to 11910.
Additional information: Founded in 1962. Other used book stores in area. Book searches offered.

Peter Pun Books
835 Bowie Road
Rockville, MD 20852
(301) 762-4062
Hours: By appointment.
Owner(s): Joseph E. Jeffs
Type of Shop: Antiquarian
Major Categories represented by at least 100 titles:

Americana	History	Poetry
Art	Military History	Rare Books
Fiction		

Specialty Categories: Americana, literary first editions, art, rare books, literary manuscripts & correspondence, Civil War.
Approximate number of volumes: 5,000
paperback: 1%
hardback : 99%
Approximate breakdown: rare: 60%
out-of-print: 39%
in-print: 1%
Special Items and Services: Literary manuscripts & correspondence, historical correspondence, some fine prints. Book searches.
Directions: Operates from home, one minute from Rockville Pike (Rt 355) and Ritchie Parkway in Rockville, Md.
Additional information: Founded in 1991. Material priced for dealer resale. 350 sq. ft. shop area.

Second Story Books
12160 Parklawn Drive
Rockville, MD 20852-1708
(301) 770-0477
Hours: Sun-Thur:10-6 Fri & Sat:10-9
Owner(s): Allan Stypeck (president)
Professional Affiliations: A.B.A.A., I.L.A.B., A.B.A., A.S.A.
Major Categories represented by at least 100 titles:
ALL CATEGORIES.
Specialty Categories: Rare books.
Approximate number of volumes: 250,000
        paperback: 30%
        hardback : 70%
Approximate breakdown: rare: 20%
        out-of-print: 60%
        in-print: 20%
Catalog will be available in the future.
Additional information: Appraisals and expert witness. 14,000 sq. ft. shop area. Second Story Books has four locations in the Baltimore-Washington area.

Yak & Yeti Books
P.O. Box 5736
Rockville, MD 20855
(301) 977-7285
Hours: By appointment only.
Owner(s): Daniel W. Edwards
Type of Shop: Specialty antiquarian.
Major Categories represented by at least 100 titles:
    Exploration   History   Travel
Specialty Categories: All subjects pertaining to Himalayan lands, Central Asia, Mongolia & Tibet.
Approximate number of volumes: 1,500 separate titles
        paperback: 5%
        hardback : 95%
Approximate breakdown: rare: 5%
        out-of-print: 70%
        in-print: 25%
Catalog available on request three times per year.
Special Items and Services: Reference library and stock open to bonafide scholars/authors for research purposes.
Additional information: Founded in 1982. "We have more titles on that geographical region of the world (Himalayas, Tibet & Central Asia) than any U.S. dealer." Located within walking distance of Washington's metrorail system.

Old Books at Savage Mill
Antique Center I, Savage Mill (P.O. Box 231)
Savage, MD 20763
(410) 531-6065
Hours: Daily:9-5
Owner(s): Steve & Rita Elkins
Type of Shop: Used & rare hardbacks, vintage paperbacks.
Major Categories represented by at least 100 titles:

Art	Gardening	Paperback
Children's	History	Poetry
Cooking	Medicine	Rare Books
Fiction	Military History	Religion
	Mystery	
	Nautical	

Other major categories: Modern first editions.
Approximate number of volumes: 8,000
    paperback: 10%
    hardback : 90%
Approximate breakdown: rare: 28%
    out-of-print: 70%
    in-print: 2%
Free catalog issued now and again.
Special Items and Services: Posters, prints. Free international book search.
Directions: Located midway between Washington & Baltimore. Exit 38A off I-95 to Historic Savage Mill. Located in Antique Center I.
Additional information: Business founded in 1981; present location since 1987. Send for copy of current catalog, quoters asked to send for copy of want list, searchers asked to send in your wants. Collections purchased. Over 200 antique dealers in Historic Savage Mill. Also restaurants, craft shops, artist studios and much more. Handicap access.

Hirschtritt's "1712"
1712 Republic Road
Silver Spring, MD 20902
(301) 649-5393
Hours: By appointment only.
Owner(s): Ralph Hirschtritt
Type of Shop: Mail order general out-of-print.
Major Categories represented by at least 100 titles:

Americana	History	Rare Books
Fiction	Nautical	Social Science
		Travel

Specialty Categories: Golf, Japan.
Approximate number of volumes: --
    paperback: --
    hardback : 2,000
Approximate breakdown: rare: 15%
    out-of-print: 85%
    in-print: 0%

Lists available. Founded in 1970.
Special Items and Services: Book searches and appraisals.

O'Boyle Books
14605 Pebblestone Drive
Silver Spring, MD 20905
(301) 384-9346
Owner(s): H. A. O'Boyle
Type of Shop: General & paperback - operated from home.
Major Categories represented by at least 100 titles:

Americana	History	Paperback
Children's	Military History	Rare Books
Collectibles	Mystery	Religion
Cooking		Romance
Fiction		
Folklore		

Approximate number of volumes: 1,500
        paperback: 300
        hardback : 1,200
Approximate breakdown: rare: 5%
        out-of-print: 85%
        in-print: 10%
Additional information: Semi-retired book collector for many years. Collected over 10,000 books then sold 90% to one dealer. Subscribes to want lists and exhibits at book fairs.

Imagination Books
946 Sligo Avenue
Silver Spring, MD 20910
(301) 589-2223
Hours: Mon-Sat:11-7 Sun:11-5 Closed Tuesdays
Owner(s): Elisenda D. Hopper
Type of Shop: General.
Major Categories represented by at least 100 titles:

Americana	Gardening	Paperback
Art	History	Philosophy
Children's	Hobbies & Crafts	Poetry
Collectibles	Military History	Political Science
Cooking	Music	Rare Books
Do-it-yourself	Mystery	Religion
Exploration	Mythology	Romance
Fiction	Nature	Science Fiction
Folklore		Science/Technology

Other major categories: Foreign language, occult, new age and black history.
Approximate number of volumes: --
        paperback: 10,000
        hardback : 10,000
Inquire to find if catalog is available.
Special Items and Services: Records. Book searches.
Directions: Georgia Avenue between Colesville Rd. & Rt 410 (East-West Hwy).

Metered parking, free on weekends.
Additional information: Founded in 1972. Under current ownership since 1991. Store has been completely reorganized. Three bookstores in Silver Spring. Good Italian restaurant across street. 1,200 sq. ft. shop area.

Silver Spring Books
938 Bonifant Street
Silver Spring, MD 20910
(301) 587-7484
Hours: Thur-Sat & Mon: 10-6:30   Sun: 10-5
Owner(s): C. Parker, W. Morgan, I. Morgan, P. DeFlumear, D. Goodwin
Professional Affiliations: Washington Romance Writers, Romance Writers of America.
Type of Shop: Five dealers - four general, one specialty.
Major Categories represented by at least 100 titles:

Americana	Gardening	Paperback
Antiques	History	Philosophy
Art	Hobbies & Crafts	Poetry
Business	Military History	Religion
Children's	Mystery	Romance
Collectibles	Nature	Science Fiction
Cooking		Science/Technology
Do-it-yourself		Social Science
Fiction		Travel
Folklore		

Specialty Categories: Black literature, science fiction, literature, religion, mystery, romance.
Approximate number of volumes: 50,000
　　　　paperback: 20%
　　　　hardback : 80%
Approximate breakdown: rare: 5%
　　　　out-of-print: 70%
　　　　in-print: 25%
Special Items and Services: Appraisals, some limited searching for books.
Directions: One block off Georgia Ave. in downtown Silver Spring. Two blocks from Silver Spring Metro Station.
Additional information: New location established in 1992. Five former partners of Imagination Books (Silver Spring, MD) - "120+ years of bookman experience." Used bookstore across street. Wheelchair access, wide aisles throughout. 1,400 sq. ft. shop area.

Atherton's Used Books
2913 Stanton Avenue
Silver Spring, MD 20910
(301) 589-3879
Hours: By appointment.
Owner(s): Pat & Jim Atherton
Type of Shop: General

Maryland - Region 2

Major Categories represented by at least 100 titles:
```
Art            Military History
Children's     Nautical
Cooking
Fiction
```
Additional information: Founded in 1978. Dealer sells at book fairs and by appointment.

Tales Retold
939 Bonifant Street
Silver Spring, MD 20910
(301) 588-1933
Hours: Mon-Sat:11-6 Sun:1-4
Owner(s): Christine Vincent
Type of Shop: General
Major Categories represented by at least 100 titles:
```
Art             History         Paperback
Business        Mystery         Philosophy
Children's                      Poetry
Collectibles                    Political Science
Cooking                         Religion
Fiction                         Science Fiction
                                Science/Technology
                                Social Science
                                Travel
```
Other major categories: "We have a little of everything."
Specialty Categories: Science fiction and fantasy.
Approximate number of volumes: 5,000
   paperback: 3,000
   hardback : 2,000
Approximate breakdown: rare: 200-300
   out-of-print: 3,000
   in-print: 1,500
Special Items and Services: Postcards, greeting cards, used records.
Directions: From I-495: take Georgia Avenue south, continue for about 1 1/2 miles to Bonifant St., turn left. Store is on left in middle of block. Parking on Bonifant Street. Located 2 blocks from Silver Spring Metro.
Additional information: Founded in 1989 by present owner. Other used book stores and good dining nearby. 1,200 sq. ft. shop area. Limited handicap access.

Ground Zero Books, Ltd.
P.O. Box 1046, Blair Station
Silver Spring, MD 20910
(301) 585-1471
Hours: By appointment.
Owner(s): R. Alan Lewis & Lynne Haims
Type of Shop: Specialty
Major Categories represented by at least 100 titles:
```
Americana       History             Political Science
Aviation        Military History    Rare Books
                Nautical            Science/Technology
```

Specialty Categories: Military science and technology, military medicine, and wars of the 20th century.
Approximate number of volumes: 40,000
        paperback: 1%
        hardback : 99%
Approximate breakdown: rare: 10%
        out-of-print: 85%
        in-print: 5%
Catalog issued free three times a year.
Special Items and Services: Posters. Appraisals and book searches.
Directions: Call first.
Additional information: Founded in 1978 by trained graduate historians.

Well Read Books
7050 Carroll Avenue
Takoma Park, MD 20912
(301) 270-4748
Hours: Mon-Fri:12-7 Weekends:11-6 Open 7 days.
Owner(s): Margaret Fletcher and Shirley Burgess
Type of Shop: General and new & used comics.
Major Categories represented by at least 100 titles:

Art	History	Paperback
Children's	Hobbies & Crafts	Philosophy
Cooking	Mystery	Poetry
Do-it-yourself		Political Science
Fiction		Religion
		Science Fiction
		Science/Technology
		Social Science
		Spectator Sports
		Travel

Directions: Old Town Takoma Park. Meter parking.
Additional information: Founded in 1989. Small shop with a carefully selected stock. Excellent science fiction, mystery and children's area. New comics every week. Small selection of back issues. Located in shopping area of Takoma Park. Nearby restaurants: Taliano's, Mark's Kitchen, Everyday Gourmet. 750 sq. ft. shop area.

The Barbarian Bookshop
11254 Triangle Lane
Wheaton, MD 20902
(301) 946-4184
Hours: Tues-Sun:12-6
Owner(s): George Bridgers
Type of Shop: General, comics and role-playing games.

Major Categories represented by at least 100 titles:

Americana	Gardening	Paperback
Art	Health-fitness	Philosophy
Business	History	Poetry
Children's	Hobbies & Crafts	Political Science
Collectibles	Military History	Religion
Cooking	Music	Romance
Do-it-yourself	Mystery	Science Fiction
Fiction	Nature	Science/Technology
		Social Science
		Spectator Sports
		Travel

Approximate number of volumes: 100,000
    paperback: 75%
    hardback : 25%
Approximate breakdown: rare: 0%
    out-of-print: 95%
    in-print: 5%
Special Items and Services: Comics, posters, role-playing games, models, nostalgia, collectibles.
Directions: Near intersections of Georgia, University, and Viers Mill Roads; behind Dunkin' Donuts, 1/2 block from Wheaton Red Line Metro.
Additional information: Store founded in 1970. Large parking lot available and restaurants nearby. 1,800 sq. ft. shop area.

Bowes Books
718 Great Mills Road
Lexington Park, MD 20653
(301) 863-6200
Hours: Mon-Sat:9-6
Owner(s): Joseph F. Bowes
Type of Shop: General
Major Categories represented by at least 100 titles:
    Americana   History
Other major categories: Civil War.
Additional information: Store carries primarily new books.

Second Looks Books
759 Solomons Island Road N., Fox Run Shopping Ctr. (PO Box 600)
Prince Frederick, MD 20678
(410) 535-6897
Hours: Mon-Wed:10-7   Thurs-Fri:10-8   Sat:10-5
Owner(s): Richard C. Due and Elizabeth A. Prouty
Type of Shop: General
Directions: Located on Rts 2/4 at Fox Run Shopping Center next to Peebles Department Store. Ample parking.
Additional information: Founded in 1991, stock still growing. Handicap access.

114   Maryland - Region 3

Lazy Moon Bookshop
14510 Main Street
Solomons, MD 20688
(410) 326-3720
Hours: Summer - 7 days:11-6   Winter - Thurs-Mon:11-6
Owner(s): Jim Gscheidig
Type of Shop: General, specialty, antiquarian, paperback.
Major Categories represented by at least 100 titles:

Americana	Gardening	Paperback
Antiques	Geography	Philosophy
Art	History	Poetry
Children's	Military History	Rare Books
Collectibles	Music	Religion
Cooking	Mystery	Romance
Exploration	Mythology	Science Fiction
Fiction	Nature	Science/Technology
Folklore	Nautical	Social Science
	Outdoor Recreation	Spectator Sports
		Travel

Specialty Categories: Nautical books, Chesapeake Bay (new and OP), military history, science fiction & mystery, classic literature, first edition fiction.
Approximate number of volumes: --
　　　　paperback: 8,500
　　　　hardback : 7,000
Approximate breakdown: rare: 10%
　　　　　　　　　out-of-print: 40%
　　　　　　　　　in-print: 50%
Catalog available in future on mystery, science fiction and first editions (fiction).
Special Items and Services: Book searches, appraisals, will special order new books.
Directions: From D.C.: Capital Beltway (I-495) to Rt 4 (Pennsylvania Ave. south). After approximately one hour turn left into Solomons before crossing the Thomas Johnson Bridge.
From Baltimore: Take Rt 3/301 south to Upper Marlboro, then south on Rt 4 (Pennsylvania Ave.) approximately 50 miles. Turn left into Solomons before crossing the Thomas Johnson Bridge.
Additional information: Founded in 1988. Previously owned Imagination Books in Silver Spring, MD from 1978 till 1991; was voted "best used bookshop" in D.C. by the City Paper in 1986. Located in an old house built in 1912 on the Patuxent River near the Chesapeake Bay. "A bit of a drive but well worth the effort." Solomons Marine Museum (one of best in the country) nearby. Plenty of good seafood restaurants. 1,200 sq. ft. shop area.

Ellie's Paperback Shack
Box 31-D Acton Square
Waldorf, MD 20601-9402
(301) 934-3140 or (301) 843-3676
Hours: Mon-Sat:10-5 or 6
Type of Shop: 80% paperback, 20% hardback.

Major Categories represented by at least 100 titles:

Children's	Gardening	Paperback
Cooking	Health-fitness	Philosophy
Do-it-yourself	History	Poetry
Education	Hobbies & Crafts	Religion
Fiction	Medicine	Romance
	Music	Science Fiction
	Mystery	Science/Technology
	Mythology	Spectator Sports
	Nature	
	Nautical	

Other major categories: Military non-fiction.
Approximate number of volumes: 20,000
       paperback: 15,000
       hardback : 5,000
Approximate breakdown: rare: --
                out-of-print: majority
                in-print: --
Special Items and Services: Takes requests for hard-to-find books.
Directions: Located twenty minutes south of Branch Ave. exit off Beltway (I-495) on Route 301 in Waldorf, MD.
Additional information: Store founded in 1977 and at same location for past 12 years. Good dining nearby. Dr. Mudd House and Suratt House not far away. 1,200 sq. ft. shop area. Handicap access.

Washington, DC

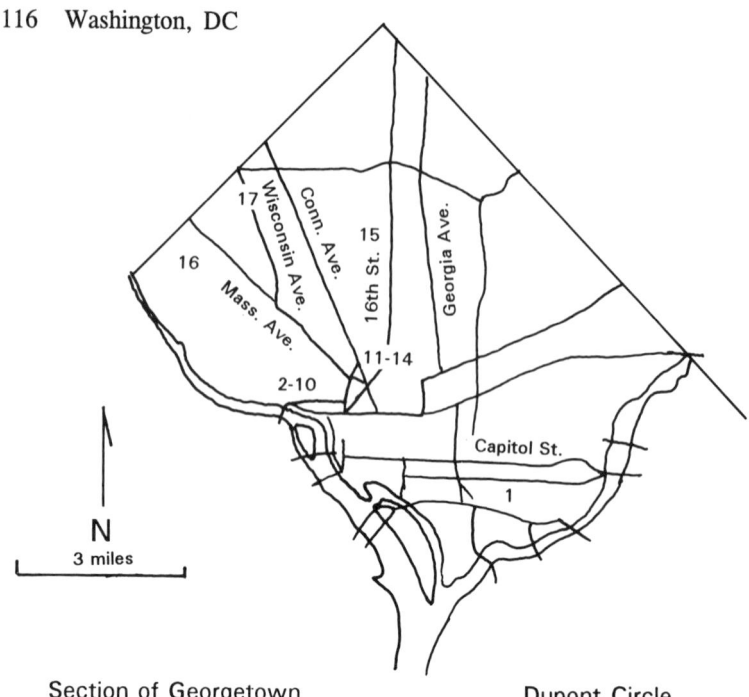

Section of Georgetown
(All streets in area are shown)

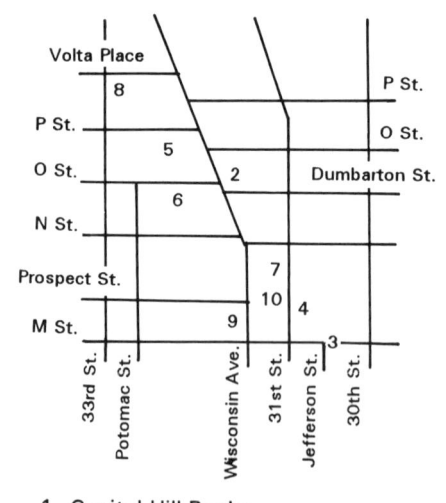

Dupont Circle
(Many streets not shown)

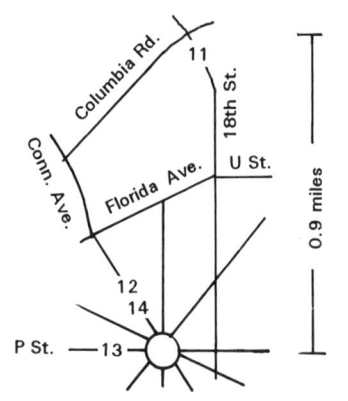

1. Capitol Hill Books
2. The Old Forest Bookshop
3. Logic & Literature Bookshop
4. Booked Up
5. Fuller & Saunders Books
6. The Lantern Bryn Mawr Bookshop
7. The Old Print Gallery
8. Ptak Science Books
9. Rock Creek Bookshop
10. William F. Hale - Books
11. Idle Time Books
12. Lambda Rising
13. Second Story Books
14. Kultura's Books & Records
15. Samuel Yudkin & Associates
16. Voyages Books & Art
17. Yesterday's Books
-- The President's Box Bookshop (mail order only)

Capitol Hill Books
657 C Street, SE
Washington, DC 20003
(202) 544-1621
Hours: Mon-Fri:11-7 Sat:9-6 Sun:11-5
Owner(s): William J. Kerr
Type of Shop: General
Major Categories represented by at least 100 titles:

Americana	Gardening	Philosophy
Art	History	Poetry
Children's	Military History	Religion
Cooking	Music	Science Fiction
Exploration	Mystery	Science/Technology
Fiction		Spectator Sports
		Travel

Other major categories: Theater, occult, metaphysical, psychiatry, classics (Latin and Greek).
Specialty Categories: Travel narratives.
Approximate number of volumes: 12,000
        paperback: 30%
        hardback : 70%
Approximate breakdown: rare: 0.05%
        out-of-print: 40%
        in-print: 60%
Additional information: Store founded in 1990. Location adjacent to Eastern Market (an old-fashioned public food market). 1,000 sq. ft. shop area.

The Old Forest Bookshop
3145 Dumbarton Street, NW
Washington, DC 20007
(202) 965-3842
Hours: Tues-Sat:11-7 Sun:Noon-6 (Closed Mondays)
Owner(s): Derrick Hsu
Professional Affiliations: W.A.B.A.
Type of Shop: Used and out-of-print books for both general and scholarly interests, specializing in literature, history and art.
Major Categories represented by at least 100 titles:

Americana	Gardening	Paperback
Art	History	Philosophy
Children's	Military History	Poetry
Cooking	Music	Science/Technology
Exploration	Nature	Travel
Fiction	Nautical	

Approximate number of volumes: --
        paperback: 3,500
        hardback : 7,000
Approximate breakdown: rare: --
        out-of-print: 50%
        in-print: 50%

Washington, DC

Special Items and Services: Postcards and classical, jazz, blues and folk LPs.
Directions: In Georgetown, near Wisconsin Ave. between N and O Streets.
Additional information: Founded in 1988. Previously located in Bethesda, MD. Several other used and rare bookshops within blocks. Georgetown is a well-known and popular shopping and dining district in DC. 1,200 sq. ft. shop area.

Logic & Literature Book Shop
3034 M Street, NW, 2nd floor
Washington, DC 20007
(202) 625-1668
Hours: Wed-Sat:1-6 Mon & Tues:By appointment.
Owner(s): Candee S. Harris
Professional Affiliations: W.A.B.A.
Type of Shop: General out-of-print and antiquarian.
Major Categories represented by at least 100 titles:

Americana	History	Philosophy
Art	Military History	Science/Technology
Exploration	Mythology	Social Science
Fiction	Nature	Travel

Specialty Categories: Classical studies (Greek & Latin), ancient & medieval history and archeology, mathematics, logic, and history of science.
Approximate number of volumes: 5,000
    paperback: 5%
    hardback : 95%
Approximate breakdown: rare: 10%
    out-of-print: 80%
    in-print: 10%
Catalog issued quarterly at $2 each.
Special Items and Services: Appraisals and searches within specialty fields shown above.
Directions: Located in center of the Georgetown area on M Street between 30th and 31st Streets. Metered parking on street and pay lot next to building.
Additional information: Ten second-hand and antiquarian shops within a six-block radius. Dozens of good restaurants of various specialty and ethnic cuisines. Climbing staircase is required to reach second floor. Catalog or mail order available for those unable to use stairs. Owner welcomes members of the trade and offers reciprocal terms.

Booked Up
1209 31st Street NW
Washington, DC 20007
(202) 965-3244
Hours: Mon-Fri:11-3 Sat:10-12:30
Owner(s): Marcia Carter and Larry McMurtry
Professional Affiliations: A.B.A.A.
Type of Shop: Antiquarian

Washington, DC   119

Major Categories represented by at least 100 titles:

Americana	History	Philosophy
Children's		Poetry
Exploration		Rare Books
Fiction		Religion
		Science Fiction
		Travel

Specialty Categories: Rare books.
Approximate number of volumes: 20,000
        paperback: --
        hardback : 100%
Approximate breakdown: rare: 75%
        out-of-print: 25%
        in-print: --
Directions: Located in Georgetown.
Additional information: Store founded in 1971.

Fuller & Saunders Books
3238 P Street, NW
Washington, DC 20007
(202) 337-3235
Type of Shop: General
Major Categories represented by at least 100 titles:

Americana	History	Poetry
Exploration	Military History	Rare Books
Fiction		Travel

Other major categories: Modern firsts, Washington, DC and vicinity, and baseball.
Approximate number of volumes: 4,000
        paperback: 10%
        hardback : 90%
Approximate breakdown: rare: 40%
        out-of-print: 60%
        in-print: --
Free catalog available.
Directions: Second floor, 100 feet west of Wisconsin Ave., south side of P Street.
Additional information: Store founded in 1985. Located in Georgetown within a ten-minute walk of nine other used and antiquarian shops. 400 sq. ft. shop area.

The Lantern Bryn Mawr Bookshop Inc.
3222 O Street, NW
Washington, DC 20007
(202) 333-3222
Hours: Mon-Fri:11-4   Sat:11-5   Sun:12-4
Type of Shop: General
Major Categories represented by at least 100 titles:

Americana	Gardening	Paperback
Art	Geography	Philosophy

(LIST CONTINUED NEXT PAGE)

Business	Health-fitness	Poetry
Children's	History	Political Science
Cooking	Hobbies & Crafts	Rare Books
Do-it-yourself	Medicine	Religion
Education	Military History	Science Fiction
Fiction	Music	Science/Technology
	Mystery	Social Science
	Nature	Spectator Sports
	Nautical	Travel
	Outdoor Recreation	

Approximate number of volumes: 15,000
    paperback: 5,000
    hardback : 10,000
Approximate breakdown: rare: 5%
    out-of-print: 35%
    in-print: 60%
Special Items and Services: CDs, records, prints, antiques and collectibles such as old silver, porcelain, crystal and paintings. Conducts book searches using "Bookman's Weekly."
Directions: Near Wisconsin Avenue in Georgetown. O Street is one-way running west to east. On-street parking available.
Additional information: Store founded in 1976. The Bryn Mawr Bookshop is a volunteer operation for the purpose of raising scholarship money for students of Bryn Mawr College in Pennsylvania. Books and collectibles are donated and all proceeds go to the College Scholarship Fund. A flight of six stairs required to enter the store. 3,000 sq. ft. shop area.

The Old Print Gallery
1220 31st Street, NW
Washington, DC 20007
(202) 965-1818
Hours: Mon-Sat:10-5:45
Owner(s): James C. Blakely, Judith Blakely, James von Ruster
Professional Affiliations: A.B.A.A., Appraisers Assn. of America
Type of Shop: Gallery selling antique prints and maps.
Catalogs issued quarterly ($3 each).
Special Items and Services: American and European antique prints and antique maps. Print/map searches, custom framing and paper conservation.
Directions: In heart of Georgetown one block north of M Street. On-street meter parking and commercial parking in covered lot at rear.
Additional information: Store founded in 1971. Shopping area and many restaurants nearby. Antiquarian bookstores and antique stores on same block.

Ptak Science Books
1531 33rd Street, NW
Washington, DC 20007
(202) 337-2878
Hours: Wed-Sat:12-6

Owner(s): J. F. Ptak
Type of Shop: Specialty - science & history of science.
Major Categories represented by at least 100 titles:
                         Medicine   Science/Technology
Approximate number of volumes: 30,000
Approximate breakdown: rare: 95% (rare & out-of-print)
                     out-of-print: --
                     in-print: 5%
Special Items and Services: Appraisals.
Additional information: Store founded in 1983.

Rock Creek Bookshop
1214 Wisconsin Avenue (P.O. Box 25692)
Washington, DC 20007
(202) 342-8046
Hours: Call ahead. Most afternoons to early evening.
Owner(s): Peter Seaborg
Type of Shop: General
Major Categories represented by at least 100 titles:
Americana	History	Philosophy
Art	Military History	Religion
Children's	Mystery	Science Fiction
Fiction	Nature	Travel

Specialty Categories: Civil War, military, U.S. history, general history, and philosophy/religion.
Approximate number of volumes: 10,000-15,000
                 paperback: 30%
                 hardback : 70%
Approximate breakdown: rare: 1-2%
                     out-of-print: 40-50%
                     in-print: 40-50%
Directions: Wisonsin Avenue & M Street in heart of Georgetown: upstairs in the third building up from M Street on the west side of Wisconsin Avenue, above Coach Leather Shop. Street parking catch-as-catch-can. Pay lots one block north, around corner on Prospect Street and two blocks south at foot of Wisconsin Avenue.
Additional information: Founded in 1986. Moved from Connecticut and Porter (Cleveland Park) three years before. The largest concentration of used bookshops in DC is here within a few blocks in Georgetown: ten within walking distance. Many restaurants, boutiques, and antique shops. 900 sq. ft. shop area.

William F. Hale - Books
1222 31st Street, NW
Washington, DC 20007
(202) 338-8272   FAX (202) 338-8420
Hours: Mon-Fri:1-6 pm
Owner(s): William F. Hale
Professional Affiliations: A.B.A.A., I.L.A.B.
Type of Shop: Antiquarian and scholarly books.

Major Categories represented by at least 100 titles:
```
Art                    Music                   Travel
```
Specialty Categories: Rare books.
Approximate number of volumes: 3,500
        paperback: --
        hardback : 99.9%
Approximate breakdown: rare: 40%
        out-of-print: 60%
        in-print: --
Catalog issued irregularly.
Special Items and Services: Appraisals and collection development.
Directions: In Georgetown, 1/3 block north (uphill) from M Street, directly opposite the Post Office. Meters along 31st Street.
Additional information: Store founded in 1975. Located next door to Old Print Gallery, across the street from Booked Up, and around the corner from Logic and Literature. There are ten bookshops in Georgetown. Handicap access with difficulty (three steps up and down). 540 sq. ft. shop area.

Idle Time Books
2410 18th Street, NW
Washington, DC 20009
(202) 232-4774
Hours: Seven days a week: 11-10
Owner(s): Jacques Morgan
Type of Shop: General
Major Categories represented by at least 100 titles:
  ALL CATEGORIES except: aviation, outdoor recreation, philosophy.
Approximate number of volumes: 30,000
        paperback: 10,000
        hardback : 20,000
Approximate breakdown: rare: less than 1%
        out-of-print: 50%
        in-print: 50%
Directions: North of Dupont Circle between 16th Street and Connecticut Ave NW. Street parking difficult but pay parking across street.
Additional information: Store founded in 1981. Store is located in a townhouse, and has three floors of books with selections in all categories. 4,500 sq. ft. shop area. Good nearby dining with a selection of 50 restaurants.

Lambda Rising (two locations)
1625 Connecticut Ave., NW   241 West Chase Street
Washington, DC 20009   Baltimore, MD 21201
(202) 462-6969   (410) 234-0069
Hours: Mon-Fri: 10am-midnight (DC); Mon-Fri: 11-8 (Balt.)
Owner(s): Deacon MacCubbin (DC), James Bennett (Balt.)
Professional Affiliations: A.B.A., C.R.A.B.S.
Type of Shop: Specialty - gay/lesbian.

Major Categories represented by at least 100 titles:

Art	Health-fitness	Paperback
Children's	History	Philosophy
Cooking	Medicine	Poetry
Fiction	Military History	Political Science
	Mystery	Rare Books
	Mythology	Religion
		Romance
		Science Fiction
		Social Science
		Travel

Other major categories: Both stores deal in gay/lesbian books with large selections of used and out-of-print books.
Approximate breakdown: rare: 30% (rare and out-of-print)
    out-of-print: --
    in-print: 70%
Catalog offered free three times a year. Mostly new titles but some listings for rare/out-of-print titles.
Special Items and Services: Book searches.
Directions: In the District, between Q&R Streets NW, 1 1/2 blocks from Dupont Circle. Limited street parking until 6:30 pm. Easy parking after that.
Additional information: Store founded in 1974. Both stores are located where there are related businesses in the neighborhoods. 1,700 sq. ft. shop area.

Samuel Yudkin & Associates
3636 16th Street, NW, Room A232 (for mail, Box A117)
Washington, DC 20010
(202) 232-6249   Home: (703) 768-1858)
Hours: 10-6 weekdays.
Owner(s): Samuel Yudkin
Professional Affiliations: Washington Rare Book Group, Washington Map Society, American Historic Print Collectors Society
Type of Shop: General
Major Categories represented by at least 100 titles:
 ALL CATEGORIES except: mythology, outdoor recreation.
Other major categories: National Geographics, other magazines, prints and maps.
Specialty Categories: First day covers.
Approximate breakdown: rare: 10%
    out-of-print: 75%
    in-print: 15%
Bimonthly auction catalog at $3.50 each or $25/year ($35/year with prices realized). Mixed bag catalog with used books and prints issued from time-to-time.
Special Items and Services: Prints, maps and first day covers. Appraisals, and auctions since 1970.
Directions: From Beltway (I-495): south on Georgia Avenue to Silver Spring. Stay in right lane, after two lights cut off to right to 16th Street. Proceed south to Woodner just south of Spring Road, take entrance into Woodner Garage - free parking.
Additional information: Founded in 1970. Samuel Yudkin, owner and president,

bookseller since 1948. Book auctions started on regular basis in 1970. At present location since 1986. Previous owner of Bonifant Books, sold in 1988. Open for purchases by appointment. Certain dates advertised for open sale each month. Copy of "Selling at Auction" available on request. Auction consignments invited. 3,500 sq. ft. shop area. Used bookstores nearby in Silver Spring and Bethesda, Md., and Adams Morgan, D.C.

The President's Box Bookshop
P.O. Box 1255
Washington, DC 20013
(703) 998-7390
Hours: Mail order only.
Owner(s): David A. Lovett
Type of Shop: Specialty antiquarian.
Specialty Categories: Specializes in rare and out-of-print books, pamphlets, and other ephemera on the assassination of American Presidents, Secret Service protection and related subjects.
Approximate number of volumes: --
        paperback: 20%
        hardback : 80%
Approximate breakdown: rare: 60%
        out-of-print: 39%
        in-print: less than 1%
Catalogs issued in spring and fall each year, and usually contain about 500 titles. Price is $3, refundable with purchase.
Special Items and Services: Appraisals and book searches in area of specialty.
Additional information: Founded in 1982.

Voyages Books & Art
4705 Butterworth Place, NW
Washington, DC 20016
(202) 244-9636
Hours: Daily:10(or 11)-6
Owner(s): William Claire
Type of Shop: Antiquarian
Major Categories represented by at least 100 titles:

```
    Americana          History            Poetry
    Antiques           Music              Rare Books
    Art                                   Spectator Sports
    Fiction
```

Specialty Categories: 20th century literature, but mainly general stock.
Approximate number of volumes: 10,000
        paperback: 1,000 vintage paperbacks.
        hardback : --
Approximate breakdown: rare: 30%
        out-of-print: 60%
        in-print: 10%

Washington, DC   125

Special Items and Services: Prints.   Searches and informal appraisals of 20th century literature.
Additional information: Founded in 1985.   Expanded slowly to five other professionally managed outlets: Alexandria, VA (Washington Antiques Center) 209 Madison at N. Fairfax, (703) 739-2484; Berkeley Springs, WV (Berkeley Springs Antique Mall), 102 Fairfax Street, (304) 258-9420; Queenstown, MD (Chesapeake Antique Center), Rt 301, (410) 827-6640; Lewes, DE (Heritage Antique Market), Rt 1, (302) 645-2309; Rehoboth Beach, DE (Affordable Antiques), 4300 Rt 1, (302) 227-5803.
Handicap access generally good except at Alexandria branch.

Yesterday's Books
4702 Wisconsin Avenue
Washington, DC 20016
(202) 363-0581
Hours: Mon-Thur:11-9   Fri-Sat:11-10   Sun:1-7
Owner(s):   Katina Stockbridge and Montez Swanner
Type of Shop: General
Major Categories represented by at least 100 titles:
   ALL CATEGORIES.
Other major categories: Womens' studies, photography, biographies, gay studies, black studies, true crime, anthropology, archeology, horror, classic literature, essays, linquistics, games, and humor.
Approximate number of volumes: --
            paperback: 50%
            hardback :   50%
Approximate breakdown: rare: 10%
              out-of-print: 30%
              in-print: 60%
Special Items and Services: Prints and records. Appraisals and book searches.
Directions: From Georgetown: come up Wisconsin Ave. about 3 miles, store on left. Parking on street and on side street of Chesapeake.
From I-495 (Beltway):   Take Wisconsin Ave. south (Route 355) for about four miles; store is on right next to Steak & Eggs.
Additional information: Store founded in 1975. An "especially cozy" store with coffee & fruit breads set out for customers, overstuffed chairs and a general air of comfort. Good dining nearby, movie theater, and a Metro Station. 1,500 sq. ft. shop area.

Second Story Books
2000 P Street, NW (Dupont Circle)
Washington, D.C. 20036
(202) 659-8884
Hours: Everyday:10-10
Owner(s):   Allan Stypeck (president)
Professional Affiliations: A.B.A.A., I.L.A.B., A.B.A., A.S.A.

Major Categories represented by at least 100 titles:
ALL CATEGORIES.
Specialty Categories: Rare books.
Approximate number of volumes: 75,000
            paperback: 35%
            hardback : 65%
Approximate breakdown: rare: 20%
            out-of-print: 60%
            in-print: 20%
Catalog will be available in the future.
Special Items and Services: Posters, prints, antiques, CDs and records. Appraisals, book searches and expert witness.
Additional information: Founded in 1979. Good dining and museums nearby. Handicap access. 2,800 sq. ft. shop area. Second Story Books has four locations in the Baltimore-Washington area.

Kulturas Books & Records
1621 Connecticut Ave., NW
Washington, DC 20036
(202) 462-2541
Hours: Mon-Sat:11-8 Sun:12-6
Owner(s): A. MacDonald
Professional Affiliations: General
Major Categories represented by at least 100 titles:

Art	History	Paperback
Children's	Music	Philosophy
Cooking	Mystery	Poetry
Fiction	Mythology	Political Science
	Nature	Rare Books
		Religion
		Science Fiction

Specialty Categories: Poetry, philosophy, art, and Marxist studies.
Approximate number of volumes: 20,000
            paperback: 15,000
            hardback : 5,000
Approximate breakdown: rare: 10%
            out-of-print: 40%
            in-print: 60%
Special Items and Services: Extensive jazz LP section.
Directions: One block north of Dupont Circle. Metro: Red Line Dupont Circle stop.
Additional information: Store founded in 1988. Located in center of town with restaurants, night life, etc. Elevator for handicapped. 1,000 sq. ft. shop area.

128 Virginia

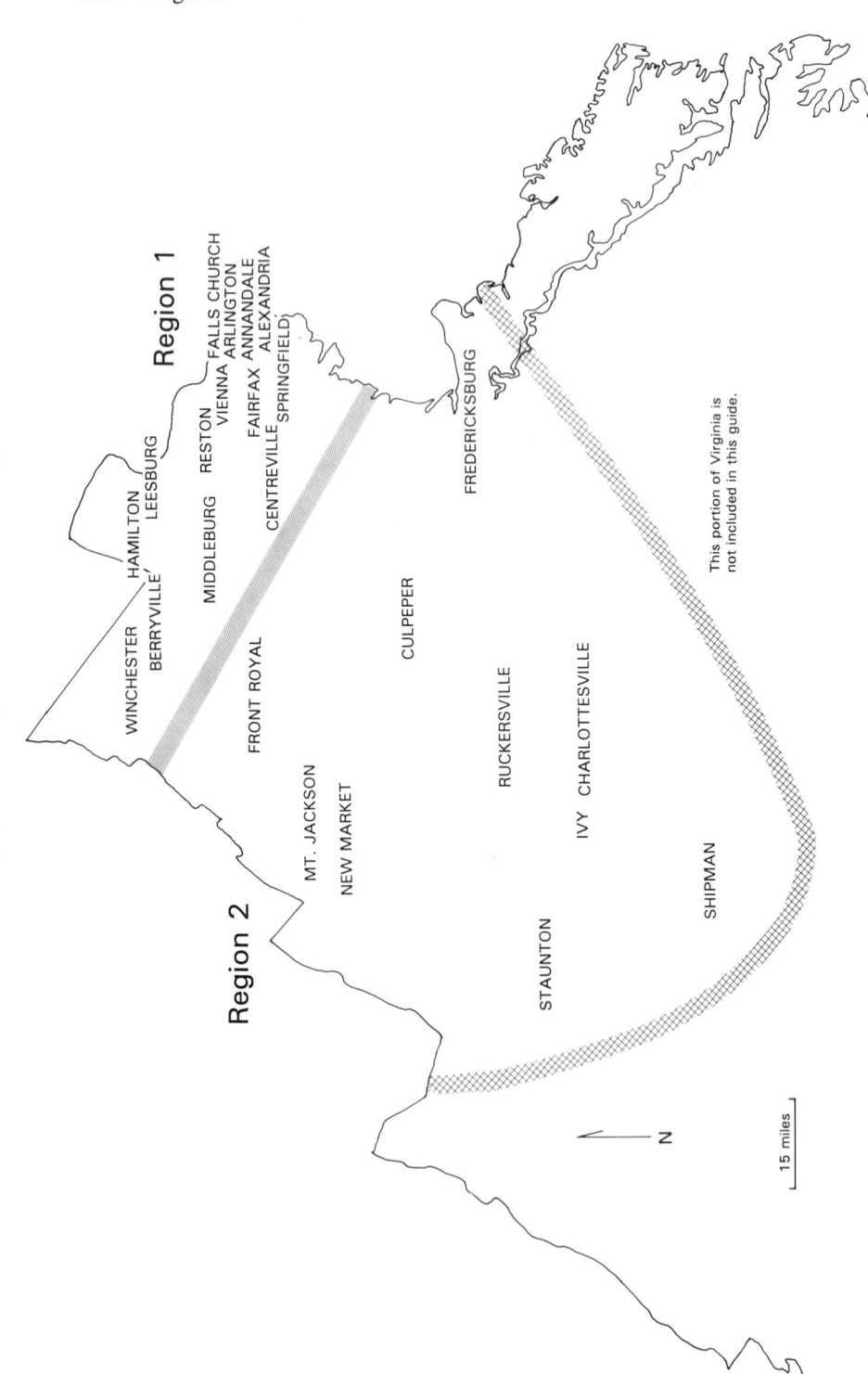

Capital Comics Center & Book Niche
2008 Mt. Vernon Ave.
Alexandria, VA 22301
(703) 548-3466
Hours: Mon-Thurs,Sat:11:30-7 Fri:12-8
Major Categories represented by at least 100 titles:

```
Children's        Mystery           Paperback
                                    Science Fiction
```

Other major categories: Literary classics. Regular categories with less than 100 titles: art, gardening, history, nature, movie-related and self-help.
Specialty Categories: Comics and cartoon books.
Approximate number of volumes: --
    paperback: 80%
    hardback : 20%
Special Items and Services: Trading cards, fantasy posters, movie and entertainer photos, role-playing games, videos, novelty items, and new books in some of the used book categories.
Directions: Three blocks west of Rt 1; about two miles south of Crystal City, Arlington, and National Airport; about one mile north of Old Town, Alexandria. Braddock Road Station is closest Metro stop.
Additional information: Store founded in 1975. There is dining within walking distance, and nearby antique shops. 500 sq. ft. shop area.

Book Stop
3640A King Street
Alexandria, VA 22302
(703) 578-3292
Hours: Mon-Fri(except Thurs):12-6 Sat:11-6 Sun:1-5 (closed Thurs)
Owner(s): Toby Cedar
Type of Shop: General
Major Categories represented by at least 100 titles:

```
Americana         Gardening           Paperback
Antiques          History             Philosophy
Art               Hobbies & Crafts    Political Science
Aviation          Military History    Religion
Business          Music               Science Fiction
Children's        Mystery             Science/Technology
Collectibles      Nature              Travel
Cooking           Nautical
Do-it-yourself    Outdoor Recreation
Fiction
Folklore
```

Specialty Categories: Music.
Approximate breakdown: rare: 2%
                out-of-print: 60%
                in-print: 38%
Special Items and Services: Appraisals and book searches.
Directions: Located in a shopping center facing Braddock Road two blocks east of I-395. Parking in front.
Additional information: Store founded in 1982. Handicap access.

From Out of the Past
6440 Richmond Highway
Alexandria, VA 22306
(703) 768-7827
Hours: Tues-Sat:11-6   Closed Sun & Mon
Owner(s): Barbara and Mike Keck
Type of Shop: General
Major Categories represented by at least 100 titles:

Americana	Gardening	Poetry
Antiques	Geography	Political Science
Art	History	Rare Books
Aviation	Hobbies & Crafts	Religion
Children's	Medicine	Science Fiction
Collectibles	Military History	Spectator Sports
Cooking	Music	Travel
Exploration	Mystery	
Fiction	Mythology	
	Nature	
	Nautical	

Approximate number of volumes: 45,000
        paperback: collectible only.
        hardback : 100%
Approximate breakdown: rare: 2,000 rare/scarce.
        out-of-print: --
        in-print: --
Special Items and Services: 1,000,000 back issue magazines filed by title and date. Ephemera (catalogs, timetables, etc.).
Directions: Located on US Route 1, 1 1/2 miles south of I-95 (Capital Beltway) at its approach to Wilson Bridge (just south of Alexandria).
Additional information: Store founded in 1974 at current location. Mt. Vernon and Old Town Alexandria are nearby. 5,000 sq. ft. shop area.

Book Rack
7857-D Heritage Drive
Annandale, VA 22003
(703) 941-6015
Hours: Mon-Thur:11-7   Fri-Sat:10-6   Sun:12-5
Owner(s): Charles P. Leach
Type of Shop: "Thousands of used paperbacks."
Major Categories represented by at least 100 titles:

Children's	Mystery	Paperback
Fiction		Romance
		Science Fiction

Other major categories: Classics, miscellaneous non-fiction. Fiction is broken down into major categories of novels, adventure, western, war, horror.
Approximate number of volumes: 15,000
        paperback: 99.5%
        hardback : 0.5%
Approximate breakdown: rare: --
        out-of-print: 10%
        in-print: 90%

Directions: Capital Beltway (I-495) to Annandale, Va. exit, east on Va. Rt 236 (Little River Turnpike) to first traffic light. Right on Heritage Drive. One-half mile to Heritage Mall on right. Book Rack (7857-D Heritage Drive) clearly visible from road.
Additional information: Founded in 1989. Book Rack is a franchise with headquarters in Fort Lauderdale, Florida. New owner in Feb. 1992. Books are sold at about one-half cover price. Store takes books in trade, giving credit of about one-quarter cover price toward purchase. Located at small, friendly shopping center: Giant, Peoples Drug, banks and restaurants. 750 sq. ft. shop area.

Book Ends
2710 Washington Blvd.
Arlington, VA 22201
(703) 524-4976
Hours: Fri-Mon:12-6 (closed Tues-Thurs)
Owner(s): Janet & Mike Deatherage
Type of Shop: General
Major Categories represented by at least 100 titles:
  ALL CATEGORIES.
Approximate number of volumes: 30,000
  paperback: 30%
  hardback : 70%
Approximate breakdown: rare: 5%
  out-of-print: 85%
  in-print: 10%
Directions: Four blocks north of Route 50, one mile north of I-395, seven blocks from Clarendon Metro stop. Parking lot in front.
Additional information: Store founded in 1979. 1,200 sq. ft. shop area.

Bookhouse
805 North Emerson Street
Arlington, VA 22205
(703) 527-7797
Hours: 12-6 daily, closed Mon.
Owner(s): Natalie & Edward Hughes
Type of Shop: Antiquarian
Major Categories represented by at least 100 titles:
  Americana   Nature
  Art
Specialty Categories: Wallace Stevens
Approximate number of volumes: 60,000
Directions: Located off the 5100 block of Wilson Blvd.
Additional information: Store founded in 1972.

Crawfords Nautical Books
5520 North 16th Street
Arlington, VA 22205
Owner(s): Gary and Susan Crawford
Type of Shop: Specialty mail-order - new and used nautical books.
Specialty categories: A variety of nautical literature, including voyages of exploration, ships, yachting adventures, windjammer voyages, pirates, shipwrecks, and the sailoring arts. Particular emphasis on the Chesapeake Bay area.
Approximate number of volumes: 300-500 used
  paperback: 0%
  hardback : 100%
Approximate breakdown: rare: a few
  out-of-print: --
  in-print: --
Free catalog of used books available upon request. New book catalog available for $3.00, refundable with first order. Mini-catalogs mailed to customers at irregular intervals.
Special Items and Services: Gift certificates.
Additional information: The Crawfords have also just opened a store, the Book Bank, in Tilghman Island, Maryland, carrying new and used books in the same area of specialty as their mail-order operation, as well as cards, magazines and handicrafts. The store was closed for the winter but will re-open in the spring of 1993. It is located in a former bank building (complete with vault), and the address is: Book Bank, 5782 Tilghman Island Road, Tilghman Island MD 21671. Directions: south on U.S. Rt 50 to Easton MD, right on MD Rt 322 (St. Michaels bypass), right on MD Rt 33 to Tilghman Island. Free parking. Tentative store hours: weekdays noon to 6 p.m., Sat-Sun 10:30 a.m. to 6 p.m.

Virginia Book Company
P.O. Box 431
Berryville, VA 22611
(703) 955-1428
Hours: Weekdays:9-3
Type of Shop: Specialty - Virginiana.
Approximate breakdown: rare: 25%
  out-of-print: 75%
  in-print: --
Annual catalog (plus others) issued.
Additional information: Founded in 1950. Museums and good dining nearby.

Richard McKay Used Books, Inc.
14114 Lee Highway
Centreville, VA 22020
(703) 830-4048
Hours: Mon-Sat:9-9 Sun:11-7
Type of Shop: General

Major Categories represented by at least 100 titles:

Art	Gardening	Paperback
Business	Geography	Philosophy
Children's	Health-fitness	Poetry
Cooking	History	Political Science
Do-it-yourself	Hobbies & Crafts	Religion
Education	Medicine	Romance
Fiction	Military History	Science Fiction
	Music	Science/Technology
	Mystery	Social Science
	Nature	Spectator Sports
	Outdoor Recreation	Travel

Approximate number of volumes: 100,000+
    paperback: 50%
    hardback : 50%
Approximate breakdown: rare: --
    out-of-print: 50%
    in-print: 50%
Special Items and Services: CDs, books on tape, videos.
Directions: Take I-66 west to exit 52, go 1/2 mile on Rt 29 south to Newgate Shopping Center on right. Located at junction of Rt 29-211 and Rt 28.
Additional information: Founded in 1983. Recently expanded. Located close to Manassas Battlefield National Park. Handicap access with wide aisles and ramp at street curb. Large parking lot. 5,000 sq. ft. shop area.

Original Historic Newspapers
3002 Winter Pine Court
Fairfax, VA 22031
(703) 591-3150
Hours: By appointment only.
Owner(s): Mark E. Mitchell
Professional Affiliations: International Society of Appraisers, Manuscript Society, National Press Club, Virginia Historical Society.
Type of Shop: Antiquarian newspapers, 1635-1980.
Specialty Categories: Historic newspapers - Civil War, American Revolution, Presidents, science, U.S. & world history and more.
Catalog issued twice per year at $2.
Special Items and Services: Appraisals. Want lists gladly accepted.
Additional information: Founded in 1981 by present owner. Original newspapers bought and sold. Buys Harpers Weekly bound volumes, collections of early newspapers 1620-1880. Manuscripts & documents also wanted.

Alexander Lauberts
1073 West Broad Street
Falls Church, VA 22046
(703) 533-1699
Hours: Wed-Sat:Noon-5
Owner(s): Alexander Lauberts
Type of Shop: General

134   Virginia - Region 1

Major Categories represented by at least 100 titles:
```
Americana            History                Rare Books
Aviation
Collectibles
```
Approximate number of volumes: 5,000
Approximate breakdown: rare: 10%
out-of-print: 90%
in-print: --
Directions: Located in shopping center at west end.
Additional information: This location opened in 1973. Prior to here, located in Georgetown, D.C. (1958), before that in Heidelberg, Germany (1945-1946), and before that in Riga, Latvia. Mr. Lauberts writes, "Some claim that I am one of the oldest book dealers in D.C., Virginia or Maryland."

Hamilton Virginia Books
412 East Colonial Highway
Hamilton, VA 22068
(703) 338-6338
Hours: Sat-Sun:10-5   Other times by chance or appointment.
Owner(s): Bob Daniels
Type of Shop: General antiquarian.
All of the major categories are represented but by less than 100 books. Shop is new, and additional books are sought.
Approximate number of volumes: 3,000
paperback: --
hardback : 100%
Approximate breakdown: rare: 2%
out-of-print: 89%
in-print: 9%
Special Items and Services: Provides search services.
Additional information: Founded in 1991. 750 sq. ft. shop area.

Let There Be Praise
9 Catoctin Circle, SE
Leesburg, VA 22075
(703) 777-6311
Hours: Mon-Sat:9:30-6   Fri:9:30-8
Owner(s): David & Diane Barker
Type of Shop: Christian full-service bookstore.
Major Categories represented by at least 100 titles:
```
Children's                          Religion
Fiction
```
Other major categories: Used videos.
Approximate number of volumes: --
paperback: 20%
hardback : 80%

Approximate breakdown: rare: 5%
out-of-print: 20%
in-print: 75%
Additional information: Founded in 1976.

Hooper's Books
103-B West Federal Street
Middleburg, VA 22117
(703) 687-5714
Hours: Tues-Sat:11-5
Owner(s): Richard Hooper
Professional Affiliations: A.B.A.A., I.L.A.B.
Type of Shop: General antiquarian.
Major Categories represented by at least 100 titles:
```
                              Rare Books
                              Travel
```
Other major categories: Fine bindings, equestrian sports, fishing, shooting.
Approximate number of volumes: --
paperback: --
hardback : 100%
Approximate breakdown: rare: 30%
out-of-print: 70%
in-print: --
Catalog issued once in a while, usually free.
Directions: One block south of Rt 50 (the main street through town) and 1 1/2 blocks west of the only traffic light in town (which is on Rt 50).
Additional information: Located in beautiful rural countryside, fine restaurants nearby. Handicap access. 700 sq. ft. shop area.

Reston's Used Book Shop
1623 Washington Plaza, Lake Anne Center
Reston, VA 22090
(703) 435-9772
Hours: Open everyday.
Owner(s): Susan Weston and Sue Schram
Type of Shop: General used book shop.
Other major categories: Covers all general categories but not necessarily by 100 copies.
Approximate number of volumes: --
paperback: 40%
hardback : 60%
Additional information: 685 sq. ft. shop area.

W. B. O'Neill - Old & Rare Books
11609 Hunters Green Court (P.O. Box 2275)
Reston, VA 22091
(703) 860-0782
Hours: Mail order & by appointment.
Owner(s): William B. O'Neill
Professional Affiliations: Modern Greek Studies Association
Type of Shop: Specialty (largely antiquarian) - books and pamphlets on the Eastern Mediterranean (modern Greece, Cyprus, Turkey, Albania, Armenia, Lebanon, Palestine), early travel, Baedeker travel guides.
Major Categories represented by at least 100 titles:

>   Exploration   Geography   Political Science
>   Folklore   History   Rare Books
>   Military History   Religion
>   Nautical   Social Science
>   Travel

Other major categories: Bibliography
Approximate number of volumes: --
>   paperback: 0%
>   hardback : 100%

Approximate breakdown: rare: 50%
>   out-of-print: 45%
>   in-print: 5%

Catalog issued annually at $7.50.
Special Items and Services: Appraisals in area of expertise.
Additional information: Opened this location in 1976. 400 sq. ft. shop area. Previously in New York (1945-50) and Arlington, Va. (1950-53).

Antiquarian Tobacciana
11505 Turnbridge Lane
Reston, VA 22094-1220
(703) 435-8133
Hours: Evenings only and weekends (by phone).
Owner(s): Ben Rapaport
Professional Affiliations: A.S.A., N.E.A.A.
Type of Shop: Antiquarian and new books on all aspects of tobacco and smoking artifacts (domestic & foreign).
Approximate breakdown: rare: 50%
>   out-of-print: 30%
>   in-print: 20%

Catalog issued 4 times per year at $1.
Special Items and Services: Antiquarian smoking prints, lithographs, and engravings. Appraisals, book searches, and want lists maintained.
Additional information: Founded in 1975 by present owner.

David Holloway, Bookseller
7430 Grace Street
Springfield, VA 22150
(703) 569-1798
Hours: By appointment only.
Owner(s): David Holloway
Type of Shop: Antiquarian/specialty.
Major Categories represented by at least 100 titles:
    Art   Mystery   Rare Books
    Collectibles
    Fiction
Specialty Categories: Modern first editions, mystery first editions, and African-American studies.
Approximate number of volumes: 5,000
                      paperback: 10%
                      hardback : 90%
Approximate breakdown: rare: 70%
                      out-of-print: 30%
                      in-print: --
Free catalog issued twice yearly.
Additional information: Located ten minutes off I-95 - call for directions. Appraisals offered.

The Manuscript Company of Springfield
P.O. Box 1151
Springfield, VA 22151-0151
(703) 256-6748
Hours: By appointment only.
Owner(s): Terry and Jeanette Alford
Type of Shop: Specialty antiquarian.
Specialty Categories: Manuscripts, historically interesting letters, diaries, documents from 18th and 19th century U.S. Some ephemera and prints.
Approximate breakdown: rare: 100%
                      out-of-print: --
                      in-print: --
Free catalog issued occasionally.
Additional information: Founded in 1974. Offers appraisals of manuscript items (collections only).

JoAnn Reisler, Ltd.
360 Glyndon Street, NE
Vienna, VA 22180
(703) 938-2967
Hours: By appointment only.
Owner(s): JoAnn & Don Reisler
Professional Affiliations: A.B.A.A., P.B.F.A.
Type of Shop: Specialty antiquarian.

138 Virginia - Region 1, Region 2

Specialty Categories: Children's and illustrated books; original illustrative art.
Approximate breakdown: rare: 100%
　　　　　　　　　out-of-print: --
　　　　　　　　　in-print: --

The Book Shelf
106 Featherbed Lane
Winchester, VA 22601
(703) 665-0866
Hours: Mon-Thurs:10-7   Fri:10-8   Sat:10-5   Sun:12-4
Owner(s): Loretta Winchester
Type of Shop: General with specialty.
Major Categories represented by at least 100 titles:

Art	Health-fitness	Philosophy
Business	History	Religion
Children's	Hobbies & Crafts	Romance
Cooking	Medicine	Science Fiction
Do-it-yourself	Military History	
Fiction	Mystery	
Folklore		

Other major categories: Autobiography, biography.
Specialty Categories: Co-dependence, recovery (12 steps), metaphysics, and Civil War.
Approximate number of volumes: --
　　　　　　　　paperback: 100,000
　　　　　　　　hardback : 5,000
Approximate breakdown: rare: 1%
　　　　　　　　　out-of-print: 25%
　　　　　　　　　in-print: 74%
Special Items and Services: Cards, posters, prints, CDs, cassettes, jewelry, incense, homeopathic remedies, massage oils, etc. Will special order new books (fast delivery).
Directions: From Washington via Rt 7: Take Rt 7 (also called Berryville Ave. in Winchester), take right on Pleasant Valley Road and right on Featherbed Lane. Store is 1/2 block on right.
From Washington via Rt 50: Come straight into Winchester on Rt 50, make left on Pleasant Valley Road and right on Featherbed Lane. Store is 1/2 block on right.
Additional information: Founded in 1984. Full service store in which dealers try their very best to find books for customers. Carries a full line of new and used books in all categories. Handicap access. Good dining and museums nearby.

The Book Room
1424 Seminole Trail, Rt 29 North, Shoppers World
Charlottesville, VA 22901
(804) 973-1525
Hours: Mon-Sat:10-7:30   Sun:12-5
Type of Shop: General, paperback, historical romance a specialty.

Major Categories represented by at least 100 titles:

Americana	Health-fitness	Paperback
Business	History	Political Science
Children's	Medicine	Religion
Education	Mystery	Romance
Fiction	Nature	Science Fiction
		Social Science
		Travel

Approximate number of volumes: 50,000
  paperback: 80%
  hardback : 20%
Approximate breakdown: rare: --
  out-of-print: 20%
  in-print: 80%

Directions: Located on Rt 29 North at north end of Charlottesville.
Additional information: Founded in 1978. Recently reorganized under new owner. Excellent dining at Copacabana (Brazilian food). Christian bookstore nearby. Handicap access. 2,000 sq. ft. shop area.

Daedalus
121 4th Street, NE
Charlottesville, VA 22901
(804) 293-7595
Hours: Mon-Sat:10-6   Closed Sunday.
Owner(s): Sandy McAdams
Type of Shop: General
Major Categories represented by at least 100 titles:

Antiques	Gardening	Paperback
Art	Health-fitness	Philosophy
Aviation	History	Poetry
Business	Medicine	Political Science
Children's	Military History	Rare Books
Cooking	Music	Religion
Do-it-yourself	Mystery	Romance
Education	Nature	Science Fiction
Fiction	Nautical	Science/Technology
		Social Science
		Spectator Sports
		Travel

Specialty Categories: Fiction and little magazines.
Approximate number of volumes: 65,000
  paperback: 30%
  hardback : 70%

Directions: Located in the middle of downtown Charlottesville two blocks from public garage.
Additional information: Founded in 1968 (5 years on Long Island, 18 years in Charlottesville). Three floors of books. Three other book dealers within two blocks. Owns another store (Daedalus East) on Chincoteague, Va.: general stock of some 5,000 books, no rare or scarce, open May through October, Fri,Sat,Sun:3-7.

The Book Broker
310 East Market Street
Charlottesville, VA 22902
(804) 296-2194
Hours: Tues-Sat:11:30-5
Owner(s): Vesta Lee Gordon
Type of Shop: Antiquarian
Major Categories represented by at least 100 titles:

Americana	History	Travel
Art	Military History	
Children's		
Cooking		

Specialty Categories: Virginia, decorative trade bindings.
Approximate number of volumes: 7,000
  paperback: 1%
  hardback : 99%
Approximate breakdown: rare: 5%
  out-of-print: 95%
  in-print: --
Catalog issued 3 to 4 times per year.
Special Items and Services: Appraisals, book searches.
Directions: In the downtown area, two blocks from the parking garage.
Additional information: Founded in 1985. Three other antiquarian shops within two blocks. Handicap access. 1,600 sq. ft. shop area. Good dining nearby.

The Book Cellar
316 East Main Street
Charlottesville, VA 22902
(804) 979-7787
Hours: Mon:10-5   Tues-Thurs:10-6 (or later)   Fri-Sat:10-8 or 9   Closed Sun
Owner(s): Claude A. Ripley
Professional Affiliations: A.B.A.
Type of Shop: General - used and publishers' mark-downs
Major Categories represented by at least 100 titles:

Antiques	Gardening	Paperback
Art	Health-fitness	Philosophy
Aviation	History	Poetry
Business	Hobbies & Crafts	Political Science
Children's	Medicine	Religion
Collectibles	Military History	Romance
Cooking	Music	Science Fiction
Do-it-yourself	Mystery	Science/Technology
Education	Mythology	Social Science
Fiction	Nature	Spectator Sports
Folklore	Outdoor Recreation	Travel

Other major categories: Computer books, photography, architecture, performing arts, drama/film, new age, biography, literary studies, black studies, women's studies, reference, humour.

Approximate number of volumes: 30,000 on display
           paperback: 65%
           hardback : 35%
Approximate breakdown: rare: --
           out-of-print: 50%
           in-print: 50%
Special Items and Services: Playing cards, books on tape. New books on subjects of local & regional interest, such as Thomas Jefferson, UVA, Civil War, etc. Accepts used books for cash or credit.
Directions: Located downtown on the pedestrian-only "mall." At lower level of the old hardware store building, now the Hardware Store Restaurant. Good parking immediately behind the building in Water Street Parking Lot - two hours free with validation.
Additional information: Founded in 1988. Store's policy is to reduce the price of books from the original, so there are many bargains & great savings for the careful browser, and a good deal of recent material at half-price or less. Two used book stores, two antiquarian book stores and two new book stores all within one block from store. Virginia Discovery Museum (children's) and many good restaurants nearby. Expanded from 1,000 sq. ft. to 1,600 sq. ft. shop area in 1992.

Heartwood Books
5 and 9 Elliewood Avenue
Charlottesville, VA 22903
(804) 295-7083
Hours: Mon-Sat:10-6
Owner(s): Paul Collinge & Sherry L. Joseph
Professional Affiliations: A.B.A.A.
Type of Shop: Scholarly and general, used and antiquarian.
Major Categories represented by at least 100 titles:

Americana	Gardening	Paperback
Art	History	Philosophy
Children's	Military History	Poetry
Collectibles	Mystery	Political Science
Cooking	Nature	Rare Books
Fiction		Religion
		Science Fiction
		Social Science

Other major categories: Literary criticism.
Specialty Categories: Virginiana, Thomas Jefferson, Civil War, scholarly, literary first editions.
Approximate number of volumes: 50,000
           paperback: 25%
           hardback : 75%
Approximate breakdown: rare: 20%
           out-of-print: 30%
           in-print: 50%
Catalog issued occassionally at $1.
Special Items and Services: Book searches, appraisals.
Directions: Located one-half block off University Avenue, across from stone wall of the old section of the university. Pay parking lot across the street.

Additional information: Founded in 1975 by present owners. "Best general used and rare shop in Virginia." Five steps into shop, narrow aisles. 3,000 sq. ft. shop area. Located across from the historic grounds of the University of Virginia.

Fantasia Comics & Records (two locations)
1419 1/2 University Avenue   1861 Seminole Trail
Charlottesville, VA 22903   Charlottesville, VA 22901
(804) 971-1029   (804) 974-7512
Hours: Mon-Sat:10:30-7 (University Ave.), Sun:12-5:30 (Seminole Trail)
Owner(s): Steven M. Miller
Type of Shop: Comics
Approximate number of volumes: 50,000+
        paperback: --
        hardback : 1%
Special Items and Services: Posters, "gaming". Over 7,000 records. New comics reserve service.
Additional information: University Ave. location founded in 1982 as "Recycled Records." 650 sq. ft. shop area. Located ten minutes from Monticello. Seminole Trail location opened in 1989, 720 sq. ft. shop area, handicap access. "Over 250 restaurants in and around Charlottesville."

Clover Hill Books
P.O. Box 6278
Charlottesville, VA 22906
(804) 973-1506
Hours: Books on display at The Book Broker.
Owner(s): Candace Carter Crosby
Type of Shop: Mail order.
Specialty Categories: 20th century British & American first edtions.
Approximate breakdown: rare: 50%
        out-of-print: 50%
        in-print: --
Catalog issued occasionally at $1.
Additional information: Founded in 1982. Also sells at antiquarian book fairs on occasion.

Ace Books & Antiques
120 West Culpeper Street
Culpeper, VA 22701
(703) 825-8973
Hours: Mon-Sat:9:30-6 Sun:Noon-5
Owner(s): James & Mary Lou Leftwich
Type of Shop: General
Major Categories represented by at least 100 titles:
ALL CATEGORIES.

Approximate number of volumes: over 250,000
    paperback: 60%
    hardback : 40%
Approximate breakdown: rare: 20%
    out-of-print: 70%
    in-print: 10%
Special Items and Services: Cards, posters, pictures, frames, records.
Directions: From Washington, D.C.: take I-495 to I-66 west, exit I-66 at Gainesville & take Rt 29 south to Culpeper.
From southern Virginia: take I-95 to Fredericksburg, then Rt 3 west to Culpeper. West Culpeper Street intersects the main street through Culpeper. Store is located 1/2 block west of the main street.
Additional information: Good dining, bed & breakfast, and Fountain Hall nearby. 6,000 sq. ft. shop area.

Collectvs Books
820 Caroline Street
Fredericksburg, VA 22401
(703) 373-6148
Hours: Sun-Thurs:11-6:30 Fri-Sat:11-9
Owner(s): Martin and Patricia Coburn
Type of Shop: General with emphasis on military history, literature, mystery, science fiction.
Major Categories represented by at least 100 titles:

Americana	History	Paperback
Art	Military History	Poetry
Children's	Mystery	Political Science
Cooking		Rare Books
Exploration		Religion
Fiction		Science Fiction
		Science/Technology
		Social Science

Approximate number of volumes: 24,000
    paperback: 10%
    hardback : 90%
Approximate breakdown: rare: 5%
    out-of-print: 85%
    in-print: 10%
Special Items and Services: Appraisals, book searches.
Directions: Follow signs to Fredericksburg Visitor Center - store located in the next block, same side of street. On-street parking and large municipal lot one block away.
Additional information: Founded in 1990. Fredericksburg Museum and three other bookstores within one block. Several good restaurants within three blocks. One block from Rappahannock River. Completely surrounded by Civil War battle parks, sites and attractions. Handicap access. 1,700 sq. ft. shop area.

Beck's Antiques and Books
708 Caroline Street
Fredericksburg, VA 22401
(703) 371-1766
Hours: Mon-Sat:10:30-5 Sun:12:30-5
   (Often later on weekend evenings and by appt.)
Owner(s): Wm. M. & Susan L. Beck
Major Categories represented by at least 100 titles:

```
Americana        Gardening            Poetry
Antiques         History              Rare Books
Art              Hobbies & Crafts
Children's       Military History
Cooking
Fiction
```

Other major categories: Virginiana, Civil War, architecture.
Approximate number of volumes: --
   paperback: --
   hardback : 5,000
Approximate breakdown: rare: 5%
   out-of-print: 90%
   in-print: 5%
Special Items and Services: Antiques. Also carries new material on Virginiana and local county history.
Directions: Take Rt 3 east from I-95 to Fredericksburg downtown historic district. Follow the signs to Fredericksburg Visitor Center at 706 Caroline Street - store is at 708 Caroline Street. Parking lots and two-hour parking on street.
Additional information: Founded in 1973. Located in historic district, six museums within two blocks, next to Visitor Center. Two other book stores on same street within two blocks. Many good restaurants. 800 sq. ft. devoted to old books.

Royal Oak Bookshop
207 S. Royal Avenue
Front Royal, VA 22630
(703) 635-7070
Hours: Mon-Sat:10-6 Sun:12-5
Owner(s): Nan Hathaway
Professional Affiliations: A.B.A.
Type of Shop: General (also carries new books and remainders).
Major Categories represented by at least 100 titles:
```
ALL CATEGORIES except: collectibles, education, exploration,
geography, rare books, spectator sports.
```
Specialty categories: Civil War, Virginiana.
Approximate number of volumes: 15,000
   paperback: 50%
   hardback : 50%
Approximate breakdown: rare: 5%
   out-of-print: 60%
   in-print: 35%

Free newsletter issued bi-annually.
Special Items and Services: "We will help you obtain any book, in print or out-of-print." Notecards, posters, audio and music cassettes, calendars, book-related items. 15% of stock is new books, with a large selection of remainders - "new books at used book prices." Always buying second-hand books. "Ask about our booklover's rebate program."
Directions: From I-66, take exit 6 (Rt 340 south) through town. Shop is on right three blocks after crossing Main Street. Access to parking in rear via side streets and alleyway.
Additional information: Founded in 1975. Same location and owner for 17 years, with a gradual expansion at the same address. Located one-half mile from the northern entrance to Skyline Drive and Shenandoah National Park. Shop carries complete information on the many special features nearby. Handicap access from parking lot in rear. 1,500 sq. ft. shop area.

Jerry N. Showalter, Bookseller
P.O. Box 84
Ivy, VA 22945
(804) 295-6413
Hours: By appointment only.
Professional Affiliations: A.B.A., International Booksellers Federation
Type of Shop: Antiquarian
Major Categories represented by at least 100 titles:

Americana	Rare Books
Fiction	

Other major categories: Manuscripts, autographs.
Specialty Categories: Southeast Americana, western Americana, southern literature.
Approximate number of volumes: 2,000
Approximate breakdown: rare: 100%
                        out-of-print: --
                        in-print: --
Additional information: Appraisals.

Nostalgia Mart
5946 Main Street (P.O. Box 745)
Mt. Jackson, VA 22842
(703) 477-2182
Hours: Thurs-Mon:10-5
Owner(s): Burton Padoll, Sheila B. Applebaum
Type of Shop: Antiquarian books, paper, collectibles, memorabilia.
Major Categories represented by at least 100 titles:

Americana	Military History	Paperback
Art	Music	Political Science
Children's	Mystery	Rare Books
Fiction		Religion
		Spectator Sports

146   Virginia - Region 2

Other major categories: Black Americana, theater & dance, sports.
Specialty Categories: J. F. Kennedy, author-autographed, black Americana, theater & dance, Civil War, Virginia, sports.
Approximate number of volumes: --
  paperback: 3,000
  hardback : 25,000
Special Items and Services: Posters. Mail order.
Directions: I-81 to exit 269 or 273, on Rt 11 (Main Street) in Mt. Jackson.
Additional information: Founded in 1989. Good dining nearby, many nice shops in town, large used bookstore nine miles away. Handicap access. 1,500 sq. ft. shop area.

Paper Treasures
9595 Congress Street (P.O. Box 1160)
New Market, VA 22844
(703) 740-3135
Hours: Summer: Sun:10 or 12-6   Mon-Sat:10-6   (often till 8 on Fri & Sat)
Winter: Sun:12-5   Mon-Sat:10-5
Owner(s): Mike Lewis
Type of Shop: General, antiquarian, paper collectibles (magazines, comics, prints, etc.)
Major Categories represented by at least 100 titles:

Americana	History	Paperback
Art	Medicine	Rare Books
Business	Military History	Religion
Children's	Music	
Collectibles	Nature	
Cooking		
Fiction		

Other major categories: "We also have eight other dealers specializing in Americana, Civil War, southern literature, cookbooks, Americana, etc."
Specialty Categories: Shenandoah Valley imprints (especially Henkel Press), Civil War, ephemera.
Approximate number of volumes: --
  paperback: 15,000
  hardback : 50,000
  other: 100,000 magazines & over 100,000 paper ephemera
Approximate breakdown: rare: 5%
  out-of-print: 94%
  in-print: 1%
Special Items and Services: All types of ephemera - post cards, comics, magazines, prints, etc. Appraisals.
Directions: I-81 to exit 264, two blocks to center of town, then five blocks south on Rt 11. Parking in front of store plus large adjoining parking lot, all free.
Additional information: Founded in 1986. Two battlefields, Endless Caverns, and several antique dealers nearby. Several good restaurants (The Galley, New Market Cafe, Southern Kitchen Restaurant). Handicap access with wide aisles (but will need help with bathrooms). 10,000 sq. ft. shop area.

M-R Books
Rt 2, Box 16F
Ruckersville, VA 22968
(804) 985-6459
Hours: Mon-Sat:9-5
Owner(s): Mildred Pedercine
Type of Shop: Paperback, comics, etc.
Major Categories represented by at least 100 titles:

Children's	Gardening	Paperback
Cooking	Hobbies & Crafts	Poetry
Fiction	Military History	Religion
	Mystery	Romance
		Science Fiction
		Spectator Sports

Approximate number of volumes: 40,000
paperback: 75%
hardback : 25%
Directions: Located on Rt 29 between Ruckersville and Charlottesville, Va. Across from Jefferson National Bank.
Additional information: Founded in 1991. Zandi's Deli next door. 1,000 sq. ft. shop area.

Buteo Books
Route 1, Box 242
Shipman, VA 22971
(800) 722-2460 or (804) 263-8671
Hours: By appointment.
Owner(s): Allen M. Hale
Professional Affiliations: A.B.A., A.O.U., W.O.S.
Type of Shop: Specializing in ornithology.
Specialty Categories: Ornithology, natural history and, as a sideline, WPA guides.
Approximate number of volumes: 6,000
paperback: 30%
hardback : 70%
Approximate breakdown: rare: 10%
out-of-print: 20%
in-print: 70%
Free catalog issued four times per year.
Special Items and Services: Bird song recordings. Appraisals, active searches.
Directions: Located about 25 miles south of Charlottesville, Va. off Rt 29.
Additional information: Founded in 1971 and purchased by present owners in 1990. Beautiful countryside, near Wintergreen resort. 500 sq. ft. shop area.

Staunton Book Review
11 South Augusta Street
Staunton, VA 24401
(703) 886-6913
Hours: Mon-Sat:10-5 (Summer hours expanded)
Owner(s): Andrew & Louise Gutterman
Type of Shop: General used & rare.
Major Categories represented by at least 100 titles:

Americana	Music	Paperback
Art	Mystery	Poetry
Children's		Religion
Cooking		Romance
Fiction		Science Fiction
		Travel

Specialty Categories: Children's, southern Americana.
Approximate number of volumes: 7,500
     paperback: 33%
     hardback : 67%
Directions: Take I-81 to exit 225, go west on Va. Rt 275 to first stop light, go south on Rt 11 to downtown. Shop located between East Beverly Street and the courthouse. Parking lots and metered parking are available, or call store for best parking.
Additional information: Business founded in 1986. Shop started as Andy's Book Shop in Littleton, New Hampshire, which was sold in 1991. This store opened in the same year. Located in historic district of Staunton. Many pre-Civil War buildings still standing. Staunton has been mentioned more than once in "Bon Appetit" for its good dining. Birthplace of Woodrow Wilson. "Main entrance and aisles provide easy access for the handicapped." 2,000 sq. ft. shop area.

Farther Afield

When we sent out questionnaires for this book, we accidentally sent several to dealers that were outside our intended region. Since they were kind enough to respond, we have included them in this section. Clarion and Shohola, Pennsylvania are located in northwestern and northeastern Pennsylvania, respectively. Rural Retreat and Wytheville are located in southwestern Virginia.

Paperback Alley
504 Main Street
Clarion, PA 16214
(814) 226-4147
Hours: Mon-Sat:9-4:30   Friday until 8:00.
Owner(s): Jacqueline Baker
Type of Shop: Used paperback only.
Major Categories represented by at least 100 titles:
   Children's   Mystery   Romance
   Fiction   Science Fiction
Other major categories: General nonfiction in all categories.
Approximate number of volumes: 14,000
            paperback: 100%
            hardback : --
Special Items and Services: Used jigsaw puzzles. Searches using AB Bookman's Weekly.
Directions: Located on Main Street. On-street parking in front of store.
Additional information: Founded in 1987. Store is at street level - no steps. 600 sq. ft. shop area. Located in Clarion County, Pa.

Alan F. Innes - Books
Box 123
Shohola, PA 18458
(717) 559-7873
Hours: Mail order only.
Type of Shop: General mail order only.
Major Categories represented by at least 100 titles:
   Americana   History   Travel
   Exploration   Nautical
   Fiction
Approximate number of volumes: 2,500
            paperback: --
            hardback : 100%
Approximate breakdown: rare: --
            out-of-print: 95%
            in-print: 5%
Additional information: Founded around 1989. Book searches offered. Free catalog issued two to three times per year. Located in Pike County, Pa.

Bookworm & Silverfish
Church Street
Rural Retreat, VA 24368
(P.O. Box 639, Wytheville, VA 24382)
(703) 686-5813
Hours: Mon-Fri:8-4
Owner(s): Jim Presgraves
Professional Affiliations: A.B.A.A.
Type of Shop: Antiquarian
Major Categories represented by at least 100 titles:

Americana	History	Political Science
Antiques	Military History	Rare Books
Art	Music	Science Fiction
Aviation	Nautical	Science/Technology
Business		Travel
Children's		
Cooking		
Education		
Exploration		

Other major categories: Genealogy, local history, Civil War.
Specialty Categories: Trade catalogs, Virginia.
Approximate number of volumes: --
        paperback: 0
        hardback : 8,000 - 10,000
Approximate breakdown: rare: 10%
        out-of-print: 85%
        in-print: 5% "by accident"
Catalog issued ten or more times per year.
Directions: From I-81: take exit 60 (for Rural Retreat), go south two miles and take a right on Buck Street, go one block and take a left onto Church Street, go 75 feet to Glassom Avenue. Stop at the first set of steps you see.
Additional information: This location founded in 1973, in book business for over 40 years. Located within one hour of Barter Theater, Highlands Festival, Chautauqua, and much more. "If you arrive with this guide in hand, take a 5% response-reward discount." Appraisals and book searches offered. Handicap access by appointment. Located in Wythe County, Va.

Complete List

The following is the list of book dealers who were sent questionnaires. Where a telephone number is present, the dealer responded to the questionnaire and is included in this guide. Where the telephone number is omitted, the dealer did not respond to the questionnaire and is not included in this guide. In such cases, confirmation that the dealer is still in business has not been obtained. The dealers are listed by state. Within a state, they are alphabetized by city, and within a city they are alphabetized by first name. See the general index for page numbers.

Pennsylvania

Abby's Book Case	1915 Susquehanna Road	Abington, PA 19001
Another Story:Books	100 North 9 Street	Allentown, PA 18102
Book Bargains	14 North 8th Street	Allentown, PA 18101 (215) 885-2232
Book Rack, The	Calasaqua Road at Airport Road South	Allentown, PA 18103
Books 'N More	1409 North Cedar Crest Blvd.	Allentown, PA 18104 (215) 439-1552
Cap's Comic Cavalcade	1980 Catasauqua Road	Allentown, PA 18103
Florence Finkel, Books	3425 Iron Bridge Road	Allentown, PA 18104
Occult Emporium, The	102 North 9 Street	Allentown, PA 18102 (215) 264-5540
Bookshelf	43 North Main Street	Ambler, PA 19002
Robert F. Batchelder	One West Butler Avenue	Ambler, PA 19002
Book Trade, The	24 Ardmore Avenue	Ardmore, PA 19003
Mystery Books	42 Rittenhouse Place	Ardmore, PA 19003 (215)642-3565
Trade-in Used Paperback Book Store	223 Pennel Road	Aston, PA 19014
Paperback Trader	1502 DeKalb Pike	Blue Bell, PA 19422 (215) 279-8855
Epistemologist, Scholarly Books	P.O. Box 63	Bryn Mawr, PA 19010 (215) 527-1065
Owl Bookshop, The	801 Yarrow Street	Bryn Mawr, PA 19010 (215) 525-6117
Title Page, The	24 Summit Grove	Bryn Mawr, PA 19010
Angler's Art, The	R D Nine, Box 203	Carlisle, PA 17013
Whistlestop Bookshop	152 West High Street	Carlisle, PA 17013
Doe Run Valley Books	640 Baltimore Pike	Chadds Ford, PA 19317 (215) 388-2826

152   Complete List

Cesi Kellinger, Bookseller	735 Philadelphia Avenue	Chambersburg, PA 17201	(717) 263-4474
Cloak & Dagger Books	868 Lincoln Way West	Chambersburg, PA 17201	(717) 267-0886
George Hall, Jr. Books	1441 Lincoln Way East	Chambersburg, PA 17201	
Mason's Rare & Used Books	115 South Main Street	Chambersburg, PA 17201	(717) 261-0541
Back Room Books	2 South Bridge Street	Christiana, PA 17509	(215) 593-7021
Paperback Alley	504 Main Street	Clarion, PA 16214	(814) 226-4147
Antonio Raimo Fine Books	401 Chestnut Street	Columbia, PA 17512	(717) 684-4111
RAC Books in Partners' Antique Center	403 North Third Street	Columbia, PA 17512	(717) 684-5364
Book House, The	Village Shops, Rt 15	Dillsburg, PA 17019	(717) 432-2720
Collector's Corner	31 EAst Lancaster Avenue	Downingtown, PA 19335	
Country Shepherd	109 East Lancaster Ave.	Downingtown, PA 19335	
Sottile's Books	Lansdowne Ave. & State Rd	Drexel Hill, PA 19026	(215) 789-6742
Hive of Industry	PO Box 602	Easton, PA 18044	
Quadrant Book Mart	20 North Third Street	Easton, PA 18042	(215) 252-1188
Zellner's Book Service	2839 Norton Avenue	Easton, PA 18042	
Motorsport Miscellania	913 Jenkintown Road	Elkins Park, PA 19117	(215) 884-8314
CML Books	RR 1, #92	Elverson, PA 19520	
Avocational	PO Box 41	Ephrata, PA 17522	
Clay Book Store	2450 West Main Street	Ephrata, PA 17522-9731	(717) 733-7253
Robert Wynne Books	3653 Lincoln Way East	Fayetteville, PA 17222	(717) 352-8485
Chester Valley Old Books	489 Lancaster Avenue, Box 1228	Frazer, PA 19355	(215) 251-9500
Dr. Walter L. Powell Antiquarian Bookman	201 Ewell Avenue	Gettysburg, PA 17325	
Robert Wynne Books	Rear 103 Carlisle Street	Gettysburg, PA 17325	(717) 334-9387
Stan Clark Military Books	915 Fairview Avenue	Gettysburg, PA 17325	(717) 337-1728
Whistlestop Bookshop	104 Carlisle Street	Gettysburg, PA 17325	
Family Album, The	RD 1, Box 42	Glen Rock, PA 17327	(717) 235-2134
Charles C. Rake Bookseller	PO Box 106	Greencastle, PA 17225	
Michael T. Shilling Bookman	152 South Washington Street	Greencastle, PA 17225	
Bookworm Bookstore, The (two locations)	Box 1341	Harrisburg, PA 17105	(717) 657-8563
MAC Books	137 S. 14th Street	Harrisburg, PA 17104	
Paperback Exchange	3988 Jonestown Road	Harrisburg, PA 17109	(717) 545-6199
Jean's Books	Box 264	Hatfield, PA 19440	(215) 362-0732

James S. Jaffe Rare Books	PO Box 496	Haverford, PA 19041	
Jaynes Booksearch	325 Valley Road	Havertown, PA 19083	
Tamerlane Books	516 Kathmere Road	Havertown, PA 19083	
R. F. Selgas, Sporting Books	P.O. Box 227	Hershey, PA 17033	(717) 534-1868
Rebecca of Sunnybook Farm	P.O. Box 209	Hershey, PA 17033	(717) 533-3039
Hobson's Choice	511 Runnymede Avenue	Jenkintown, PA 19046	
Medical Manor Books Antiquarian	PO Box 647	Jenkintown, PA 19046	
Palinurus Antiquarian Books	101 Greenwood Avenue	Jenkintown, PA 19046	
Griffin Bookshop, The	430 Main Street	Johnstown, PA 15901	
Thomas Macaluso Rare and Fine Books	130 South Union Street	Kennett Square, PA 19348	(215) 444-1063
Gene's Books	King of Prussia Plaza	King of Prussia, PA 19406	
Used Book Store, The	474 West Main Street	Kutztown, PA 19530	(215) 683-9055
Photographic Memory	Box 64	Lafayette Hill, PA 19444	
Antiquarian Map & Book Den	217 East New Street	Lancaster, PA 17602	
Book Bin Bookstore	14 West Orange Street	Lancaster, PA 17603	(717) 392-6434
Book Bin, The	27 North Prince Street	Lancaster, PA 17603	
Book Haven, The	146 North Prince Street	Lancaster, PA 17603	(717) 393-0920
Cerebro	P.O. Box 1221	Lancaster, PA 17603	
Chestnut Street Books	11 West Chestnut Street	Lancaster, PA 17603	(717) 393-3773
Wholesale Rug	2448 Lincoln Hwy East	Lancaster, PA 17602	
Rosamond L. Dupont - Books	RD1, Box 4	Landenberg, PA 19350	
Hyman's Books for Little People	69 Oakwyn NE Terrace	Langhorne, PA 19047	
Book Swap	Hillcrest Shopping Center	Lansdale, PA 19446	
Johnson & Roth Used Books	121 East Cumberland Street	Lebanon, PA 17042	(717) 272-2511
Paperback Exchange	1005-A Market Street	Lemoyne, PA 17043	(717) 761-2430
Antiquarian Map & Book Den	217 East New Street	Lititz, PA 17543	(717) 626-5002
Virginia Scaccia Serine	6 Mann Street	Mansfield, PA 16933	
William Thomas - Bookseller	P.O. Box 331	Mechanicsburg, PA 17055	(717) 766-7778
Windsor Park Books & News	5252 Simpson Ferry Road	Mechanicsburg, PA 17055	(717) 795-8262
William Hutchison	P.O. Box 909	Mendenhall, PA 19357	(215) 388-0195
Light of Parnell Bookshop	3362 Mercersburg Road	Mercersburg, PA 17236	(717) 328-3478
Charles Agvent	RD 2, Box 377A	Mertztown, PA 19539	(215) 682-4750

Complete List 153

154 Complete List

Mosher Books	P.O. Box 111	Millersville, PA 17551-0111	(717) 872-9209
Philip R. Bishop	PO Box 111	Millersville, PA 17551	
CML Books	The Market Place, Rts 10 & 23, RD 1	Morgantown, PA 19543	(215) 286-7297
Walter Amos, Bookseller	The Market Place, Rts 10 & 23, RD 1	Morgantown, PA 19543	(215) 286-0510
Derek White	85 Trenton Avenue	Morrisville, PA	
William L. Zeigler	10 Lincolnway West	New Oxford, PA 17350	
Bridge Street Old Books	129 West Bridge Street	New Hope, PA 18938	(215) 862-0615
Miscellaneous Man	Box 1000	New Freedom, PA 17349	(717) 235-4766
Newtown Book & Record Exchange	102 S. State Street	Newtown, PA 18940	(215) 968-4914
J. Cheny	P.O. Box 901	Newtown, PA 18940	
S & C Najarian	852 Milmar Road	Newtown Square, PA 19073	(215) 353-5165
Bookworm, The	510 Chester Pike	Norwood, PA 19074	(215) 534-2446
Paoli Book Exchange	11 Paoli Plaza	Paoli, PA 19301	
Art Carduner Booksearch	6228 Greene Street (Box 4197)	Philadelphia, PA 19144	(215) 843-6071
Bauman Rare Books	1215 Locust	Philadelphia, PA 19107	
Bikes & Books	6228 Greene Street	Philadelphia, PA 19144	
Bob's Book Shop	206 South 13th Street	Philadelphia, PA 19107	(215) 546-7015
Book Mark	2049 West Rittenhouse Square	Philadelphia, PA 19103	(215) 735-5546
Book Shop, The	3828 Morrell Avenue	Philadelphia, PA 19114	(215) 632-7835
Book Swap, Inc.	1916 Welsh Rd.	Philadelphia, PA 19115	
Book Trader, The	501 South Street	Philadelphia, PA 19147	(215) 925-0219
Bookhaven	2202 Fairmount Avenue	Philadelphia, PA 19130	(215) 235-3226
Books & Coffee	7167 Germantown Avenue	Philadelphia, PA 19119	
Bump in the Night Books	133 Elfreths Aly	Philadelphia, PA 19106	
Carmen D. Valentino, Rare Books & Mss.	2956 Richmond Street	Philadelphia, PA 19134	(215) 739-6056
Catherine Barnes	2031 Walnut Street, 3rd floor	Philadelphia, PA 19103	(215) 854-0175
Christopher D. Lewis	2016 Walnut Street	Philadelphia, PA 19103	
David & Luba Haynes Books	2210 Trenton Avenue	Philadelphia, PA 19125	
David J. Holmes, Autographs	230 South Broad Street, 3rd floor	Philadelphia, PA 19102	(215) 735-1083
Factotum Books	1709 South Street	Philadelphia, PA 19146	(215) 985-1929
Fountainhead Books	6347 Cottage Street	Philadelphia, PA 19124	
Friend's General Conference	1216 Arch Street, Suite 2-B	Philadelphia, PA 19107	

Complete List   155

Name	Address	City	State	Zip	Phone
George S. MacManus Company	1317 Irving Street	Philadelphia	PA	19107	(215) 735-4456
Giovanni's Room	345 South 12th	Philadelphia	PA	19107	
Hibberd's Books	1310 Walnut Street	Philadelphia	PA	19107	(215) 222-1576
House of Our Own	3920 Spruce Street	Philadelphia	PA	19104	
James G. Tanner	4333 Main Street	Philadelphia	PA	19127	(215) 561-6422
John F. Warren, Bookseller	124 South 19th Street	Philadelphia	PA	19103	
Joseph Fox	1724 Sansom St	Philadelphia	PA	19103	(215) 877-8656
Kathleen Rais & Company	3901 Conshohocken Avenue, Suite 2310	Philadelphia	PA	19131	
Lame Duck Used Books	218 South 45th Street	Philadelphia	PA	19104	
Manor House Publications	3501 Newberry Road	Philadelphia	PA	19154	
Marlo Bookstore	2339 Cottman Avenue	Philadelphia	PA	19149	
Miriam and William Crawford Books	P.O. Box 42587	Philadelphia	PA	19101	Not provided.
Ninth Street Market Books & Records	1022 South 9th Street	Philadelphia	PA	19147	(215) 922-2352
Old Original Bookfinders	1018 Pine Street	Philadelphia	PA	19107	
Patricia Libby	226 W. Rittenhouse Sq.	Philadelphia	PA	19103	(215) 981-0777
Philadelphia Drama Bookshop	2209 Walnut Street	Philadelphia	PA	19103	(215) 242-4750
Philadelphia Print Shop, Ltd., The	8441 Germantown Avenue	Philadelphia	PA	19118	(215) 744-6734
Philadelphia Rare Books & Mss. Co., The	P.O. Box 9536	Philadelphia	PA	19124	
PRB&M	PO Box 9536	Philadelphia	PA	19119	
Ray Riling Arms Books Company	6844 Gorsten Street	Philadelphia	PA	19107	(215) 922-6643
Reedmor Magazine Company, Inc.	1229 Walnut Street, 2nd floor	Philadelphia	PA	19143	(215) 726-5493
Richard T. Rosenthal	4718 Springfield Avenue	Philadelphia	PA	19103	(215) 545-6072
Rittenhouse Medical Book Store	1706 Rittenhouse Square	Philadelphia	PA	19107	(215) 592-8380
Russakoff's Books and Records	259 South 10th Street	Philadelphia	PA	19130	
Spring Garden Book Supply	1537 Spring Garden Street	Philadelphia	PA	19118	
SummerhouseBooks	8127 Germantown Ave.	Philadelphia	PA	19017	
W. Graham Arader III	1308 Walnut Street	Philadelphia	PA	19103	(215) 735-8811
Whodunit	1931 Chestnut Street	Philadelphia	PA	19103	
William H. Allen, Bookseller	2031 Walnut Street	Philadelphia	PA	19103	(215) 563-3398
Zavelle Book Store	1900 North Broad	Philadelphia	PA	19121	
Book Bin, The	PO Box 344	Phoenixville	PA	19460	
Bookworm	742 South Main Street	Phoenixville	PA	19460	

156 Complete List

Name	Address	City, State ZIP	Phone
Antiquarians	2091 Newville Road	Plainfield, PA 17081	
Americanist	1525 Shenkel Road	Pottstown, PA 19464	(215) 323-5289
S. F. Collins' Bookcellar	266 Concord Drive	Pottstown, PA 19464	(215) 323-2495
Book Stop, The	Shillington Shopping Center	Reading, PA 19607	
Dell's Book Outlet	1018 Windsor Street	Reading, PA 19612-3156	(215) 376-7957
Larry W. Soltys	330 South 17 1/2 Street	Reading, PA 19602	(215) 372-7670
Museum Books & Prints	P.O. Box 7832	Reading, PA 19603	
Whale of a Bookstore	1001 Oley Street	Reading, PA 19604	(215) 373-3660
T.W. Clemmer	236 Manor Dr.	Richboro, PA 18954	
RAC Books	Box 296, RD #2	Seven Valleys, PA 17360	(717) 428-3776
Robert Wynne	227 Lurgan Avenue	Shippensburg, PA 17257	
Alan F. Innes - Books	Box 123	Shohola, PA 18458	(717) 559-7873
Thomas S. DeLong	RD 6, Box 336	Sinking Spring, PA 19608	(215) 777-7001
Book Place, The	Rt. 73 & Rt. 113, P.O. Box 236	Skippack, PA 19474	(215) 584-6966
Meadowbrook Hollow Books & Bits	8842 Furnace Road	Slatington, PA 18080	(215) 767-7542
Indian Path Books	Route 23 & Bethel Church Road	Spring City, PA 19475	(215) 495-3001
BOOKSOURCE, LTD	15 S. Chester Road, P.O. Box 43	Swarthmore, PA 19081	(215) 328-5083
Thomas Heller, Inc.	PO Box 356	Swathmore, PA 19081	
Ye Olde Book Treasury	234 Dickinson Avenue	Swathmore, PA 19081	
Blase Book Barn	P.O. Box 217	Telford, PA 18969	
Volume Control	955 Sandy Lane	Warminster, PA 18974	(215) 674-0217
David Lib. of the Amer. Rev.	P.O. Box 748	Washington Crossing, PA 18977	
Beattie Books	105 West Wayne Avenue	Wayne, PA 19087	(215) 687-3347
Konigsmark Books	309 Midland Avenue, Box 543	Wayne, PA 19087-0543	(215) 687-5965
Kenton & Audrey Broyles Historical Coll.	P.O. Box 42	Waynesboro, PA 17268	(717) 762-3068
Baldwin's Book Barn	865 Lenape Road	West Chester, PA 19382	
Bill & Val's Comics	128 East Gay Street	West Chester, PA 19380	(215) 358-0359
Elizabeth L. Matlat - Antiques	Rt 202, Brandywine Summit Center	West Chester, PA 19381	(215) 430-0529
Maiden Voyage Rare Books	120 East Virginia Avenue	West Chester, PA 19380	
Second Reading Bookstore	124 South High	West Chester, PA 19382	
Book Place, The	1814 Valley Forge Road	Worcester, PA 19490	(215) 887-0228
David C. Lachman	127 Woodland Road	Wyncote, PA 19095	

Earl Moore	PO Box 243	Wynnewood, PA 19096	
Book Barter, The	1960 Carlisle Road	York, PA 17404	(717) 843-6516
Comix Connection	Delco Plaza, 1201 Carlisle Road	York, PA 17404	(717) 845-7760
Inscribulus Books	236 N. George Street	York, PA 17405	(717) 846-2866
First Capitol Books and Antiques	343 West Market Street	York, PA 17401	(717) 757-6977
Frank Fogleman/Bookseller	701 South Vernon Street	York, PA 17402	
Marie Fetrow	1777 West Market Street	York, PA 17404	
McIlnay's Books	306 West Market Street	York, PA 17401	(717) 846-0315
Paperback Trade, The	165 S. Richland Ave.	York, PA 17405	
RAC 8 Books in 1st Capitol Bks & Antiques	343 West Market Street	York, PA 17401	(717) 846-2866
RAC Books in York Antique Mall	236 North George Street	York, PA 17401	(717) 845-7760
Tollgate Bookstore	2559 South Queen Street	York, PA 17402	

Delaware

Between Books	Philadelphia Pike & Harvey Road	Claymont, DE 19703	
Bookseller, The	764 Townsend Blvd.	Dover, DE 19901	(302) 678-5935
Books Incorporated	3826 Kennett Pike	Greenville, DE 19807	
Oak Knoll Books	414 Delaware Street	New Castle, DE 19720	(302) 328-7232
John P. Reid	307 Main Street	Stanton, DE 19804	(302) 995-6580
Around Again Books	1717 Marsh Road	Wilmington, DE 19803	(302) 478-3333
Aviation Books	705 West 38th Street	Wilmington, DE 19802	(302) 764-2427
Hollyoak Bookshop	214 West Seventh Street	Wilmington, DE 19801	
Dale A. Brandreth, Books	P.O. Box 151	Yorklyn, DE 19736	(302) 239-4608

New Jersey

Galaxy Book Trader	121 West Merchant Street	Audubon, NJ 08106	(609) 546-6283
Novel Idea, A	Dutch Neck Village/RD 2, Trench Road	Bridgeton, NJ 08302	(609) 451-3280
Caney Booksellers	One Cherry Hill, Suite 220	Cherry Hill, NJ 08002	
Between the Covers	575 Collings Avenue	Collingswood, NJ 08107	
Collingswood Book Trader	757 Haddon Avenue	Collingswood, NJ 08108	
Heinoldt Books	1325 W. Central Ave.	Egg Harbor, NJ 08215	(609) 965-2284
People's Bookshop, The	160 Main Street	Flemington, NJ 08822	(908) 788-4953

Complete List

Name	Address	City, State ZIP	Phone
Pollywog Paperback Bookswap	23 Church Street	Flemington, NJ 08822	(908) 782-6900
Between the Covers Rare Books	132 Kings Highway East	Haddonfield, NJ 08033	(609) 354-7665
Old Cookbooks - H. T. Hicks	P.O. Box 462	Haddonfield, NJ 08033	(609) 854-2844
Ray Boas, Bookseller	407 Haddon Avenue	Haddonfield, NJ 08033	(609) 795-4853
Booktrader of Hamilton	104 Flock Road	Hamilton, NJ 08619	(609) 890-1455
Elisabeth Woodburn, Books	PO Box 398	Hopewell, NJ 08525	(609) 466-0522
La Scala Autographs, Inc.	PO Box 368	Hopewell, NJ 08525	
Bookbizniz	58 Marc Drive	Howell, NJ 07731	
Phoenix Books	49 North Union Street	Lambertville, NJ 08530	(908) 901-8870
South Jersey Magazine	PO Box 847	Millville, NJ 08332	(609) 397-4960
Wind Chimes Book Exchange	210 N. High Street	Millville, NJ 08332	
Murphy's Loft Books & Prints	53 North Main Street	Mullica Hill, NJ 08062	(609) 327-3714
White Papers, c/o Wolf's Antiques	36 S. Main Street, PO Box 129	Mullica Hill, NJ 08062	(609) 467-2004
Ted's Engine House	6307 Westfield Avenue	Pennsauken, NJ 08110	
Bryn Mawr Book Shop	102 Witherspoon Street	Princeton, NJ 08542	
Micawber Books, Inc.	110 Nassau Street	Princeton, NJ 08542	(609) 921-7479
Witherspoon Art & Bookstore	12 Nassau Street	Princeton, NJ 08542	
Sporting Book Service	PO Box 177	Rancocas, NJ 08073	
Mrs. Joann V. White	R.R. 2 Box 404	Swedesboro, NJ 08085	
Autographs & Collectibles	124 Pickford Avenue	West Trenton, NJ 08628	(609) 530-1350
Brian Kathenes Autographs & Coll.	PO Box 77296	West Trenton, NJ 08628	

Maryland

Briarwood Books	88 Maryland Ave.	Annapolis, MD 21401	(410) 268-1440
Elm Spy Books	Box 9753	Arnold, MD 21012	(410) 544-9014
19th Century Shop, The	1047 Hollins Street	Baltimore, MD 21223	(410) 539-2586
Allen's Book Shop	416 East 31st Street, 2nd floor	Baltimore, MD 21218-3410	(410) 243-4356
Arista Book Service	2222 Park Ave.	Baltimore, MD 21217	
ASABI International	4610 York Road	Baltimore, MD 21212	(410) 323-2355
Balser Shirley, Prints & Books	PO Box 5803	Baltimore, MD 21208	
Baltimore Book Company, Inc.	2112 North Charles Street	Baltimore, MD 21218	(410) 659-0550
Book Arbor	PO Box 20885	Baltimore, MD 21209	(410) 367-0338

Complete List 159

Name	Address	City, State ZIP	Phone
Book Miser	24 West 25th Street	Baltimore, MD 21218	(410) 256-9220
Book Miser	518 St. Paul Street	Baltimore, MD 21202	(410) 448-1015
Bryn Mawrket	109 West Melrose Ave.	Baltimore, MD 21210	(410) 323-7767
Butternut and Blue	3411 Northwind Road	Baltimore, MD 21234	
Camelot Books	2403 Hillhouse Road	Baltimore, MD 21207	
Cecil Archer Rush - Fine Books-Fine Arts	1410 Northgate Road	Baltimore, MD 21218-1549	
Chirurgical Bookshop	1211 Cathedral Street	Baltimore, MD 21201	(410) 661-2974
D. R. Sandy	P.O. Box 15317	Baltimore, MD 21220	(410) 225-0277
Drusilla's Books	859 North Howard Street	Baltimore, MD 21201	(410) 234-0069
Lambda Rising	241 West Chase Street	Baltimore, MD 21201	
Genealogical Publishing Company, Inc.	1001 North Calvert Street	Baltimore, MD 21202	(410) 298-1758
Geppi's Comic World, Inc.	7019 Security Blvd.	Baltimore, MD 21207	
Granny's Attic	22 West 25th Street	Baltimore, MD 21218	
Hardford Coin Co., Inc.	2160 East Joppa Road	Baltimore, MD 21234	(410) 235-6810
Kelmscott Bookshop, The	32 West 25th Street	Baltimore, MD 21218	(410) 234-0069
Lamda Rising Baltimore	241 West Chase Street	Baltimore, MD 21201	
Mindbridge, Ltd.	1786 Merritt Blvd.	Baltimore, MD 21222	
New Era Book Shop	408 Park Ave.	Baltimore, MD 21201	(410) 539-6364
Normal's Books & Records	429 E Thirty-first Street	Baltimore, MD 21218	
Perfect Ending, The	1004 Reisterstown Road	Baltimore, MD 21208	(410) 448-5340
Rug Book Shop, The	2603 Talbot Road	Baltimore, MD 21216	(410) 367-8194
Russel Sandy Antiquarian Bookseller	P.O. Box 15317	Baltimore, MD 21220	
Second Story Books	3302 Greenmount Ave.	Baltimore, MD 21218	(410) 467-4344
Sherlock Book Detective	PO Box 1174	Baltimore, MD 21203	
Tales From the White Hart	3360 Greenmount Avenue	Baltimore, MD 21218	(410) 889-0099
Tiber Bookshop	8 West 25th Street	Baltimore, MD 21218	(410) 243-2789
AOC Books	6601 Lybrook Court	Bethesda, MD 20817	
Bartleby's Books	4823 Fairmont Ave.	Bethesda, MD 20814	(301) 654-4373
Book Cellar, The	8227 Woodmont Ave.	Bethesda, MD 20814	(301) 654-1898
Continental Divide Trail Society	PO Box 30002	Bethesda, MD 20824	(301) 493-4080
Curious Books	7921 Norfolk Ave.	Bethesda, MD 20814	(301) 656-2668
Dar-Danelles Books	9305 Ewing Drive	Bethesda, MD 20817	

Complete List

Name	Address	City, State ZIP	Phone
Federal Circuit Div. of Shellenard, Inc.	7100 Crail Drive	Bethesda, MD 20817	(301) 229-7102
Georgetown Book Shop	7770 Woodmont Ave.	Bethesda, MD 20814	(301) 907-6923
Iranbooks	8014 Old Georgetown Road	Bethesda, MD 20814	(301) 986-0079
Leonard S. Blondes Use Law Books	7100 Crail Drive	Bethesda, MD 20817	
Mystery Bookshop Bethesda	7700 Old Georgetown Road	Bethesda, MD 20814	(301) 657-2665
Old Forest Bookshop, The	7921 Norfolk Avenue	Bethesda, MD 20814	
Old World Mail Auctions	5614 Northfield Road	Bethesda, MD 20817	
Paper Memories	5308 Portsmouth Road	Bethesda, MD 20816	
R. Quick, Bookseller	7155 Wisconsin Avenue	Bethesda, MD 20815	(301) 654-5030
Schweitzer Japanese Prints, Inc.	6313 Lenox Road	Bethesda, MD 20817	(301) 229-6574
Second Story Books	4836 Bethesda Ave.	Bethesda, MD 20814	(301) 656-0170
Stone Ridge School	9101 Rockville Pike	Bethesda, MD 20814	
Magic Page, The	7416 Laurel-Bowie Road	Bowie, MD 20715	
Old Hickory Bookshop	20225 New Hampshire Avenue	Brinklow, MD 20862	(301) 924-2225
Stewart's Used Bookstore	6504 Old Branch Avenue	Camp Springs, MD 20748	(301) 449-6766
Castle Bookshop, Ltd., The	611 Frederick Road	Catonsville, MD 21228	(410) 788-0207
Ashe & Deane Fine Books	P.O. Box 15601	Chevy Chase, MD 20825	(301) 588-9590
Encore Books, Inc.	7335 Old Alexandria Ferry Road	Clinton, MD 20735	
Book Rack, The	12 Scott Adam Road	Cockeysville, MD 21030	
Book Nook	9933 Rhode Island Ave.	College Park, MD 20740	(301) 474-4060
Mary Chapman Bookseller	PO Box 304	College Park, MD 20740	
Maryland Book Exchange	4500 College Avenue	College Park, MD 20740	
Mike's Best Sellers	8608 Baltimore Blvd.	College Park, MD	
Cover to Cover	7284 Cradlerock Way	Columbia, MD 21045	
Culpepper, Hughes & Head	9770 Basket Ring Road	Columbia, MD 21045	(301) 730-1484
John Gach Books, Inc.	5620 Waterloo Road	Columbia, MD 21045	(410) 465-9023
Second Edition Used Books	6490M Dobbin Road	Columbia, MD 21045	(410) 730-0050
Steven C. Bernard - First Editions	15011 Plainfield Lane	Darnestown, MD 20874	(301) 948-8423
Books on the Beach	5809 Maryland Route 256	Deale, MD 20751	
Mindridge Books, Ltd.	1786 Merritt Blvd	Dundalk, MD	
Book Shelf, The	57 Mayo Road	Edgewater, MD 21037	
Carol's Used Book Shop	2002 Pulaski Highway	Edgewood, MD 21040	(410) 798-0595

Complete List 161

Name	Address	City, State ZIP	Phone
Stone House Books	71 Stone House Lane	Elkton, MD 21921	
Deeds Book Shop	8012 Main Street/P.O. Box 85	Ellicott City, MD 21041	(410) 465-9419
Turtle Hill Books	3420 Sylvan Lane	Ellicott City, MD 21043	(410) 465-7213
White's Antiques	277 W. Patrick Street	Frederick, MD 21701	
Wonder Book and Video	1306 West Patrick Street	Frederick, MD 21702	(301) 694-5955
Book Alcove, Inc.	15976 Shady Grove Road	Gaithersburg, MD 20877	(301) 977-9166
Cheryl's Cookbooks	18705 Capella Lane	Gaithersburg, MD 20877	(301) 977-8033
Doris Frohnsdorff	P.O. Box 2306	Gaithersburg, MD 20886	(301) 869-1256
Olde Soldier Books, Inc.	18779-B North Frederick Road	Gaithersburg, MD 20879	(301) 963-2929
Ron Van Sickle Military Books	935-A Russell Avenue	Gaithersburg, MD 20879	
Book Nook II	143 Delaware Avenue, N.E.	Glen Burnie, MD 21061	(410) 766-5758
Esad Adventure Company	210 South Crain Highway	Glen Burnie, MD 21061	
Delmarva Book Shop	300 Drummer Drive	Grasonville, MD 21638	(410) 827-9400
Barnwood Books	103 South Potomac Street	Hagerstown, MD 21740	
Courtyard Bookshop	313 St. John Street	Havre De Grace, MD 21014	(410) 939-5150
Hiram Larew Books	3312 Gumwood Drive	Hyattsville, MD 20783	
Children's BookAdoption Agency	P.O. Box 643	Kensington, MD 20895-0643	(301) 565-2834
John C. Rather	PO Box 273	Kensington, MD 20895	
Lionel Epstein - Bookseller	9909 Old Spring Road	Kensington, MD 20895	(301) 949-8622
Attic Books	100 Washington Blvd.	Laurel, MD 20707	(301) 725-3725
Bonanza Books	8821 Cardinal Court	Laurel, MD 20273	
Comic Classics	365 Main Street	Laurel, MD 20707	(410) 792-4744
John W. Knott, Jr.	8453 Early Bud Way	Laurel, MD 20723	
Vintage Paperback Exchange, The	8821 Cardinal Court	Laurel, MD 20723	
Bowes Books	718 Great Mills Road	Lexington Park, MD 20653	(301) 369-0484
Frazier Americana	10509 Water Point Way	Mitchellville, MD 20721	(301) 863-6200
Eleanor Weller, Charlotte's Web Antiques	16135 Old York Road	Monkton, MD 21111	(301) 336-3616
B&B Smith, Booksellers	P.O. Box 158	Mount Airy, MD 21771	(410) 771-4239
News Shop	13 South Main Street	North East, MD 21901	(410) 549-1227
Bookcom	8265 Maryland Rt. 3 North	North Millersville, MD 21108	
T. A. Borden	17119 Old Baltimore Road	Olney, MD 20832	(301) 774-4669
This 'N' That Antiques	16650 Georgia Avenue	Olney, MD 20832	

Complete List

Name	Address	City, State ZIP	Phone
BookQuest	135 Village Queen Drive	Owings Mills, MD 21117	(410) 581-0394
Books From X to Z	8513 Summit Road	Pasadena, MD 21122-3046	(410) 360-9602
Mindbridge Books Ltd.	9847 Belair Road	Perry Hall, MD 21128	
Fields of Pikesville	1401 Reisterstown Road	Pikesville, MD 21208	
Willis Van Devanter Books	PO Box 277	Poolesville, MD 20837	
Old Quenzel Store	PO Box 326	Port Tobacco, MD 20677	
Second Looks Books	759 Solomons Island Road N.	Prince Frederick, MD 20678	(410) 535-6897
Dial Organization Year Book	12000 Reisterstown Road	Reisterstown, MD 21136	
Riverdale Bookshop	4701 Queensbury Road	Riverdale, MD 20737	
Antiquarian Bookworm	1307 Templeton Place	Rockville, MD 20852	
Book Alcove, Inc.	5210 Randolph Road	Rockville, MD 20852	
Peter Pun Books	835 Bowie Road	Rockville, MD 20852	(301) 762-4062
Q. M. Dabney & Company	11910 Parklawn Drive	Rockville, MD 20852	(301) 881-1470
Quill & Brush	Box 5365	Rockville, MD 20848	(301) 460-3700
Richard Alexander Books	5901 Montrose Road, # 807N	Rockville, MD 20852	(301) 816-2944
Robert A Madle SF-Fantasy Books	4406 Bestor Drive	Rockville, MD 20853	
Second Story Books	12160 Parklawn Drive	Rockville, MD 20852-1708	(301) 770-0477
Yak & Yeti Books	P.O. Box 5736	Rockville, MD 20855	(301) 977-7285
Dragonstar Craft	PO Box 2039	Savage, MD 20763	
Old Books at Savage Mill	Antique Center I	Savage, MD 20763	(410) 531-6065
Shepherd's Nook	558 Baltimore-Annapolis Blvd.	Severna Park, MD 21146	
Atherton's Used Books	2913 Stanton, Avenue	Silver Spring, MD 20910	(301) 589-3879
Dale Music Co. Book Dept.	8240 Georgia Ave.	Silver Spring, MD 20910	
Ground Zero Books	P.O. Box 1046, Blair Station	Silver Spring, MD 20902	(301) 585-1471
Hirschtritt's "1712"	1712 Republic Road	Silver Spring, MD 20910	(301) 649-5393
Imagination Books	946 Sligo Avenue	Silver Spring, MD 20905	(301) 589-2223
O'Boyle Books	14605 Pebblestone Drive	Silver Spring, MD 20905	(301) 384-9346
Peter Koffsky	1708 Glenkarney Place	Silver Spring, MD 20902	
Silver Spring Books	938 Bonifant Street	Silver Spring, MD 20910	(301) 587-7484
Tales Retold	939 Bonifant Street	Silver Spring, MD 20910	(301) 588-1933
Lazy Moon Bookshop	14510 Main Street	Solomons, MD 20688	(410) 326-3720
Jerome Shochet	6144 Oakland Mills Road	Sykesville, MD 21784	(410) 795-5879

Complete List   163

Well Read Books	7050 Carroll Avenue	Takoma Park, MD 20912	(301) 270-4748
Taneytown Antique Shoppes	7 Frederick Street	Taneytown, MD 21787	(410) 756-4262
E. Christian Mattson	1 Center Road A1	Towson, MD 21204	(410) 825-8967
Francis, Ltd.	205 East Joppa Road	Towson, MD 21204	
Greetings & Readings	809 Taylor Avenue	Towson, MD 21204	(410) 821-6286
Jean-Maurice Poitras & Sons	107 Edgerton Road	Towson, MD 21204	
Mattson E. Christian Bookseller	1 Centre Road	Towson, MD 21204	
Smith College Club of Baltimore Used Bks	7300 York Road	Towson, MD 21204	(410) 821-6241
Ellie's Paperback Shack	Box 31-D Action Square	Waldorf, MD 20601-9402	(301) 934-3140
Family Line Publications	63 East Main Street	Westminster, MD 21157	
Paperback Exchange Book Store, The	100 Manchester Avenue	Westminster, MD 21157	(410) 848-0828
Barbarian Bookshop, The	11254 Triangle Lane	Wheaton, MD 20902	(301) 946-4184
Bonifant Books, Inc.	11240 Georgia Avenue	Wheaton, MD 20902	
Books of Colonial America	3611 Janet Road	Wheaton, MD 20906	
M-C Associates	11910 Lafayette Dr.	Wheaton, MD 20902	

Washington, D.C.

Adams Bookstore	2912 M Street, NW	Washington, DC 20007	
American Book Centres	Box 39090	Washington, DC 20016	
Another World	1504 Wisconsin Avenue, NW	Washington, DC 20007	
Bickerstaff & Barclay	P.O. Box 46259	Washington, DC 20050	
Bird-in-Hand Bookstore	PO Box 15258	Washington, DC 20003	
Book Market	2603 Connecticut Avenue, NW	Washington, DC 20008	(202) 965-3244
Booked Up	1209 31st Street NW	Washington, DC 20007	(202) 544-1621
Capitol Hill Books	657 C Street, SE	Washington, DC 20003	
Dabney Bindery	PO Box 42026	Washington, DC 20015	
Estate Book Sales	2914 M Street, NW	Washington, DC 20007	(202) 337-3235
Fuller & Saunders Books	3238 P Street, NW	Washington, DC 20007	
Ginza Things Japanese	1721 Connecticut Ave. NW	Washington, DC 20009	
Idle Time Books	2410 18th Street, NW	Washington, DC 20009	(202) 232-4774
Joshua Heller Rare Books, Inc.	PO Box 39114	Washington, DC 20007	
Key Bridge News Stand	3326 M Street, NW	Washington, DC 20007	
Kultura's Books & Records	1621 Connecticut Ave., NW	Washington, DC 20036	(202) 462-2541

Lambda Rising	1625 Connecticut Ave., NW	Washington, DC 20009	(202) 462-6969
Lantern Bryn Mawr Bookshop, The	3222 O Street, NW	Washington, DC 20007	(202) 333-3222
Latin American Books	PO Box 39090	Washington, DC 20016	
Logic & Literature Book Shop	3034 M Street, NW, 2nd floor	Washington, DC 20007	(202) 625-1668
National Intelligence Book Center	1700 K Street NW, No. 607	Washington, DC 20006	
Old Forest Bookshop, The	3145 Dumbarton Street, NW	Washington, DC 20007	(202) 965-3842
Old Print Gallery, The	1220 31st Street, NW	Washington, DC 20007	(202) 965-1818
Oscar Shapiro	3726 Connecticut Ave., NW	Washington, DC 20008	
President's Box Bookshop, The	P.O. Box 1255	Washington, DC 20013	(703) 998-7390
Ptak Science Books	1531 33rd Street, NW	Washington, DC 20007	(202) 337-2878
Richard Samuel West	1650 Aronne Pl, NW	Washington, DC 20009	
Rock Creek Bookshop	1214 Wisconsin Avenue	Washington, DC 20007	(202) 342-8046
Samuel Yudkin & Associates	3636 16th Street, NW	Washington, DC 20010	(202) 232-6249
Second Story Books	2000 P Street, N.W.	Washington, DC 20036	(202) 659-8884
Secondhand Prose	5010 Connecticut Avenue	Washington, DC 20008	
Voyages Books & Art	4705 Butterworth Place, NW	Washington, DC 20016	(202) 244-9636
William F. Hale - Books	1222 31st Street, NW	Washington, DC 20007	(202) 338-8272
Yesterday's Books	4702 Wisconsin Avenue	Washington, DC 20016	(202) 363-0581

Virginia

Air, Land & Sea	1215 King Street	Alexandria, VA 22314	(703) 578-3292
Book Stop	3640A King Street	Alexandria, VA 22302	(703) 548-3466
Capital Comics Center & Book Niche	2008 Mt. Vernon Ave.	Alexandria, VA 22301	
Donna Lee's Books	206 Queen Street	Alexandria, VA 22314	
From Out of the Past	6440 Richmond Highway	Alexandria, VA 22306	(703) 768-7827
Jennie's Book Nook	15 West Howell Avenue	Alexandria, VA 22301	
Old Mill Books	PO Box 21561	Alexandria, VA 22320	
Book Rack	7857-D Heritage Drive	Annandale, VA 22003	(703) 941-6015
Flanagan's	7120 Little River Turnpike	Annandale, VA 22003	
Book Ends	2710 Washington Blvd.	Arlington, VA 22201	(703) 524-4976
Barcroft Books	3621 Columbia Pike	Arlington, VA 22204	
Bookhouse	805 North Emerson Street	Arlington, VA 22205	(703) 527-7797
Crawfords Nautical Books	5520 North 16th Street	Arlington, VA 22205	Not provided

Complete List 165

Name	Address	City, State ZIP	Phone
Virginia Book Company	P.O. Box 431	Berryville, VA 22611	(703) 955-1428
Burke Centre Books & Comics	5741 Burke Centre Parkway	Burke, VA 22015	
Richard McKay Used Books, Inc.	14114 Lee Highway	Centreville, VA 22020	(703) 830-4048
Abintra, The Bookseller	412 First Street, North	Charlottesville, VA 22901	
Book Broker, The	310 East Market Street	Charlottesville, VA 22902	(804) 296-2194
Book Cellar, The	316 East Main Street	Charlottesville, VA 22902	(804) 979-7787
Book Room, The	1424 Seminole Trail	Charlottesville, VA 22901	(804) 973-1525
Clover Hill Books	P.O. Box 6278	Charlottesville, VA 22906	(804) 973-1506
Daedalus	121 4th Street, NE	Charlottesville, VA 22901	(804) 293-7595
Fantasia Comics & Records	1419 1/2 University Avenue	Charlottesville, VA 22903	(804) 971-1029
Fantasia Comics & Records	1861 Seminole Trail	Charlottesville, VA 22901	(804) 974-7512
Franklin Gilliam	112 4th Street, NE	Charlottesville, VA 22901	
Heartwood Books	5 and 9 Elliewood Avenue	Charlottesville, VA 22903	(804) 295-7083
Terry Marston	625 Monticello Road	Charlottesville, VA 22901	
Ace Books and Antiques	120 West Culpeper Street	Culpeper, VA 22701	(703) 825-8973
Dick Brani	PO Box 1806	Culpeper, VA 22701	
Greenmantle Books	P.O. Box 1777	Culpeper, VA 22701	
Original Historic Newspapers	3002 Winter Pine Court	Fairfax, VA 22031	(703) 591-3150
Richard A. Johnson	9702 Flintridge Court	Fairfax, VA 22032	
Alexander Lauberts	1073 West Broad Street	Falls Church, VA 22046	(703) 533-1699
Hole in the Wall Books	905 West Broad Street	Falls Church, VA 22046	
Beck's Antiques and Books	708 Caroline Street	Fredericksburg, VA 22401	(703) 371-1766
Collectvs Books	820 Caroline Street	Fredericksburg, VA 22401	(703) 373-6148
Royal Oak Bookshop	207 S. Royal Ave.	Front Royal, VA 22630	(703) 365-7070
Hamilton Virginia Books	412 East Colonial Highway	Hamilton, VA 22068	(703) 338-6338
Downtown Books	49-B West Water Street	Harrisonburg, VA 22801	
Franklin Farm Book & Comics	13320-C Franklin Farm Road	Herndon, VA 22071	
Jerry N. Showalter, Bookseller	P.O. Box 84	Ivy, VA 22945	(804) 295-6413
Ben Franklin Booksellers, Inc.	27 South King Street	Leesburg, VA 22075	
Let There Be Praise	9 Catoctin Circle, SE	Leesburg, VA 22075	(703) 777-6311
Jack R. Levien	PO Box 31	McDowell, VA 24458	
MCL Associates	PO Box 26	McLean, VA 22101-0026	

166 Complete List

Name	Address	City, State ZIP	Phone
Hooper's Books	103-B West Federal Street	Middleburg, VA 22117	(703) 687-5714
Nostalgia Mart	5946 Main Street, P.O. Box 745	Mt. Jackson, VA 22842	(703) 477-2182
Paper Treasures	9595 Congress Street, P.O. Box 1160	New Market, VA 22844	(703) 740-3135
E. Wharton & Company	3232 History Drive	Oakton, VA 22124	
Loudoun Books	P.O. Box 884	Purcellville, VA 22132	
Antiquarian Tobacciana	11505 Turnbridge Lane	Reston, VA 22094-1220	(703) 435-8133
Book Alcove, Inc.	2337 Hunters Woods Plaza	Reston, VA 22091	
Book Shelf, The	2355-B Hunters Woods Plaza	Reston, VA 22091	
Reston's Used Book Shop	1623 Washington Plaza	Reston, VA 22090	(703) 435-9772
W. B. O'Neill - Old & Rare Books	11609 Hunters Green Court	Reston, VA 22091	(703) 860-0782
M-R Books	Rt 2, Box 16F	Ruckersville, VA 22968	(804) 985-6459
Bookworm & Silverfish	Church Street	Rural Retreat, VA 24368	(703) 686-5813
Buteo Books	Route 1, Box 242	Shipman, VA 22971	(800) 722-2460
Manuscript Company of Springfield, The	P.O. Box 1151	Springfield, VA 22151-0151	(703) 256-6748
David Holloway, Bookseller	7430 Grace Street	Springfield, VA 22150	(703) 569-1798
Staunton Book Review	11 South Augusta Street	Staunton, VA 24401	(703) 886-6913
Crest Books	46950 Community Plaza, No. 103	Sterling, VA 22170	
JoAnn Reisler, Ltd.	360 Glyndon Street, NE	Vienna, VA 22180	(703) 938-2967
Book Shelf, The	106 Featherbed Lane	Winchester, VA 22601	(703) 665-0866

Specialty Index

Those dealers appearing with an asterisk are specialists, while those without are general book dealers who also specialize.

African-American (see also Black)
  *ASABI International 74
  Between the Covers Rare Books 64
  *David Holloway, Bookseller 137
Agriculture
  *Book Arbor 73
  Taneytown Antique Shoppes 87
America - Southeast, West, South
  *Jerry N. Showalter, Bookseller 145
America - Rocky Mountains, Southwest
  *Continental Divide Trail Society 96
American Revolution
  *Autographs & Collectibles 69
  *Stan Clark Military Books 46
Americana
  *Camelot Books 72
  *Heinoldt Books 62
  Peter Pun Books 106
  *Philadelphia Rare Books & Manuscripts Co. 11
  Staunton Book Review 148
  Thomas Macaluso Rare and Fine Books 21
  William Hutchison 22
  *William Thomas - Bookseller 48
Antiques
  *Eleanor C. Weller, Charlotte's Web Antiques 85
  *Inscribulus Books 54
Archeology
  Logic & Literature Book Shop 118
  *B&B Smith, Booksellers 86
Architecture
  *Beattie Books 28
  Book Mark 5
  *Eleanor C. Weller, Charlotte's Web Antiques 85
  Kelmscott Bookshop, The 76
  William Hutchison 22

Art
  Cecil Archer Rush - Fine Books - Fine Arts 78
  *Cesi Kellinger, Bookseller 44
  *Eleanor C. Weller, Charlotte's Web Antiques 85
  Georgetown Book Shop 93
  *Inscribulus Books 54
  *John F. Warren, Bookseller 6
  Kelmscott Bookshop, The 76
  Kultura's Books & Records 126
  Peter Pun Books 106
  *Robert Wynne Books 46, 47
  Thomas Macaluso Rare and Fine Books 21
Art, European
  *Factotum Books 14
  Old Forest Bookshop, The 117
Assassinations of American Presidents
  *President's Box Bookshop 124
Autographs, letters, manuscripts
  *Autographs & Collectibles 69
  Carmen D. Valentino, Rare Books & Mss. 12
  *Catherine Barnes 5
  Charles Agvent 39
  *David J. Holmes, Autographs 3
  *Manuscript Company of Springfield, The 137
  Nostalgia Mart 145
  Peter Pun Books 106
  *Philadelphia Rare Books & Manuscripts Co. 11
Automotive
  *Motorsport Miscellania 20
Aviation
  *Aviation Books 58
Baedeker travel guides
  *W. B. O'Neill - Old & Rare Books 136
Baseball cards
  *Geppi's Comic World, Inc. 72
Baseball
  Butternut and Blue 80
  Chestnut Street Books 38

Specialty Index

Baseball (cont'd)
Georgetown Book Shop 93
Baum, Frank L.
*S. F. Collins' Bookcellar 25
Bibles
*David C. Lachman 30
*Philadelphia Rare Books & Manuscripts Co. 11
Biography
*Autographs & Collectibles 69
Curious Books 94
*Robert Wynne Books 46, 47
Taneytown Antique Shoppes 87
Black literature (see also African-American)
Silver Spring Books 110
Black studies/Black interest (see also African-American)
*Culpepper, Hughes & Head 81
Book Nook II 84
Mason's Rare & Used Books 45
Ninth Street Market Books & Records 15
Nostalgia Mart 145
Bookbinding
Oak Knoll Books 57
Books about books/bibliographies
Oak Knoll Books 57
Boxing
*Jerome Shochet 87
Brandywine School
Sottile's Books 19
Thomas Macaluso Rare and Fine Books 21
Business (see also Stock markets)
*Books From X to Z 87
Cartography (see also Maps, atlases)
*Antiquarian Map & Book Den 39
Catholicism
CML Books 41
Chesapeake Bay
Delmarva Book Shop 101
Lazy Moon Bookshop 114
Chess
*Dale A. Brandreth, Books 59
Children's
Book House, The 45
Bookworm Bookstore, The 34

*Children's BookAdoption Agency 102
Deeds Book Shop 82
*Drusilla's Books 71
*E. Christian Mattson 88
*Inscribulus Books 54
*JoAnn Reisler, Ltd. 137
Meadowbrook Hollow Books & Bits 43
*Perfect Ending, The 72
Ray Boas, Bookseller 64
*Rebecca of Sunnybook Farm 36
*Robert Wynne Books 46, 47
Sottile's Books 19
Staunton Book Review 148
Taneytown Antique Shoppes 87
White Papers (two locations) 68
China
*Schweitzer Japanese Prints 95
Christian
*Let There Be Praise 134
Civil War
*Autographs & Collectibles 69
Book Shelf, The 138
Book Trader, The 14
Book House, The 45
Book Haven, The 37
Bridge Street Old Books 23
Butternut and Blue 80
*Frazier Americana 104
Heartwood Books 141
Nostalgia Mart 145
*Olde Soldier Books, Inc. 100
Paper Treasures 146
Peter Pun Books 106
Rock Creek Bookshop 121
Royal Oak Bookshop 144
*Stan Clark Military Books 46
Taneytown Antique Shoppes 87
William Hutchison 22
Classics, 19th century (see also Literature)
*19th Century Shop, The 79
Classics, Greek & Latin
Logic & Literature Book Shop 118
*B&B Smith, Booksellers 86
Collectible toys
*Perfect Ending, The 72

Specialty Index

Comics
  *Cap's Comic Cavalcade 31
  *Capital Comics Center & Book Niche 129
  *Comic Classics 102
  *Comix Connection 53
  *Fantasia Comics & Records (two locations) 142
  *Galaxy Book Trader 61
  *Geppi's Comic World, Inc. 72
  *M-R Books 147
  *Paperback Trader 17
  *Reedmor Magazine Company 9
Cooking
  Allen's Book Shop 78
  *Americanist, The 25
  *Chervyl's Cookbooks 100
  Ninth Street Market Books & Records 15
  *Old Cookbooks - H. T. Hicks 65
Cyprus
  *W. B. O'Neill - Old & Rare Books 136
Darwin, Charles
  *19th Century Shop, The 79
Decorative trade bindings
  Book Broker, The 104
Decorative arts
  *Back Room Books 31
  *Eleanor C. Weller, Charlotte's Web Antiques 85
  William Hutchison 22
Delaware
  Sottile's Books 19
Dentistry
  Antonio Raimo Fine Books 32
Dickens, Charles
  *E. Christian Mattson 88
Dogs
  *Kathleen Rais & Company 12
Doyle, Arthur Conan
  *E. Christian Mattson 88
Drama/music/film/cinema
  *Philadelphia Drama Bookshop 6
Economics
  *Lionel Epstein - Bookseller 102
Egypt
  *New Era Book Shop 71

Espionage/military intelligence/POW
  *Elm Spy Books 91
Essays
  Curious Books 94
Ethiopia
  *New Era Book Shop 71
Exploration/travels
  *Robert Wynne Books 46, 47
Fiction
  *Comic Classics 102
  Daedalus 139
  Frank Fogleman/Bookseller 53
  Lazy Moon Bookshop 114
  Meadowbrook Hollow Books & Bits 43
Fine bindings
  Antonio Raimo Fine Books 32
  *Mosher Books 40
First editions
  Between the Covers Rare Books 64
  Charles Agvent 39
  *Clover Hill Books 142
  *David Holloway, Bookseller 137
  Heartwood Books 141
  Lazy Moon Bookshop 114
  *Maiden Voyage Rare Books 29
  Peter Pun Books 106
First day covers
  Samuel Yudkin & Associates 123
Fishing
  Book Trader, The 14
  Bridge Street Old Books 23
  *R. F. Selgas, Sporting Books 35
  *Turtle Hill Books 83
  William Hutchison 22
Fore-edge paintings
  Antonio Raimo Fine Books 32
  *E. Christian Mattson 88
Franklin, Benjamin
  *19th Century Shop, The 79
Freemasonry
  Mason's Rare & Used Books 45
Gardens (see also Horticulture)
  *Book Arbor 73

Specialty Index

Gardens (cont'd)
*Eleanor C. Weller, Charlotte's Web Antiques 85
*Inscribulus Books 54
Gay/lesbian
*Lambda Rising (two locations) 122
Geography
*Robert Wynne Books 46, 47
Golden Books
*Drusilla's Books 71
*Rebecca of Sunnybook Farm 36
Golf
Hirschtritt's "1712" 108
Great civilizations
*New Era Book Shop 71
Greece
*W. B. O'Neill - Old & Rare Books 136
Grey, Zane
Thomas S. DeLong 43
Henkel Press
Paper Treasures 146
Himalayan lands: Central Asia, Mongolia, Tibet
*Yak & Yeti Books 107
Hispanica
*Philadelphia Rare Books & Manuscripts Co. 11
History
McIlnay's Books 51
Old Forest Bookshop, The 117
Rock Creek Bookshop 121
History, American
*Lionel Epstein - Bookseller 102
Rock Creek Bookshop 121
History, ancient
Logic & Literature Book Shop 118
*B&B Smith, Booksellers 86
History, medieval
Logic & Literature Book Shop 118
History, of business
Ray Boas, Bookseller 64
History, of science
Logic & Literature Book Shop 118
*Ptak Science Books 120
History, Spanish
Book Trader, The 14

Horror
Book Nook II 84
*Comic Classics 102
*Tales From the White Hart 74
Horticulture (see also Gardens)
*Elisabeth Woodburn, Books 66
Humanities
*William H. Allen, Bookseller 4
Illustrated books
Book Haven, The 37
Cecil Archer Rush - Fine Books - Fine Arts 78
*JoAnn Reisler, Ltd. 137
Oak Knoll Books 57
*S. F. Collins' Bookcellar 25
Sottile's Books 19
Thomas Macaluso Rare and Fine Books 21
Incunabula/early books
*Back Room Books 31
*Philadelphia Rare Books & Manuscripts Co. 11
Japan
Hirschtritt's "1712" 108
*Schweitzer Japanese Prints, Inc. 95
Kennedy, John F.
Nostalgia Mart 145
King Arthur
Frank Fogleman/Bookseller 53
Ku Klux Klan
*Kenton & Audrey Broyles Historical Collection 51
Landscape architecture
*Book Arbor 73
Languages
Book Bin Bookstore 37
Cecil Archer Rush - Fine Books - Fine Arts 78
Law
*Federal Circuit Div. of Shellenard, Inc. 95
*Lionel Epstein - Bookseller 102
Letters - see Autographs
Literary criticism
Curious Books 94
Literature (see also Classics)
Bookworm Bookstore, The 34
CML Books 41
Deeds Book Shop 82

Specialty Index 171

Literature (cont'd)
Kelmscott Bookshop, The 76
Lazy Moon Bookshop 114
McIlnay's Books 51
Old Forest Bookshop, The 117
Silver Spring Books 110
Thomas Macaluso Rare and Fine Books 21
Voyages Books & Art 124
William Hutchison 22
Literature, English
Kelmscott Bookshop, The 76
Magazines
Baltimore Book Company, Inc. 75
Daedalus 139
From Out of the Past 130
*Reedmor Magazine Company, Inc. 9
Manuscripts - see Autographs
Maps/atlases (see also Cartography)
*Antiquarian Map & Book Den 39
*Camelot Books 72
*Old Print Gallery, The 120
Marxist studies
Kultura's Books & Records 126
Maryland
Allen's Book Shop 78
Deeds Book Shop 82
Kelmscott Bookshop, The 76
Taneytown Antique Shoppes 87
Mathematics/logic
Logic & Literature Book Shop 118
Medical
*Jean-Maurice Poitras & Sons 88
*Rittenhouse Medical Book Store 7
Mediterranean
*W. B. O'Neill - Old & Rare Books 136
Mediterranean archeology
*B&B Smith, Booksellers 86
Mencken, H. L.
Kelmscott Bookshop, The 76
*19th Century Shop, The 79
Metaphysics
Book Shelf, The 138

Military history
Attic Books 103
Bookworm Bookstore, The 34
Castle Bookshop, Ltd., The 80
CML Books 41
Georgetown Book Shop 93
*Ground Zero Books 111
Lazy Moon Bookshop 114
Ray Boas, Bookseller 64
Rock Creek Bookshop 121
*Stan Clark Military Books 46
Stewart's Used Bookstore 97
Mosher books
*Mosher Books 40
Mountain climbing
William Hutchison 22
Music (see also Sheet music)
Allen's Book Shop 78
Book Stop 129
Mystery/suspense
Book House, The 45
*Cloak & Dagger Books 44
Lazy Moon Bookshop 114
*Mystery Bookshop Bethesda 92
*Mystery Books 16
Silver Spring Books 110
Used Book Store, The 36
Natural history
Book Bin Bookstore 37
*Buteo Books 147
*Robert Wynne Books 46, 47
Nautical (see also Yachting)
*Crawfords Nautical Books 132
Lazy Moon Bookshop 114
New age/occult
Book Nook II 84
Newell, Peter
*S. F. Collins' Bookcellar 25
New Jersey
Ray Boas, Bookseller 64
Newspapers
*Original Historic Newspapers 133
Non-fiction
Ray Boas, Bookseller 64
On-line computer database for book-hunting
*BookQuest 86
Orient
T.A. Borden 104

Specialty Index

Ornithology (birds)
*Buteo Books 147
Paper collectibles/ephemera
*Miscellaneous Man 50
Paper Treasures 146
Paperback, vintage
Book House, The 45
Castle Bookshop, Ltd., The 80
Old Books at Savage Mill 108
*Vintage Paperback Exchange, The 104
Paperbacks
*Around Again Books 59
*Book Rack 130
*Booktrader of Hamilton 165
*Bookworm, The 24
*Comic Classics 102
*Galaxy Book Trader 61
*M-R Books 147
*Newtown Book & Record Exchange 23
*Novel Idea, A 61
*Paperback Trader 17
Pennsylvania
Book House, The 45
Book Haven, The 37
Quadrant Book Mart 33
Sottile's Books 19
*William Thomas - Bookseller 48
Pennsylvania Dutch/German/Amish
Book Haven, The 37
Pennsylvania imprints
Book Haven, The 37
Persian (Farsi)/Iran
*Iranbooks 91
Philadelphia
*Factotum Books 14
Sottile's Books 19
Philosophy
Allen's Book Shop 78
Kultura's Books & Records 126
Rock Creek Bookshop 121
Tiber Bookshop 77
Photography
*Richard T. Rosenthal 13
Poetry
Frank Fogleman/Bookseller 53
Kultura's Books & Records 126

Porter, Gene Stratton
Thomas S. DeLong 43
Potter, Beatrix
*Doris Frohnsdorff 101
Prints
*Old Print Gallery, The 120
Private press
*Mosher Books 40
Psychology/psychiatry/psychoanalysis
*John Gach Books, Inc. 81
Pyle, Howard
Sottile's Books 19
Quilting
Book Trader, The 14
Rackham, Arthur
*S. F. Collins' Bookcellar 25
Railroads
Allen's Book Shop 78
Rare books
*19th Century Shop, The
*Beattie Books 28
Between the Covers Rare Books 64
Book Trader, The 14
*Booked Up 118
*Cesi Kellinger, Bookseller 44
David Holloway, Bookseller 137
*David J. Holmes, Autographs 3
*Doris Frohnsdorff 101
*Jerry N. Showalter, Bookseller 145
*Maiden Voyage Rare Books 29
*Mosher Books 40
Peter Pun Books 106
*Richard T. Rosenthal 13
*S. F. Collins' Bookcellar 25
Second Story Books 77, 91, 107, 125
*W. B. O'Neill - Old & Rare Books 136
*William F. Hale - Books 121
Wonder Book and Video 84
Recovery
Book Shelf, The 138
Religion (see also Theology)
Bookworm Bookstore, The 34
*Robert Wynne Books 46, 47
Rock Creek Bookshop 121
Silver Spring Books 110
Tiber Bookshop 77

Specialty Index   173

Romance
  *Novel Idea, A 61
  Silver Spring Books 110
Rugs
  *Rug Book Shop, The 74
Scholarly
  BOOKSOURCE, LTD 27
  *Epistemologist, Scholarly
    Books 18
  Heartwood Books 141
  Old Forest Bookshop, The 117
  *William F. Hale - Books 121
Science fiction/fantasy
  Attic Books 103
  Book House, The 45
  Book Nook II 84
  Bookworm Bookstore, The 34
  *Comic Classics 102
  Frank Fogleman/Bookseller 53
  Lazy Moon Bookshop 114
  Reedmor Magazine Company 9
  Silver Spring Books 110
  Tales Retold 111
  *Tales From the White Hart 74
  Used Book Store, The 36
Science/technology
  *Ptak Science Books 120
  Tiber Bookshop 77
Sheet music
  S & C Najarian 24
Shenandoah Valley
  Paper Treasures 146
Sherlock Holmes
  Frank Fogleman/Bookseller 53
Signed books
  Between the Covers Rare
    Books 64
  *Catherine Barnes 5
  *David J. Holmes, Autographs 3
  *Maiden Voyage Rare Books 29
Smith, Jessie Willcox
  Sottile's Books 19
Social science
  *Books From X to Z 87
Sporting (see also Fishing)
  *Eleanor C. Weller, Charlotte's
    Web Antiques 85
  William Hutchison 22
Sports
  Nostalgia Mart 145
  *Robert Wynne Books 46, 47

Stamp collecting
  Book Trader, The 14
Stock markets
  Delmarva Book Shop 101
Theater & dance (see also Drama)
  Nostalgia Mart 145
Theology (see also Religion)
  *David C. Lachman 30
Tobacco
  *Antiquarian Tobacciana 136
Trade catalogs
  Bookworm & Silverfish 150
Travel
  Capitol Hill Books 117
  Kelmscott Bookshop, The 76
  *W. B. O'Neill - Old & Rare
    Books 136
Turkey
  *W. B. O'Neill - Old & Rare
    Books 136
Twain, Mark
  *19th Century Shop, The 79
Vampires
  *Tales From the White Hart 74
Virginia
  Book Broker, The 104
  Heartwood Books 141
  Nostalgia Mart 145
  Royal Oak Bookshop 144
  *Virginia Book Company 132
Werewolves
  *Tales From the White Hart 74
White, Stewart Edward
  Thomas S. DeLong 43
Wine
  Between the Covers Rare
    Books 64
Women's studies
  Book Nook II 84
World War II
  *William F. Hale - Books 121
  *Stan Clark Military Books 46
  *Volume Control 27
WPA Guides
  *Buteo Books 147
Wyeth, N. C.
  Sottile's Books 19
Yachting & ships (see also Nautical)
  Delmarva Book Shop 101

By Appointment Dealers

Antiquarian Map & Book Den
Art Carduner Booksearch
Atherton's Used Books
Aviation Books
Back Room Books
Beattie Books
Buteo Books
Butternut and Blue
Camelot Books
Carmen D. Valentino, Rare Books & Manuscripts
Catherine Barnes
Cecil Archer Rush - Fine Books - Fine Arts
Cesi Kellinger, Bookseller
Charles Agvent
Children's BookAdoption Agency
Continental Divide Trail Society
D. R. Sandy
David C. Lachman
David Holloway, Bookseller
David J. Holmes, Autographs
Doris Frohnsdorff
E. Christian Mattson
Eleanor C. Weller, Charlotte's Web Antiques
Elisabeth Woodburn, Books
Elm Spy Books
Epistemologist, Scholarly Books
Frazier Americana
Ground Zero Books
Heinoldt Books
Hirschtritt's "1712"
Jean-Maurice Poitras & Sons
Jerry N. Showalter, Bookseller

JoAnn Reisler, Ltd.
John Gach Books, Inc.
Kathleen Rais & Company
Kenton & Audrey Broyles Historical Collections
Konigsmark Books
Light of Parnell Bookshop
Lionel Epstein - Bookseller
Manuscript Company of Springfield, The
Meadowbrook Hollow Books & Bits
Mosher Books
O'Boyle Books
Old Hickory Bookshop
Original Historic Newspapers
Peter Pun Books
Philadelphia Rare Books & Manuscript Company, The
Q. M. Dabney & Company
Quill & Brush
Rebecca of Sunnybook Farm
Richard T. Rosenthal
Rug Book Shop, The
S & C Najarian
S. F. Collins' Bookcellar
Schweitzer Japanese Prints, Inc.
Stan Clark Military Books
Steven C. Bernard - First Editions
T.A. Borden
Thomas S. DeLong
Turtle Hill Books
Vintage Paperback Exchange, The
William Thomas - Bookseller
Yak & Yeti Books

Mail Order Service

The following dealers offer mail order service. Some also operate an open shop, or see customers by appointment.

Alan F. Innes - Books
Ashe & Deane Fine Books
Bookbizniz
Chervyl's Cookbooks
Clover Hill Books
Culpepper, Hughes & Head
Elm Spy Books
Frank Fogleman/Bookseller
Frazier Americana
Hirschtritt's "1712"
Jerome Shochet
Larry W. Soltys
Maiden Voyage Rare Books
Miriam and William Crawford Books
Miscellaneous Man
Q. M. Dabney & Company
R. F. Selgas, Sporting Books
RAC Books
Richard Alexander Books
Rug Book Shop, The
S. F. Collins' Bookcellar
Turtle Hill Books
Vintage Paperback Exchange, The
Volume Control
W. B. O'Neill - Old & Rare Books

General Index

19th Century Shop, The 79
Abby's Book Case 16
Ace Books and Antiques 142
Agvent, Charles 39
Alexander, Richard, Books 105
Allen's Book Shop 78
Allen, William H., Bookseller 4
Americanist 25
Amos, Walter, Bookseller 40
Antiquarian Map & Book Den 39
Antiquarian Tobacciana 136
Arader ,W. Graham, III 3
Around Again Books 59
ASABI International 74
Ashe & Deane Fine Books 97
Atherton's Used Books 110
Attic Books 103
Autographs & Collectibles 69
Aviation Books 58
Back Room Books 31
Baltimore Book Company, Inc. 75
Barbarian Bookshop, The 112
Barnes, Catherine 5
Bartleby's Books 94
Beattie Books 28
Beck's Antiques and Books 144
Bernard, Steven C. - First Eds. 98
Between the Covers Rare
    Books 64
Boas, Ray, Bookseller 64
Bob's Book Shop 8
Book Alcove, Inc. 99
Book Arbor 73
Book Bargains 30
Book Bin Bookstore 37
Book Broker, The 104
Book Cellar, The 92
Book Cellar, The 140
Book Ends 131
Book Haven, The 37
Book House, The 45
Book Mark 5
Book Nook 98
Book Nook II 84
Book Place, The 26
Book Rack 130
Book Room, The 138
Book Shelf, The 99
Book Shelf, The 138

Book Shop, The 10
Book Stop 129
Book Trader, The 14
Bookbizniz 66
Booked Up 118
Bookhaven 11
Bookhouse 131
BookQuest 86
Books From X to Z 87
Bookseller, The 57
BOOKSOURCE, LTD 27
Booktrader of Hamilton 65
Bookworm & Silverfish 150
Bookworm Bookstore, The (two
    locations) 34
Bookworm, The 24
Borden, T. A. 104
Bowes Books 113
Brandreth, Dale A., Books 59
Briarwood Books 90
Bridge Street Old Books 23
Broyles, Kenton & Audrey,
    Historical Collection 51
Bryn Mawr Book Shop 68
Buteo Books 147
Butternut and Blue 80
Camelot Books 72
Cap's Comic Cavalcade 31
Capital Comics Center & Book
    Niche 129
Capitol Hill Books 117
Carduner, Art, Booksearch 13
Castle Bookshop, Ltd., The 80
Chervyl's Cookbooks 100
Chester Valley Old Books 20
Chestnut Street Books 38
Children's BookAdoption
    Agency 102
Clark, Stan, Military Books 46
Clay Book Store 34
Cloak & Dagger Books 44
Clover Hill Books 142
CML Books 41
Collectvs Books 143
Collins', S. F., Bookcellar 25
Comic Classics 102
Comix Connection 53
Continental Divide Trail
    Society 96

General Index

Courtyard Bookshop 85
Crawford, Miriam & William,
  Books 3
Culpepper, Hughes & Head 81
Crawfords Nautical Books 132
Curious Books 94
Dabney, Q. M. & Company 106
Daedalus 139
Deeds Book Shop 82
Dell's Book Outlet 42
Delmarva Book Shop 101
Delong, Thomas S. 43
Doe Run Valley Books 18
Drusilla's Books 71
Ellie's Paperback Shack 114
Elm Spy Books 91
Epistemologist, Scholarly
  Books 18
Epstein, Lionel - Bookseller 102
Factotum Books 14
Family Album, The 47
Fantasia Comics & Records (two
  locations) 142
Federal Circuit Div. of Shellenard,
  Inc. 95
First Capitol Books and
  Antiques 52
Fogleman, Frank/Bookseller 53
Frazier Americana 104
Frohnsdorff, Doris 101
From Out of the Past 130
Fuller & Saunders Books 119
Gach, John, Books, Inc. 81
Galaxy Book Trader 61
Georgetown Book Shop 93
Geppi's Comic World, Inc. 72
Ground Zero Books 111
Hale, William F. - Books 121
Hamilton Virginia Books 134
Heartwood Books 141
Heinoldt Books 62
Hirschtritt's "1712" 108
Holloway, David, Bookseller 137
Holmes, David J., Autographs 3
Hooper's Books 135
House of Our Own 7
Hutchison, William 22
Idle Time Books 122
Imagination Books 109
Indian Path Books 26
Innes, Alan F. - Books 149

Inscribulus Books 54
Iranbooks 91
Jean's Books 21
Johnson & Roth Used Books 38
Kellinger, Cesi, Bookseller 44
Kelmscott Bookshop, The 76
Konigsmark Books 28
Kultura's Books & Records 126
Lachman, David C. 30
Lambda Rising (two locations) 122
Lantern Bryn Mawr
  Bookshop, The 119
Lauberts, Alexander 133
Lazy Moon Bookshop 114
Let There Be Praise 134
Light of Parnell Bookshop 49
Logic & Literature Book Shop 118
M-R Books 147
Macaluso, Thomas, Rare and
  Fine Books 21
MacManus, George S., Co. 8
Maiden Voyage Rare Books 29
Manuscript Company of
  Springfield, The 137
Mason's Rare & Used Books 45
Matlat, Elizabeth L. - Antiques 29
Mattson, E. Christian 88
McIlnay's Books 51
McKay, Richard, Used Books,
  Inc. 132
Meadowbrook Hollow Books &
  Bits 43
Miscellaneous Man 50
Mosher Books 40
Motorsport Miscellania 20
Mystery Books 16
Mystery Bookshop Bethesda 92
Najarian, S & C 24
New Era Book Shop 71
Newtown Book &
  Record Exchange 23
Ninth Street Market Books &
  Records 15
Nostalgia Mart 145
Novel Idea, A 61
O'Boyle Books 109
O'Neill, W. B. - Old &
  Rare Books 136
Oak Knoll Books 57
Old Books at Savage Mill 108
Old Cookbooks - H. T. Hicks 65

General Index

Old Forest Bookshop, The 117
Old Hickory Bookshop 96
Old Print Gallery, The 120
Olde Soldier Books, Inc. 100
Original Historic Newspapers 133
Owl Bookshop, The 17
Paper Treasures 146
Paperback Alley 149
Paperback Exchange 35
Paperback Exchange 48
Paperback Exchange Book Store, The 90
Paperback Trader 17
People's Bookshop, The 62
Perfect Ending, The 72
Peter Pun Books 106
Philadelphia Drama Bookshop 6
Philadelphia Print Shop, Ltd., The 10
Philadelphia Rare Books & Manuscripts Co., The 11
Phoenix Books 66
Poitras, Jean-Maurice & Sons 88
Pollywog Paperback Bookswap 63
President's Box Bookshop, The 124
Ptak Science Books 120
Quadrant Book Mart 33
Quick, R., Bookseller 95
Quill & Brush 105
RAC 8 Books in 1st Capitol Books & Antiques 51
RAC Books 50
RAC Books in Partners' Antique Center 32
RAC Books in York Antique Mall 54
Raimo, Antonio, Fine Books 32
Rais, Kathleen & Company 12
Rebecca of Sunnybook Farm 36
Reedmor Magazine Company, Inc. 9
Reid, John P. 58
Reisler, JoAnn, Ltd. 137
Reston's Used Book Shop 135
Rittenhouse Medical Book Store 7
Rock Creek Bookshop 121
Rosenthal, Richard T. 13
Royal Oak Bookshop 144
Rug Book Shop, The 74

Rush, Cecil Archer - Fine Books-Fine Arts 78
Russakoff's Books and Records 9
Sandy, D. R. 79
Schweitzer Japanese Prints, Inc. 95
Second Edition Used Books 82
Second Looks Books 113
Second Story Books 77, 91, 107, 125
Selgas, R. F., Sporting Books 35
Shocket, Jerome 87
Showalter, Jerry N., Bookseller 145
Silver Spring Books 110
Smith College Club of Baltimore Used Books 89
Smith, B&B, Booksellers 86
Soltys, Larry W. 41
Sottile's Books 19
Staunton Book Review 148
Stewart's Used Bookstore 97
Tales From the White Hart 74
Tales Retold 111
Taneytown Antique Shoppes 87
Thomas, William - Bookseller 48
Tiber Bookshop 77
Turtle Hill Books 83
Used Book Store, The 36
Valentino, Carmen D., Rare Books & Manuscripts 12
Vintage Paperback Exchange, The 104
Virginia Book Company 132
Volume Control 27
Voyages Books & Art 124
Warren, John F., Bookseller 6
Well Read Books 122
Weller, Eleanor C., Charlotte's Web Antiques 85
Whale of a Bookstore 42
White Papers 68
Wind Chimes Book Exchange 67
Windsor Park Books & News 49
Wonder Book and Video 84
Woodburn, Elisabeth, Books 66
Wynne, Robert, Books 46, 47
Yak & Yeti Books 107
Yesterday's Books 125
Yudkin, Samuel & Associates 123

Turtle Hill Books
3420 Sylvan Lane
Ellicott City, MD 21043
(410) 465-7213

About Turtle Hill Books

Turtle Hill Books, the publisher of this guide to used book dealers, sells out-of-print fishing books by mail order and by appointment. A free catalog is available on request. We have a PERMANENT WANT for used/rare/scarce fishing books. We offer competitive prices and would be pleased to respond to your quotes. Please be descriptive including date, edition/printing, publisher, condition, defects, and presence/absence of dust jacket.

Turtle Hill Books will be offering a wide selection of new guide books/maps to outdoor activities for the mid-Atlantic region, starting in April 1994. Activities covered will include hiking, camping, fishing, cross-country skiing, bicycling, canoeing, cliff-climbing, spelunking, touring, travel, fossil/mineral hunting, and birding. We also have two fishing titles under way which are scheduled to be published in March and May of 1994. This book is our second publication, the first being *P.B.'s Quick Index to Bird Nesting*. Please write or call if you would like to receive our free catalog covering new books (guide books to the mid-Atlantic), as well as Turtle Hill publications.

Additional Copies
Additional copies of *A Guide to Used Book Dealers of the Mid-Atlantic* may be ordered directly from the publisher for $9.95 each. Please include $2.00 shipping and handling for the first book and 50 cents for each additional book. Shipping is by surface mail (book rate) and may take one to two weeks. Maryland residents add 5% sales tax ($0.50 per book). Prices are subject to change without notice. Wholesale discount schedule is available upon request.

Please send
A Guide to Used Book Dealers of the Mid-Atlantic

_____ copy(s) at $9.95 each = $ _____ . _____
Shipping and handling = $ _____ . _____
Sales tax (Maryland residents only) = $ _____ . _____
Total enclosed = $ _____ . _____

To _____

_____

_____

Shipping and handling:
$2.00 for the first book and 50 cents for each additional book. Shipping is by surface mail (book rate). Maryland residents add 50 cents per book (5% sales tax).

Make check payable to:
Turtle Hill Books
3420 Sylvan Lane
Ellicott City, MD 21043
(410) 465-7213

- -

Please send
A Guide to Used Book Dealers of the Mid-Atlantic

_____ copy(s) at $9.95 each = $ _____ . _____
Shipping and handling = $ _____ . _____
Sales tax (Maryland residents only) = $ _____ . _____
Total enclosed = $ _____ . _____

To _____

_____

_____

Shipping and handling:
$2.00 for the first book and 50 cents for each additional book. Shipping is by surface mail (book rate). Maryland residents add 50 cents per book (5% sales tax).

Make check payable to:
Turtle Hill Books
3420 Sylvan Lane
Ellicott City, MD 21043
(410) 465-7213